10 Great Curricula

Lived Conversations of Progressive, Democratic Curricula in School and Society

10 Great Curricula

Lived Conversations of Progressive, Democratic Curricula in School and Society

edited by

Thomas S. Poetter
Miami University

With

Susan L. M. Bartow
Lara A. Chatman
Daniel Ciamarra
Christopher L. Cox
Dawn Mann
Kevin J. Smith
Kevin M. Talbert
Mary A. Webb
Amy Fisher Young

Information Age Publishing, Inc.
Charlotte, North Carolina • www.infoagepub.com

Library of Congress Cataloging-in-Publication Data

10 great curricula : lived conversations of progressive, democratic
curricula in school and society / edited by Thomas S. Poetter with Susan L.
M. Bartow ... [et al.].
    p. cm.
  Includes bibliographical references.
  ISBN 978-1-61735-611-7 (pbk.) -- ISBN 978-1-61735-612-4 (hardcover) --
ISBN 978-1-61735-613-1 (ebook)
  1. Curriculum planning--Social aspects. 2. Curriculum planning--Political aspects.
3. Education--Philosophy. I. Poetter, Thomas S. (Thomas Stewart), 1962-
II. Bartow, Susan L. M. III. Title: Ten great curricula.
  LB2806.15.A12 2011
  375'.001--dc23   2011035153

Printed in the United States of America

CONTENTS

FOREWORD

10 Great Curricula is a collection of stories written by educators who have come to understand curricula differently as a result of their engagement with a graduate course and its instructor. The book represents the best of what can be found in teaching and learning, in general, and in the quest for meaningful ways to understand curricula in particular.

As a longtime educator, I have often reflected upon what it means to educate. What I find in *10 Great Curricula* is an intelligent and genuine effort by Tom Poetter to do just that. For me, this book succeeds largely because it documents the results of an effort to seriously engage students (i.e., the book's chapter authors) in a truly educative experience. Those who understand themselves as teachers will, I believe, see this clearly. In my mind, this book takes the reader on a journey into examples and discussions of "great curricula" still alive and at work in the world today while also providing a strong evidence trail of how one might successfully approach the task of introducing students to the important work of curriculum studies.

Kevin Talbert's *Preface* sets the stage nicely. I can practically trace the course syllabus in my mind's eye, beginning with Tom's *Introduction* and winding through each essay—the framework, the readings, the conversations about topics, the requirements (expectations) that each student somehow "engage" the inquiry through a serious presence (whether this be a site visit or an attempt to collect archival data—or both). While reading these chapters, and especially the exchanges that follow them, I recognize the course reading list and Tom's optimistic passion for the explicit parameters he's set. I can easily imagine his pushing and pulling students for more depth and insight via in-class conversations, and his nurturing of students' drafts via verbal and written feedback. And I can see, easily, the extent to which these contributors have grown and transformed as a result of all of this pedagogical activity that fed into their narrative efforts. I trust that most teacher-readers will see much the same.

The study of—and ability to theorize—curriculum is central to not only understanding but also *acting upon* education and schooling. What we find in *10 Great Curricula* (as a representation of Tom's class) is a similar belief: that exploring, pondering, questioning and understanding curriculum is a necessary step toward behaving in ways that reflect one's personal educational experience (we might also call this "actionable enlightenment"). The study of curriculum is about taking responsibility for—and accepting the associated risks related to—inviting students at all levels to ask questions and explore new ideas and information without knowing where such inquiry might lead them. At its best, the practice of curriculum studies is about contemplating the possible within the conventional educational context of expectations for unambiguous and predetermined results. It is about imagining not only who we are and how we have come to be this way, but also what we can do about matters of educational importance. Finally, and to a large extent unspoken, curriculum studies should ultimately raise questions about our willingness to accept the consequences of our actions, as teachers, for the greater good.

Crazy as it might seem, I have gleaned all of this from my reading of *10 Great Curricula*. Perhaps it is because I have known and respected Tom Poetter for many years as a thinker, writer, and friend. Tom and I have historic ties, as well: I knew and took classes with his doctoral advisor, Norm Overly, at Indiana University, and can easily recognize Norm's influence in Tom's work. Like Norm, Tom is deeply committed to the world of ideas as they pertain to how one lives life. Within the holy triumvirate of higher education, "service" is no less important that "teaching" and "research/ scholarship" to Tom Poetter. More important, "service" is understood to represent actions beyond the walls of the academy and to coincide with one's personal life. You can see this in Tom's overall course design and specific contributions to this volume, both in terms of his particular chapters and also in his feedback to each author's chapter. Tom Poetter is an academician who strives to move students to both critically interrogate and also act upon the "big ideas" that he proffers in class.

From a different perspective, part of the overall value of *10 Great Curricula* stems from the obvious effort that the contributors to this book have put into their chapters (and, as a corollary, into the course, itself). These folks, like most graduate students, live challenging and complicated lives already, what with work, family, and the rest, and it is not simple or easy for them to pursue graduate studies with these sorts of labor-intensive commitments. Graduate coursework is infamous for its focus on reading lots of books and articles, listening to lectures and (to a lesser extent) having discussions, and producing a final paper for the instructor. Writing for an audience beyond the instructor is atypical, and "writing for publication" is rare, since doing so requires students to synthesize formal course content within the context of a journey narrative told to others: What was the journey? Where and why did I take it? What did I learn that might be of relevance to the reader? Add to this the enormous amounts of time and labor involved with this particular writing process (drafting, sharing, critiquing, editing, re-drafting, etc.) and we can understand the rarity of this endeavor. In short, these chapters represent unusual sacrifices made by their authors during a semester of study with Tom in pursuit not only of satisfying a course requirement but of contributing to this book as well. More important, these chapters succeed in inviting us to share and learn from their individual journeys.

I find a great deal of hope and enthusiasm in the pages of *10 Great Curricula*, despite the difficult national context in which these contributors work and study. International, national, and local news make clear that education writ large is caught in a real bind between competing narratives of budget-cutting and efficiency/accountability, on one hand, and creating/enabling meaningful life-long learning opportunities and a thirst for knowing and understanding the world on the other. It is my hope that educators elsewhere will, like the student authors featured here, find genuinely transformative opportunities such as this that invite them to think and act purposefully in their work. More than ever, it seems, we need educational leaders who will commit to making schooling more intellectually substantive and personally (and actionably) relevant to themselves and their student in the future. You will meet some of these educators in these pages!

J. Dan Marshall, PhD
Professor Emeritus
Pennsylvania State University

PREFACE

This project was completed as part of a doctoral seminar on curriculum studies at Miami University, Oxford, Ohio. In the introduction to this volume, Tom Poetter outlines the origins of the course and his vision and hopes for it and our work as scholars on this curriculum project. He notes that the point was for us as doctoral students to "think curricularly about the world." While the focus was on curricula that he/we identified as "great," in reality, this project was not about "greatness" at all; to think so would miss the point. Instead, "Great" is a heuristic scaffold that Tom used as a prompt to help us theorize about curriculum. As a student and a relative novice to curriculum theorizing (aside from my 8 years as a public school teacher), I found the scaffolding helpful. As a researcher, I felt particularly attuned to potential "curricular moments" as I read, listened, and learned throughout the course and beyond.

As a doctoral student in curriculum, I find I often struggle to explain when family and friends ask, "What does that mean, curriculum?" Truth be told, curriculum is a tangled and expansive field. Sometimes, I do not even know clearly what it means to study curriculum. Participating in this project helped solidify my understanding. I now understand that "thinking curricularly" supposes a number of possible ways of "reading the world," to borrow from Brazilian education activist Paulo Freire. What we have offered in this volume is an attempt to read a curricular landscape through the lens of "greatness." We understand that just as our list of great curricula is not exhaustive or final, neither do we suggest that the way we have read each topic is the only valid way. We welcome the multiple readings that other theorizers might engage in. Indeed, we suggest that engaging in these sorts of theoretical exercises is precisely what will resuscitate the field from the imminent death that Joseph Schwab postulated more than four decades ago. Our desire is that as you read, you imagine the possibilities for your own articulation of these topics as curricula. Perhaps, you will envision another device for thinking about phenomena in a curricular way. We await your sequel to this volume.

Kevin Talbert
Oxford, Ohio
April 2011

LIST OF CONTRIBUTORS

Susan L. M. Bartow, MA (Miami University, 1984), BS (Miami University, 1975), Doctoral Candidate and Teaching Assistant, Department of Educational Leadership, Miami University, Oxford, Ohio. Former science teacher, McGuffey Foundation School, 1988–2008, and Head, McGuffey Foundation School, 2008–2010

Lara A. Chatman, MEd (Freed-Hardeman University, 2007), BA (University of Tennessee @ Martin, 1995), Doctoral Candidate and Graduate/Teaching Assistant, Department of Educational Leadership, Miami University, Oxford, Ohio. Former Academic Advisor, Southwest Tennessee Community College, Memphis, Tennessee

Daniel J. Ciamarra, MEd (Xavier University, 2005), BA (Northern Kentucky University, 2001), Doctoral Candidate and Teaching Assistant, Department of Educational Leadership, Miami University, Oxford, Ohio. Former middle grades math and science teacher

Christopher L. Cox, MSEd. (Southern Illinois University-Edwardsville, 1996), BS (Western Michigan University, 1992), Doctoral Candidate in the Department of Educational Leadership and Research Assistant for the Ohio Evaluation and Assessment Center for Mathematics and Science Education, Miami University, Oxford, Ohio. Former mathematics curriculum coordinator, Kalamazoo Public Schools, Kalamazoo, Michigan, and over 10 years of teaching students in secondary mathematics classrooms

Dawn Mann, MAT (Miami University, 2002), BS (Miami University, 1997), Doctoral Candidate in the Department of Educational Leadership, Miami

University, Oxford, Ohio, and High School Teacher, Fairfield Senior High School, Fairfield, Ohio

Thomas S. Poetter, PhD (Indiana University, 1994), MDiv (Princeton Theological Seminary, 1988), BA (Heidelberg College, 1985), Professor of Curriculum Studies, Miami University, Oxford, Ohio

Kevin J. Smith, PhD (Miami University, 2010), MEd (Miami University, 2005), BS (Utah State University, 2004), Teacher, Mason City School District, Mason, Ohio

Kevin M. Talbert, MEd (Miami University, 2008), BA (Ohio Northern University, 1999), Doctoral Candidate and Teaching Assistant, Department of Educational Leadership, Miami University, Oxford, Ohio. Former high school social studies teacher and co-director of drama at Shawnee High School, Lima, Ohio, 1999–2007

Mary A. Webb, MAT (Goucher College, 1996), B.S. (Park University, 1989), Doctoral Candidate in the Department of Educational Leadership, Miami University, Oxford, Ohio, and Middle School Mathematics Teacher, North College Hill Middle School, North College Hill, Ohio

Amy Fisher Young, MAT (Miami University, 2007), BA (Miami University, 2002), Doctoral Candidate in the Department of Educational Leadership and Research Assistant for the ESOL MIAMI Project, Miami University, Oxford, Ohio. National Board Certified English Teacher and former High School English Teacher, Talawanda Schools, Oxford, Ohio

INTRODUCTION

Thomas S. Poetter

10 GREAT CURRICULA: BEGINNING THOUGHTS

The idea for this book began bubbling in me more than a decade ago while I was teaching a doctoral seminar in curriculum planning at Miami University. The seminar was made up of nine doctoral students in curriculum, so it was basically of the same size and possessing a similar make-up as the one who co-wrote this volume with me in just the past few years. To be more specific about make-up, the classes were filled with very bright, mostly career teachers/administrators interested in pursuing a doctorate in curriculum at Miami University. In order to get at the concepts for examining the acts of curriculum planning and the leadership of it, especially as curriculum planning takes place (or could take place) in schools with many stakeholders, I presented examples of what I was calling "great" curriculum. The two examples of great curriculum I chose to present to that class were The United States Holocaust Memorial Museum in Washington, D.C., and The National Aeronautics and Space Administration (NASA).

Before laying out any frameworks for how programs or institutions like these are "curricular," I asked the students to suspend their judgment and questions and just listen to my descriptions of the curricula. As a teacher, I was hoping to build with them new understandings about curriculum, thinking that maybe if they started with less familiar examples outside of schools, that core concepts would emerge and take hold that might some-day influence the quality of schooling in their own settings.

Deep down, I wanted students to learn how to think curricularly, that is to theorize, to new generate ideas, to critique, and to recognize possibilities as a result of their interaction with curriculum and curriculum ideas. That is, to "curricularize." I wanted students to spring into classic questions in curriculum studies, asking "What knowledge is of the most worth? How can it be conceptualized and delivered in educational settings, and even in those not usually associated with "education," let alone "schooling"? How can subsequent learning (or not) of the curriculum be assessed, understood? And who decides all of this (where is the power and how does it work?) and how does it impact learners and society when delivered well or poorly?" (questions adapted from Spencer, 1932; referenced in Holmes, 1994)

I wanted the class to get to the questions by thinking about curriculum in the world in different, less conventional ways. I wanted the students to practice thinking about curricula that may have seemed unfamiliar to them and lay outside the typical subject areas dominant in today's public schools, like math, social studies, language arts, science, foreign language, art, and music. As a result, I thought, they would build a stronger understanding of curriculum in general and maybe a deeper base from which to spring later into curriculum work they would do with school colleagues in the future typically in the subject areas, maybe even the following week!

Maybe they would have insights as a result of working on the unfamiliar that would transform their future work in more familiar curriculum settings in schools. And perhaps, the examples that had been "invisible" to them, meaning that they had never thought that a corporation or a museum had curriculum oozing and seething from its very core and in its ways of being in the world, would illuminate their way forward. So, a starting point in that long ago class was listening to me curricularize about The United States Holocaust Memorial Museum and NASA as "great" curricula.

Over the years, I kept thinking, "Exploring curricula of this sort and the concept of 'great curricula' could constitute the core of a full seminar." And that is what happened some years later when the coauthors of this volume met with me for a semester-long seminar designed for us to explore together how community-based and school-based progressive, democratic curricula are "great."

WHAT IS GREAT, ANYWAY?

Kevin Talbert takes a stab at defining what we mean by "great" in the preface. I think he gets at some key ideas, including the notion of the use of "great" as a heuristic device that opens up the curriculum field for deeper, closer analysis. Kevin Smith, author of the chapter on the One-Room Schoolhouse, also wonders out loud about "great":

> But what do I mean by great? Great often is understood as "the best" or something close to it. However, there are so many things we call great that don't really mean they're the best or that they're something we would want to experience (such as when people refer to "the great war"). With that in mind, I don't position the concept of "great" solely in terms of "good and bad." Instead, I think of it as possessing a type of significance or distinctiveness, and in terms of curriculum, I think of it as a quality that helps us to engage in curricular theorizing that is active, meaningful, and robust—to think about curriculum in complex and compelling ways.

So, it is safe to say early on that "great" primarily works for us as a device, one that I put to work for intellectual and pedagogical purposes for students in the course. I did mean for the use of the moniker to provoke students to question more deeply and to inquire in a scholarly way into existing curricula in schools and in the world that could be called "great." Ultimately, whether or not you, the reader, think the examples are "great" in the end depends upon what we say about them and about your own sensibilities. Our main approach is to examine aspects of "great" throughout the book as the reader interacts with the text. In our epilogue, we will try to make sense of patterns, themes, and areas of contestation that the chapters reveal.

To be honest, though, especially from my point-of-view as the course instructor and the main narrative voice here, there are some fundamental ideas that form a conception of great, both in terms of the perceived qualities and effects of the curricula and for their value as curriculum examples for enhancing pedagogy in a course on curriculum and for stimulating inquiry. One idea is that a curriculum is great if it helps the inquirer to understand curriculum better and to develop deeper insights into curriculum work from his or her perspective.

Also, I usually think of "great" curriculum as having a progressive bent. In that early class years ago, I wanted to show how the Holocaust Museum and NASA put people and the projects at the center of their work, and deeper, how they embodied moral commitments to means and ends that had value beyond the work at hand, that is, though large corporate entities of certain types, their missions and the programmatic embodiment of their purposes in action were uniquely progressive. They focused on humanity, its qualities of perseverance and value, on its penchant for striving, reaching, and achieving beyond all odds, beyond evil, beyond the heavens.

In terms of advancing humankind, their ends were to reach beyond the possible and embody the seemingly impossible at the heart of the 20th and 21st centuries: humanity as agent for good, for using its know-how and spirit to better lives for all, beginning with one and branching out to many. The Holocaust Museum begins each visitor's tour with an introduction to one victim of the holocaust. And one person, though backed by a nation and a world looking on with a collective wonder, took the first steps on the surface of the moon, not 20 soldiers repelling from the lunar module with machine guns; one pilot, a civilian, brave and lucky, who grew up in the Midwest among people I knew, who spoke immortal words for himself and a nation, a world, and planted a flag, and hopes for peace, equality, and opportunity in one furiously complex moment of pride and accomplishment, simultaneously framed by war, revolution, and despair.

I chose The Holocaust Museum and NASA as curricula to present as "great" because these curricula had a profound personal impact on me, shaping who I am as a progressive citizen and educator, more or less. As I experienced them, they shaped who I am and how I see the world, while simultaneously having a profound impact on the wider world in ways that were transformational. I chose these curricula to present to students because they represented a range of curriculum endeavors and I felt they could yield lessons about curriculum planning that would serve at least as a motif or heuristic guide in the course and perhaps also about actual principles of engagement in the work. These curricula stood as examples of how good we can be together, as citizens and as a society.

I also knew that they would generate discussion as examples of curriculum planning taking place outside of schools. I wanted students to consider the broader world as curricular, and some of the examples of curriculum in the world as deeply illustrative of excellence in educational/curricular work. I thought if students saw the wider brush strokes of curriculum outside the school doors, that they might bring that world back through their own school and community portals of entry and thereby enhance the educational experiences of their constituents on the inside. And I hoped they might enhance their work with the community outside of school as an educative body, one that has a profound import in terms of what goes on inside schools and that often embodies the great, progressive hopes for the good life as they get lived out by citizens creating freedom and opportunity daily in a socially and politically democratic republic.

Also, I realized that thinking of programs or institutions this vast, this technical, this political, and even this unwieldy, made for an excellent intellectual exercise in curriculum studies. Not only would the work of thinking curricularly about these entities create possible connections to studying curriculum theory and practice, but it also might lessen the distance between our thinking about untouchable, vast, even corporate endeavors and the fact that they are all made out of human efforts, regardless of their technical complexity or our seeming distance from them. Personalizing the vastness—and understanding not only the constituent parts but also the larger purposes of major undertakings like a museum about genocide or a federal agency with wings—has always been a way of thinking about curriculum for me. After all, our graduates could be working as educationists in settings like these as soon as next year! I wanted them to populate these positions at least with the experience of critiquing the world and of valuing it through a progressive lens.

How does curriculum study of this sort shape our experience of that curriculum, or give us grounds to resist or remake it given whatever power base we have to spring from as scholar, consumer, activist, teacher, preacher, politician, etc.? And regarding something as controversial, for instance, as McDonald's employee training curriculum—breathtakingly effective and problematic on so many levels, from its approaches to training of employees, to its marketing of food products, to the management of its public image given numerous assaults [some of them curricular, see Kincheloe's *The Sign of the Hamburger* (Kinchloe, 2002)]—what educational value can be attached or gleaned from a study of it? What might make it great, or not?

Ultimately, I would ask, what impact has the curriculum had? Has it been "great"? Meaning, has it had a significantly positive impact on individuals and of many more people in terms of reach, magnitude? Does the curriculum in practice and the lived experience of it by students stand as clear examples of the progressive in action? And have those experiencing the curriculum on multiple levels been changed for the "better"?

So, ultimately, an aspect of "great" at play in all of the chapters is the degree to which curriculum experiences, depicted in the lives of those who actually experience them in some way, do several very unique, educationally progressive things:

- open us up to seeing ourselves as more fully human, both individually and in relation to others;
- create a world of institutions, cultures, and communities that are more democratic; and
- establish more clearly the criteria for fairness, justice, tolerance, diversity, and opportunity in the world for individuals and for societies.

We will use the lenses provided by these criteria in our closing pages, looking back and interpreting the narratives provided about each curriculum.

TWO EARLY EXAMPLES OF "GREAT"

Briefly, and by way of introduction, I want to frame with some more detail and in a narrative way the two early examples of what I called "great" curriculum for the first time back in the late 1990s, the United States Holocaust

Memorial Museum and NASA. In this volume, Dawn Mann explores the lived curriculum of the museum. None of my coauthors decided to take on NASA for this book. That might come in a later volume. I consider the two examples as foundational springboards to our introduction of "great" curriculum, and our inquiries into how and why they are examples of "great" curricula.

I had visited the Holocaust Museum in the late 1990s, and it had shaken me personally. Walking through it for the first time, I experienced its stark, realistic depiction of the holocaust preceding and during World War II, that is, specifically, the systematic attempt by Adolph Hitler to exterminate all Jews as part of his master plan for world domination. I understood from my own experience of the museum the depth and breadth to which the curators went to assure that the museum could be appreciated and experienced by a broad range of citizens and that each visitor would feel touched personally by the experience.

Creating a museum of this sort took a great deal of planning. It was obvious to me as I experienced it in person as a visitor and then reflected on it later, how much went into planning just how the visitor would enter the museum, how he or she would be engaged, the images he or she would be exposed to, the ideas, concerns, and lessons that would be taught as the tour progressed. And much more than a voyeur at the perimeter of the most heinous events of the twentieth century, the visitor to the museum, any one who experienced its total program and came out in the end onto the sunlit streets of D.C., became a witness to the humanity that was sacrificed and that remained out of the dark rubble of civilizations and lives. And if touched, the participant becomes a living proponent of the central commitment of the museum and of the movement behind it: "Never again."

The second example, NASA, felt and still feels personal to me. I know NASA is a vast, political, difficult institution, one of the most troubled and vital civilian agencies of our federal government. But my parents knew the great patriot, pilot, scientist, and citizen Neil Armstrong and his parents and grandparents personally. Neil spent part of his childhood in my hometown, St. Marys, Ohio, and attended second through sixth grade in St. Marys Public Schools. My father, who was the pastor of Neil's grandparents' church in St. Marys, was called to sit with the family when one of Neil's early Mercury missions went badly and everyone feared the worst. Neil returned the ship safely to earth and to accolades for his bravery, cunning, and expertise as a pilot. Then Mom and Dad were invited to sit with the Armstrong family while they watched the moon launch in July 1969 on a special feed with a secret service agent overseeing the event. We were guests of the Armstrongs at the parade honoring Neil in Wapakoneta, Ohio, after the successful return of the moonwalk mission to earth.

I felt connected to the space missions of the late twentieth century, because at least one of the people involved in it, Armstrong, grew up where I grew up (Poetter, 1994a); his kin knew mine. Young Neil took flying lessons as a young man in the airspace directly overhead—quite literally in the beautiful, azure Ohio sky that my childhood gaze soaked up as I grew. And this was the same sky the Wright Brothers shared with Neil and history. Growing up just down the road in Dayton, Orville and Wilbur Wright dreamed of putting flying machines into this very sky. They were not figments of an imagination, but real, fleshy, human people, not massive institutions. People dreamed up navigation, and made it happen with their brains, brawn, and skills. This connection has had a profound impact on me, and led me to believe that I could accomplish anything I wanted, especially if a boy just down the road could fly in the air, or wonder of wonders, fly a machine to the moon, land safely on it, walk on its surface, and return home unscathed.

Think of the power of that, for the times and even for today. Certainly President Obama and other figures carry that kind of weight today, to some degree, at least (see Chris Cox's chapter here, "The Inauguration of an American President"). Any personal connection to people and history, no matter how tenuous or distant, can have a profound impact on the knower, perhaps inspiring, lifting, challenging, and shaping him or her, at least in part. And so even from a distance, sometimes, we touch greatness as we live and perhaps, as a result, *become it* in a curricular way.

CLARIFYING OUR WORK AS CURRICULUM INQUIRERS SO YOU CAN READ ON

Many years ago, as a doctoral student at Indiana University, I read Eisner's book *The Educational Imagination* (Eisner, 1979) for the first time. I could not put the book down, especially through the last chapters, which were devoted to the curriculum inquiries (examples of "educational criticism") by Eisner's own curriculum doctoral students at Stanford. The closing pieces by Eisner's students, I recall as if it were yesterday, were so memorable. Porro's chapter "The Low Achiever's Game" and Barone's chapter "Things of Use and Things of Beauty" particularly captivated me. They stood, for me, as examples of the types of scholarly pieces that doctoral students could write if given permission to do so, as well as the skills and support to make it happen. I have used them over and over again across the years in coursework as examples of what graduate students are capable of doing as scholars while they are in a doctoral program.

I even thought to myself while reading them years ago as a doctoral student at IU, "I think I can do this." It was a marvelous inspiration to me as a young curriculum inquirer. I felt confident that a qualitative, narrative-like approach to educational inquiry, scholarship, and research could lead somewhere, maybe toward recognition by a scholarly field and the academy, and certainly toward a sense of my own self as a curriculum inquirer exploring my interests and concerns in the wider world of educational thought and practice.

It is a fact that my reading in the early 1990s made an approach to curriculum scholarship as an inquirer possible. Several pieces guided me, most of which were written in the 1960s and 1970s. I remember reading Philip Jackson's *Life in Classrooms* (Jackson, 1968) and thinking about it as a breakthrough piece since it counted as curriculum research and people read it and learned from it. It seemed timeless, almost 30 years old when I read it for the first time. It became more than a textbook, more than a case study. It was a window into school life that had not been opened before. Jackson's inquiry sparked conversation and new questions, and new waves of inquiry in the field.

This is perhaps what Joseph Schwab (1969) hoped would happen after he declared the curriculum field "moribund" and called for more practical research about classroom practices, curriculum work, and students lives together and with teachers in schools in his classic paper "The language of the practical." What Schwab hoped for was a wider, broader, more relevant field of curriculum inquiry for which multiple, talented stakeholders described and interpreted curriculum for real. No longer would a singular theoretical framing be adequate for interpreting educational phenomena; now curriculum inquirers would be expected to bring multiple frames to bear on the complex interactions and cases of educational practices in schools and institutions. The field needed more of this kind of work to make sense of itself and to say something productive to the wider educational community of curriculum practice in schools.

John Goodlad's *Curriculum Inquiry* (Goodlad, 1979)—which he has called the "best, most under read book of my career" (Goodlad, 2007, personal communication)—stands as a critically important work for the field and for me in terms of framing areas for curriculum inquiry that educational professionals and others should and must take up as scholarly pursuits. I used Goodlad's description of the "experiential domain of the curriculum" to frame my dissertation, an inquiry into the complex curriculum experiences of women on an intercollegiate volleyball team at a major Midwestern university (Poetter, 1994b).

And, of course, always present has been the critical voice of Bill Pinar, as well as those of the reconceptualists and other critical, postmodern curriculum theorists and workers (Sears, Marshall, & Schubert, 2000), especially as it is embodied in the challenges presented to get at the deeper, more personal questions surrounding curriculum and context as expressed in

Pinar's early work on "currere" (Pinar, 1975), the systematic and artistic recovery of meaning.

As a result of the influence of these texts, in particular, and my experiences pushing the envelope of student inquiry, my entire career has been spent supporting the efforts of doctoral students in curriculum to inquire into questions and events and situations of interest to them, to observe, collect data, and make sense of the phenomena at hand by using multiple theoretical frameworks in order to say something meaningful about their inquiries that illuminate their field and the educational community on a wider scale beyond themselves. The end result has always been to pursue publication of the written depictions of these inquiries (Poetter, 2010).

The operative word in this pedagogical commitment is inquiry; it is a word descriptive of a process that is not less rigorous than research, but more pliable, less rigid, more open and fluid than "research" or even "scholarship." Anyone can be an inquirer, you do not have to possess a special degree to do it. And you do not have to call it "research" in order for the work to be appreciated and read. Other criteria beyond methods, validity, reliability, etc., matter in inquiry. In our chapters, the inquiries conducted have been taken on carefully, and with vigorous spirit. They do not, however, take place over a long period of time nor do they involve complex statistical methods of control. They are not examples of highly predictive experimental or quasi-experimental research. But, they are examples of depth-filled curriculum inquiries into the complex, exciting curriculum worlds surrounding 10 great curricula, some of which you know well and some not so well. And in each treatment, the author brings not only theoretical framings from our course together on curriculum, but also other, multiple framings as they inquire more deeply into the topic, and curricularize.

At any rate, we predict that by the end of the book you will have more questions than answers, more insights than theorems, and more ideas than you did before you joined us on this curriculum inquiry journey. We hope the dividend is enhanced understanding and practice of curriculum; we also hope you have as much fun reading as we have had inquiring and writing along the curricular way.

USING MARSH AND WILLIS' CONCEPTIONS OF *PLANNED, ENACTED*, AND *LIVED* CURRICULA TO FRAME OUR INQUIRIES

Beyond the fact that these curricula had positive, personal impacts on me as a human being, I wanted students of curriculum in the seminar that produced this book to consider that institutions inside and outside schools do curriculum work and are in and of themselves, in a sense, curricular entities, as I have mentioned earlier. They produce curriculum, implement it, and become it. This understanding takes shape on several conceptual levels; the coauthors of this book used Marsh and Willis (2007) to frame their theorizing about these areas. Marsh and Willis' notions of *planned*, *enacted*, and *lived* curriculum helped us think together and more deeply about the curricular phenomena described in this book. In general, my plan was to have each student engage a curriculum as it is "lived" by its participants, perhaps for them to become participant-inquirers in the curriculum at hand, which many of them did. Following are brief descriptions of what Marsh and Willis mean by *planned*, *enacted*, and *lived*.

Planned Curriculum

In terms of the curricula as planned, these great curricula were produced by an entity and implemented in the world on purpose, with a great deal of planning and study of how the curriculum should work. The educational purposes of the curriculum producer are revealed in the curriculum created and implemented, reflecting the deeply held values and purposes of the entity. It can be illuminative to study this aspect of great curriculum because a description of the curriculum can be insightful as an example of curriculum and its impact on the world for those studying it, or paying attention to it for whatever reason. The planned curriculum is often the initial entry into a curriculum experience, a place for making sense of what is intended and how those intentions might be played out. Sometimes the inquirer can get her hands on the curriculum, if it is written down formally. Or the planned curriculum may be discernible through observation of it.

The Enacted Curriculum

Those inside the organization producing the curriculum and those who experience the curriculum create unique and shared lived experiences through the enactment of the curriculum. Many perceptions swirl around the enactment of the planned curriculum, as it stays on course or takes twists and turns in experience of both those delivering the curriculum and those experiencing it. The enacted curriculum consists of both what is planned and how it is implemented but also how the planned takes shape in the world through lived experience. That which is enacted consists of the complex embodiment of both the planned and lived. People inside and outside of the organization, culture, and or community of practice make sense of the enacted curriculum as they experience it themselves or see it play out in front of them on the palette of human experience and history.

The Lived Curriculum

Individuals and society make sense of curriculum as it is lived by the actors of it in human experience. Getting beneath the technical surface of enactment are the human questions surrounding experience such as "What did the curriculum feel like? What meaning is gleaned from experience of the curriculum?" Over the course of my career in teaching, scholarship, and service, the notion of the lived curriculum has been and continues to be of keen interest to me. I understand that curriculum developers and teachers and students have ideas about what should happen and try to make it so when they enact programs. But I want to ask, "So what?" Ultimately, I want to know about what actually happened, that is, what was lived and experienced, not just about what was intended or planned or even what people thought was enacted. I want to know what participants thought and felt about the experience of the curriculum and what they believe was learned, and how that learning has changed their lives or not (Poetter, 1994a). And on occasion, if at all possible, inquirers get to experience the curriculum by living it out, first hand. Several of us were able to do that for this book and take this perspective in our depictions of the curricula at hand. So, as inquirers, we attempt to interpret the lived experiences of participants in the curricula we study, as well as portray, when possible, to what extent and how we as scholar-inquirers lived the curriculum at-hand.

I suppose that conceptions of meaning and transformation that are idiosyncratic to the curriculum under inquiry are of most interest to me as a person and scholar. In this book, as a result of this commitment, the authors try to depict conceptions of "great" curricula as planned, enacted, and lived and we especially try to mine insights from the lived experience of "great" curricula.

Also, it is important to add here that we do not make hard distinctions between curriculum and pedagogy, choosing instead to see the continuum of curriculum acts that are planned, enacted, and lived as curricular in nature, with pedagogical aspects. But where does curriculum turn into pedagogy and vice versa? In our view, the curricular and the pedagogical are constantly turning on each other in a dialectic. It is not necessary for us to parse them out, or to worry about what to call something, curricular or pedagogical, at some point of the process. The assumption I am teaching, that carries through this book, is that it is all about curriculum anyway. Pedagogues might disagree.

WHAT WE TRY TO DO IN THIS BOOK

First of all, we want to address curriculum issues for those who will exercise school or corporate leadership in curriculum planning and enactment.

We hope our examples of great curriculum spur deeper insights into the work at hand and engage the reader in our inquiries in ways that illuminate possibilities in the reader's own life and work.

Our intention is to draw you in, in terms of your interest in examining these great curricula with the authors, so you can interact with curriculum issues and problems as you curricularize them in your own work by taking a holistic view of the curriculum enterprise, asking: What is actually at stake? Who is participating? Who benefits the most? What are experiences of those internally? How does the world outside see the curriculum as it is planned, enacted, and lived? What has been learned (or not) by those participating in the curriculum? How can the curriculum be improved? What is happening in a hidden fashion that should be surfaced, understood, and critiqued? How can hidden and implicit byproducts be brought to the fore or eliminated, if negative? (Eisner, 1994, pp. 73–74) How can education of the participants be nurtured up and possibly mis-educational situations be avoided? (Dewey, 1902)

Second, we want to work as hard as we can to answer the question, "So what?" when we write about these "great" curricula. That is, we want you as the reader to easily see the value of the "great" curricula engaged in this book, while simultaneously questioning them and critiquing them even more deeply for yourself. Ultimately, we want our depictions here to inform your thinking and your work wherever you are located professionally: school, business, agency, public/private institution.

Third, this can only happen if the curriculum under study helps us get at answers to classic curriculum questions. Throughout the text we come back to classic Herbartian questions such as "What knowledge is of the most worth?" A curriculum is "great," perhaps any curriculum that is educative is "great" (i.e., according to Dewey, if it leads to growth and not corruption), when it helps the reader understand curriculum, teaching, learning, students, and the educational institution at hand better, more completely. Therefore, we take time at the end of each chapter to discuss the ramifications, from our perspectives, of the curriculum under study for school and community leadership. We do this by supplying a curriculum response by Tom or one of the chapter authors and a Final Word by each chapter author at the end of each chapter. The goal of each section is to delve deeper into the practical applications for each chapter for school and community life and leadership.

Fourth, if our study and depictions transcend the descriptive, expository mode and become more narrative, we think our inquiries will be more complete and descriptive than if we had just written up case study-like reports. We think the best way to get deeper is to write in a narrative manner about the lived curriculum. Therefore, the writing in the following chapters is more narrative-like, more journalistic, personal and story-like than most textbook writing on education topics. We are doing this on purpose to capitalize on our strengths and to make a point: The story captures the curricular in unique ways that illuminate meaning and possibility in ways superior, typically, than straight expository prose.

Fifth, and to this end, we want to make our writing more engaging and human. We want to tell all of our stories in ways that will be illuminating to the reader, hold your interest, and keep you moving through our inquiries with us to the end.

And sixth, we hope that the various examples in the book spur reactions across the table, new thinking, conflict, and insight just as the studies we performed to get here did for us in our classroom. If in the end you are inspired or troubled to take up your own inquiries, by describing and bringing alive examples of lived curriculum in the world, then we will have been in part successful in bringing about Schwab's hope for more layers of curriculum inquiry oriented toward the practical arts in curriculum practice and research (1969).

HOW THE BOOK CAME TO BE

Nine students showed up the first day of my course entitled "10 Great Curricula" in the Spring semester of 2009. I had a list of 10 "great" curricula to study in my class notes. I shared the list with the class and asked them what they thought about studying "great" curricula. I shared some examples of what I was thinking about "great," and the students weighed in on how they saw my examples resonating with their emerging definitions, interests, and concerns. We had not engaged any of the reading for the course yet, including Marsh and Willis' fourth edition of *Curriculum: Alternative approaches, ongoing issues* (2007), which would be the anchor text in the course, so they did not know anything yet about the framework of planned, enacted, and lived the authors employed in their book.

The class discussed my list of curricula for possible study and started to make decisions about where they would land. Did they have a favorite from the list they would like to pursue? Several did. Were there other good examples that I was missing (of course) that could take the place of one of the curricula on my list? Yes. No problem. I wanted the class to have somewhere to start, but I was not wedded to the curricula named on my list. To me, they were all examples of "great," progressive curriculum, but I did not expect that each one of them would resonate with a member of the class and then miraculously get covered in the book. But, remarkably, students settled on almost all of the 10 examples.

The 10 examples I originally listed included several corporate curricula: McDonalds and NASA. I listed several schools that had remained progressive even in the midst of the accountability onslaught brought onto schools, children, teachers, families, and society by No Child Left Behind (NCLB) and state's appetite for testing and control. These schools resisted the status quo, in their founding and current practices, and pushed notions of child-centeredness. The examples included Eagle Rock School and Central Academy. I listed Bronx Science because of its fame as a competitive, rigorous comprehensive high school typically serving the underserved students in New York City.

I also listed community organizations with "great" curricula, like Little League International and The United States Holocaust Memorial Museum and a public events/institution, Freedom Summer 1964/Freedom Schools, to which Miami University has a unique historical tie. In terms of other school tie-ins, I listed the one-room schoolhouse, examples of which actually still exist in practice across the U.S. in isolated instances. I tossed around but did not list The Algebra Project, but one student ultimately decided to study it because she found it interesting personally and irresistibly "great" for studying. I originally thought Sesame Street's progressive advancement of social issues in its television programming would yield a great chapter, but a student could not make the necessary connections to get close enough to the show. In an attempt to balance in and out of school examples in the book, she worked with me on a chapter about the National Network for Educational Renewal, John Goodlad's 25 year-old progressive network of school/university partnerships.

After several weeks, students settled on the following curricula that we present to you in this volume as subjects of inquiry:

- The One-Room Schoolhouse
- Little League International
- Eagle Rock School, Estes Park, Colorado
- McDonald's Corporation
- Central Academy, Middletown, Ohio
- The Inauguration of Barack Obama
- The Algebra Project
- The United States Holocaust Memorial Museum
- The National Network for Educational Renewal (NNER)
- Freedom Summer 1964 and 2009

One significant curriculum not chosen for inquiry was NASA, which was hard for me to let go of, but no one in the room wanted to pursue it. One student tried to pursue Bronx Science but could never get permission to visit the school and gave up on it. No doubt big city politics got in the way of access.

We know ... It is a fact that it is rather bold to call anything "great," or to name a certain number of "great" things to study as definitively so. It is rather like naming the Seven Wonders of the World. The lists shift; it all ulti-mately depends on what you are talking about as wonders and who is doing the talking! Nonetheless, it is fun to conjecture, and inquire. We realize that some may be turned off by our list, our choices. That is okay. We realize that there could be any number of combinations and lists and inquiries done as top 10s! This one is ours. As I have always told my students, I am a lifelong fan of the Cincinnati Reds baseball club. I was raised on the Reds. As a result, I have developed a nearly equal disdain for the New York Yankees. That does not mean that I do not realize and understand from time to time that the Yankees are great. I may not like it, but there is no doubt about it.

We are glad you are coming along with us for the journey. Maybe you can name and describe your own top 10 curricula. Maybe they will be a com-pletely different sort, and defensible according to different criteria.

REFERENCES

Dewey, J. (1902). *The child and the curriculum*. Chicago, IL: University of Chicago Press.

Eisner, E. (1979, 1994). *The educational imagination: On the design and evaluation of school programs* (1st ed.). New York, NY: Macmillan.

Goodlad, J. (1979). *Curriculum inquiry: The study of curriculum practice*. New York, NY: McGraw Hill.

Goodlad, J. (2007). Personal communication with the author.

Holmes, B. (1994). Herbert Spencer (1820–1903). *PROSPECTS: The Quarterly Review of Comparative Education, 24*(3/4), 533–554.

Jackson, P. (1968). *Life in classrooms*. New York, NY: Holt, Rinehart, and Winston.

Kincheloe, J. (2002). *The sign of the burger*. Philadelphia: Temple University Press.

Marsh, C., & Willis, G. (2007). *Curriculum: Alternative approaches, ongoing issues* (4th ed.). Upper Saddle River, NJ: Pearson Merrill Prentice Hall.

Pinar, W. (1975). The method of "currere." Paper presented at the Annual Meeting of the American Educational Research Association (AERA), Washington, D.C.

Poetter, T. (2010). Taking the leap, mentoring doctoral students as scholars: A great and fruitful morass. *Teaching & Learning: The Journal of Naturalistic Inquiry, 24*(1), 22–29.

Poetter, T. (1994a). Making a difference: Miss Conner and Bunker Hill School. *Teaching Education, 6*(1), 149–154.

Poetter, T. (1994b). Making meaning in the experiential domain of the curriculum (Unpublished doctoral dissertation). Bloomington, IN: Indiana University.

Schwab, J. (1969). The practical: A language for curriculum. *School Review* (November edition), pp. 1–23.

Marshall, J. D., Schubert, W. H., & Sears, J. T. (2000). *Turning points in curriculum: A contemporary curriculum memoir*. Columbus, OH: Prentice Hall.

Spencer, H. (1932). *Education: Intellectual, moral and physical*. London: Williams and Norgate (reprint of 1861 book).

CHAPTER 1

THE ONE-ROOM SCHOOLHOUSE TODAY: LIVING HISTORY, LOOKING FORWARD

Kevin J. Smith

PAST, PRESENT, AND FUTURE IN THE ONE-ROOM SCHOOLHOUSE

In March of 2003, our close, perhaps old-fashioned, and possibly quirky, young family decided to get rid of our TV. Now, instead of watching television, we spend time playing games, hiking, or sometimes simply sitting around the kitchen table talking. Even in today's fast-paced and technologically saturated world, we have found there is a certain special-something about living contemporarily with the remnants of the past. I am not talking about rejecting the future, or becoming hopelessly enamored of the past, I am simply saying that we think there are some great experiences to be had as a family when we consider the lived experiences and practices of those

10 Great Curricula: Lived Conversations of Progressive, Democratic Curricula in School and Society, pp. 1–28
Copyright © 2011 by Information Age Publishing

before us and discover ways to incorporate these aspects of social life and interaction into our current ways of living. I even decided to apply this approach to the ways in which I would conduct research for this chapter on the one-room schoolhouse.

Several years ago, I spent 4 months in Carmarthen, Wales, lecturing at Trinity College University and conducting research for my dissertation at a local secondary school. I was interested in how culture is communicated through the curriculum at that school, and in order to gather data for the study, I needed a vast array of electronic devices. I packed a laptop computer, a digital camera, and video recorder, as well as CDs, DVDs, flash drives, and audio recording/editing software. It was the qualitative researcher's equivalent of "packing for bear." Traveling with this equipment, either through airports or even walking to the research site, got old fast and there was a tremendous amount of time and energy that went into collecting and maintaining the data with this equipment. In considering this experience, I asked myself, "How can I make this new project different?" The focus of my research for this chapter was to gain an understanding of how curriculum is experienced in a contemporary one-room schoolhouse, a concept that resonated with me both personally and intellectually. Considering this theme, and my previous research experience, I decided to take a different approach to this project by going "old school."

Instead of checking a suitcase filled with electronic equipment and dragging a carry-on bag with my computer onto the plane to visit a one-room schoolhouse site for my inquiry, I stripped down to the bare essentials. I grabbed a plastic shopping bag and filled it with extra socks, underwear, and a few toiletries. I would be wearing a suit to the research site, so I grabbed an extra shirt and a tie, folded them nicely, and slipped them into the bag. I glanced at my computer, and then grabbed a couple of pens and a small, college-ruled composition notebook—the kind with the imperial to metric conversion tables on the inside of the front cover, and I was on my way. You might ask yourself, "Did this help?" or "Was it necessary?" and I'd have to say that I'm not sure on both accounts, but I can say that simply making the acknowledgement that I wanted to engage the topic of my research in an atypical manner, a manner which tried in some respect to align myself with the notion of doing things "the old way," helped me to orient myself to this research project with a reflective and questioning disposition. Now, I'm not suggesting that a plastic shopping bag is a historically authentic form of luggage—but it did make me a feel a little like Tom Sawyer; like I had wrapped-up all of my belongings in a bandana, tied it to a pole, and slung it over my shoulder. As a result, in some small way, I felt I was placed into a particular frame of mind that helped me to focus on what the purpose of my research was and why I felt it was important.

MY GOALS AND PREPARING TO MEET THE SCHOOL

The purpose of this study is not to argue that schools should return to a "golden age" of education (or even that one ever existed), or that one-room schooling is somehow methodologically superior to contemporary approaches to delivering school experiences. Rather, I wanted to look at a specific educational setting and discover what elements of that setting—whether practices, places, or people (or a combination of all three)—made that curriculum "great." But what do I mean by great? Great often is understood as "the best" or something close to it. However, there are so many things we call great that do not really mean they are the best or that they are something we would want to experience (such as when people refer to "the great war"). With that in mind, I do not position the concept of "great" solely in terms of "good and bad." Instead, I think of it as possessing a type of significance or distinctiveness, and in terms of curriculum, I think of it as a quality that helps us to engage in curricular theorizing that is active, meaningful, and robust—to think about curriculum in complex and compelling ways. From this type of complicated consideration, I developed a list of questions that I used in exploring the concept of "great" in terms of curriculum and the school experience in the one-room school I would study:

- What is it about the lived experience at this school that creates a significant contribution the students' personal, academic, and civic development?
- What happens at this school in terms of the planned, enacted, and lived (Marsh & Willis, 2006) curriculum that makes school a meaningful, engaging, and efficacious experience?
- What is the purpose of education according to the educators in the school and members of the local community, and how does this understanding of education shape the students' educational experience?
- Does the community value the school, and if so, how do they illustrate their care and why?

These questions were derived from Marsh and Willis (2007) who suggested there are three fundamental question-types used when thinking about curriculum. These question-types can best be summarized as being concerned with (1) what knowledge is worth knowing; (2) how a curriculum should be developed; and (3) how a curriculum should be experienced. Marsh and Willis then categorize these questions into three relative domains: the planned curriculum, the enacted curriculum, and the lived curriculum (2007, p. 4). The questions guiding my research were built upon this framework and were developed prior to my arrival at the one-room school. These questions evoke age-old themes in education, and I am sure each question could be the subject of its own chapter. Nonetheless, these questions shaped my inquiry and approach to collecting my data, and although I may not have been able to answer each question to the fullest extent possible, asking these questions did lead to other inquiries that illuminated my understanding of how education in this one-room schoolhouse takes place. In addition, new questions emerged from my time spent at the school.

So those were my goals in undertaking this project, but how did I prepare myself in terms of orienting myself to the discourse of the one-room school and in meeting those goals? It's a complex topic, the one-room school, because it possesses an iconic disposition in terms of both Americana and education. When I first considered researching a one-room school, my mind instantly conjured up images of the frontier town in *Little House on the Prairie*, and apart from the generalized nostalgia of the one-room schoolhouse that is occasionally referred to when discussing American education, that is really all I knew about this type of schooling. I needed to learn more about one-room schools, not only in terms of the characteristics of the buildings, locations, students and teachers, but more specifically, in terms of what were the educational *experiences* of students and teachers the one-room schools. How did the lived curriculum "happen?"

An interesting article by Barker and Muse (1986) details the decline of the one-room schoolhouse in America and provides a description of the remaining schools and their locations. However, these descriptions focus largely on demographic data including categories such as the number of students per school, the percentage of female teachers working in these schools, the geographical locations of the schools, and the educational attainment of the teachers. In fact, many of the academic articles I found treated the one-room school in this way, that is by taking a scientific and somewhat sterile perspective that is useful to some degree, but largely eliminates the social aspects of teaching and learning in a one-room school. There are hundreds of books regarding one-room schools covering topics ranging from architecture, to religion, and even to political issues. From these works, I found a handful of sources that provided me with a distinct representation of life in a one-room school, a perspective that the academic articles I encountered could not provide.

These works included historical/autobiographical accounts such as *The Thread That Runs So True* (Stuart, 1998) and *A Schoolteacher in Old Alaska* (Jacobs, 1997). In addition to accounts of teaching in a one-room schoolhouse, curricular texts like Jackson's *Life in Classrooms* (1967) and Kaestle's historical *Pillars of the Republic* (1983) helped me in making theoretical and historical connections to the topic at hand. In addition, I also looked for additional resources online and within my own community. There are dozens of historical societies throughout the U.S. striving to locate and maintain one-room schoolhouses as historical landmarks and museums, but these groups tend to focus on buildings that have not had students or teachers learning and teaching in them for decades. I needed to stay focused on resources that would help me meet my goal of understanding the one-room school as a living curricular experience.

ARRIVING AT THE ONE-ROOM SCHOOLHOUSE

I arrived at the airport with my plastic bag in hand, picked up my rental car, and went straight to my hotel. When I arrived, I tossed my "luggage" onto the bed and called the teacher at the schoolhouse. She gave me directions to the school and we made arrangements for my visit the next morning, but I could not wait until the next day. I was eager to see the school and village, so I thanked her for her help and was soon out the door and back on the road. The schoolhouse was roughly an hour away from my hotel and in that time I thought a lot about curriculum and how I was to approach this project. My little blue car wound its way up the old highway, which was undergoing major construction, and I paused frequently to give the construction vehicles the right of way. I was in a thoughtful mood and did not even think about turning on the radio. I sat in near silence as I made my way to the school, and it was during this somewhat Zen-like state that I began to reflect upon my life as a teacher, and more specifically my interactions with curriculum.

This pleasant drive in the New England sun was a perfect opportunity to take Freire's advice and reflect upon my own methods, practices, and pedagogy as I actively engaged in my efforts to develop a more conscientious approach to understanding of curriculum (Freire, 2006). As a result, I began to reflect upon the circumstances of my life, both in and out of the classroom, that have enriched my understanding of curriculum. Thinking about curriculum in this way allowed me to "get inside the past" (Clandinin & Connelly, 1988, p. 20) and to explore a history of personal moments that contribute to my identity, performance, and cognizance as a teacher and learner. Pinar (1995) uses the term *currere* to describe the autobiographical connections among a person's curricular experiential history, their present understanding, and their expectations and projections for the future, and it is through the retelling and application of the theories derived from these interactions that we can actively and meaningfully participate in the praxis of understanding curriculum both as teacher/students and students/ teachers.

The hour I spent driving to the research site was helpful in allowing me a chance to autobiographically construct my own orientation to curriculum (Pinar, 1995), but I knew that I would need to adopt a different approach to writing about my observations at the one-room school. Instead of drawing solely upon my own account of the curriculum that was generated through my past experiences and present understandings, I would need to collect data regarding the curriculum as it was experienced in this school. I thought about how I would need to recount my observations and the responses to my questions and interpret important passages, cues, and themes that inform how the teachers and students at the one-room schoolhouse experience curriculum (Kreuger, Evans, Korsmo, Stanley, & Wilder, 2005). I would then incorporate those elements with my own understandings in communicating what makes a particular curriculum great. I wondered exactly how I was going to accomplish all of this when I saw the exit sign in the distance that would lead me to the village school.

I soon reached the exit and turned off of the highway onto a quiet country road. There were a series of small towns on my way to the village, and each town held its own particular New England charm. As I entered the village, the schoolhouse stood on the right side of the road. Its redbrick exterior stood out in stark contrast to the whitewashed siding of the municipal building that stood next to it. I slowly pulled onto the gravel parking area and stepped out of my car. I could hear the voices of young children through the series of six tall windows that lined the sides of the school. Over 200 years ago, the windows would have provided the main source of light for the scholars sitting on the hard, wooden benches. The school had always housed young students, and today the school accommodated Grades 1–3 with a kindergarten class held in the municipal building next door. I wondered what other aspects of the school had remained the same over the course of more than 200 years. I looked up and noticed a small enclosure on top of the building near the edge of the roof. It must have once held the school bell that called the children to school in the morning and sang to them on their way home at the end of the day. A diminutive porch protruded from the side of the building with the number *1780* displayed in bright, silver numbers. This school was constructed in 1780 and was undoubtedly one of the many common schools, or public schools, that were spreading throughout the new United States (Kaestle, 1983). I must admit I was a bit awestruck by the fact that this school had been in continuous use, serving the residents of this small country village, for over 200 years. If only these walls could speak. And they did.

The next day I arrived at the school to observe the classroom and to speak with the teacher and community members. As soon as I entered the building, I stepped into a small kitchen area. The walls were lined with cabinets and pegs for the students to hang their coats and backpacks. On the far side of the room were two bathrooms, and between these doors were a sink and a counter along with a refrigerator and a stove. To my right was a doorway that led to the classroom area. The walls were painted white, and the windows along each wall were outlined in a sage-green paint. The floor was covered with a burgundy/maroon carpet that was slightly aged. The ceiling appeared to be painted tongue and groove slats with a series of large, unpainted wooden beams that ran perpendicular to the tongue and groove planks. Thick iron bolts held the wooden beams in place.

The classroom was lined with bookshelves and chalkboards. There was an eclectic collection of desks, chairs, and tables in the classroom representing many different eras of education in this little schoolhouse. The teacher's desk was nestled in a corner of the room. On the far side of the room, opposite to the teacher's desk, were two computers for student use. As I soaked in the details of the room, I thought to myself how similar, yet different, this school was to a contemporary educational environment. Of all the reading, I had done in preparation for this trip, there were a number of books that held a particular significance for me as I stood in this school, including Stuart's *A Thread That Runs So True*, Kaestle's *Pillars of the Republic*, and Jackson's *Life in Classrooms* (Jackson, 1968). There were elements from all of these texts that flooded to mind as I soaked in the ambiance of this little one-room school.

Both Stuart and Kaestle provided a kind of personal-historical perspective on schooling that was beneficial considering the nature of this school, but for some reason Jackson and his treatment of the "hidden curriculum" in *Life in Classrooms* resonated with me in profound ways during my visit to this tiny village school. When we encounter the words "hidden curriculum," it is easy to think of the "hidden" as something insidious— lurking silently, hidden-away and waiting with a dark and sinister purpose. However, the hidden curriculum is comprised of both good and bad elements, as well as just about everything in between, and it is an aspect of education that cannot be excised from the school experience. Although there are a number of ways to approach and interpret the curriculum of this school, I will draw heavily on Jackson's *Life in Classrooms* because that text featured prominently in my mind during my time at the one-room school.

EXPERIENCING THE CURRICULUM OF A ONE-ROOM SCHOOL

While I was at the school, I furiously collected data as I observed and interacted with the people working and learning there. In the first chapter of his book, Jackson (1968) describes the standardized nature of education. He mentions an over-emphasis on what Marsh and Willis (2007) would call the planned curriculum, as well as the expected behavior of the students in regard to the enacted curriculum. I referred to Jackson often as I analyzed my data because I felt that his project was similar to mine to some degree and would provide a meaningful perspective on the lived curriculum of the one-room school. So far, I have written about my visit to this school chronologically. However, in what follows, I will separate my experiences into sections based on certain themes that emerged from my data. I believe these themes help to describe certain aspects of the village school and speak to the notion of a "great" curriculum.

ASPECTS OF THE HIDDEN CURRICULUM

I did not know what to expect prior to entering the one-room school. I assumed that since it was a building well over 200 years old that there would be some striking differences in regard to what I have come to know as elementary education. As I stepped through the threshold of the little school and into the small kitchen area, I immediately thought of a passage from Jackson's *Life in Classrooms*, "Even the odors of the classroom are fairly standardized. If a person stumbled into a classroom blindfolded, his (sic) nose alone, if he used it correctly, would tell him where he was" (Jackson, 1968, p. 7). The smell of the school *was* the same as those found in my daughter's school of more than 600 pupils. There is a particular odor that elementary schools seem to share. It is pungent, but not particularly unpleasant. The scent of the carpet, the walls and furniture, and even the school supplies (like glue and ink) mix with the faint smell of the students' perspiration in creating a slightly acrid aroma that is softened by the teacher's air fresheners, cleaning products, and mom's fabric softener. I do not want to suggest that all schools smell pleasant, that would be an overly romanticized notion of the school experience. I, for one, specifically remember times as an elementary student when the classroom smelled like soured sawdust and urinal cakes. However, the students at this school were lucky enough to be spared that particular sensation (at least for today) and they energetically went about their business seemingly oblivious to the sights and smells that I found so intriguing.

Even the sounds of the school were roughly the same, although different in volume. Prior to the start of school, the students chattered excitedly to each other about all sorts of things—video games, music, and, of course, which of their classmates was the subject of a weekly crush. When I peered from the kitchen into the classroom, I saw the familiar trappings of an elementary classroom that I mentioned above; whiteboards and chalkboards lined the walls. Colorful posters and examples of students' work could be found there as well. Desks, chairs, and worktables were arranged into small groups and a variety of bookshelves were placed throughout the room, holding just about every type of book and magazine that you would expect to find in a classroom.

In the middle of this somewhat cluttered room stood the teacher managing and directing the lively but ordered chaos of the first few minutes of the day. The teacher was animated and engaged with the kids in the room. She smiled a lot, and spoke in a clear voice that could cut through the din of preschool excitement without sounding abrasive or cross. She seemed to me to be a woman who was very comfortable in her role as teacher. In any educational environment, these elements (and others) come to represent pieces of the hidden curriculum of a school, which represents the unnamed types of knowledge that exist in education and are veiled by our all too narrow focus on what we think is important in education (Jackson, 1968). These elements present a portion of the whole-school experience and help communicate to us what schooling is, and how it looks, feels, and even smells. These elements help communicate how we are to act and be acted upon in the classroom. These elements, to a degree, even shape the way we interact with what is taught in schools and how we come to understand this knowledge.

This classroom is a particularly busy room. With students from three different grade-levels, two paraprofessionals, a teacher, and the occasional volunteer(s), this small room seemed to almost burst with activity. stood in the kitchen area waiting to speak to a member of the community about the school when I heard the teacher tell the students to settle down. A few moments later the familiar strains of the Pledge of Allegiance could be heard coming from the classroom. This was the beginning of what seemed to be a well-practiced series of rituals in the classroom. The students seamlessly moved from preparing for school, to reciting the Pledge of Allegiance, to listening to the teacher describe the upcoming events of the day.

This is part of the "daily grind" that Jackson (1968) discusses. Minds and bodies are conditioned into a course of action that facilitates what we have come to know as "school" and it is a common element that is repeated day in and day out throughout thousands of schools in American without much notice. As I thought about the opening of the school day, I also thought about the role of teacher-power as a component of the schooling experience, and how it is often taken for granted. Even with all of this activity, there were focused loci of control and power in the room. Obviously, the teacher exerted her power and influence in ways including her methods of instruction, classroom management, and even curricular design. The paraprofessionals also possessed their own power and authority, but they each exercised this power and authority in varying ways. I wondered how the reality of working in a one-room school has influenced the ways in which they exercise their power. This line of questioning brought me back to Jackson (1968) and his description of the four responsibilities of a teacher:

(1) deciding who speaks and who does not; (2) acting as supply sergeant; (3) granting of special privileges; and (4) officially keeping time (pp. 11–14). I wondered how these seemingly standardized responsibilities of being a teacher would be articulated in this environment and how the execution of these responsibilities in this environment can inform my own praxis as a teacher/student–student/teacher (Freire, 2006) in the classroom.

POWER, AUTHORITY, AND VOICE

Deciding who speaks and who does not is a necessary role of a teacher yet, as Jackson suggests, there is the possibility that the implications of this responsibility go unnoticed. Many social, political, and cultural factors can contribute to the ways in which teachers decide who speaks and who does not, and these factors directly relate to the teacher's philosophy of power and authority in the classroom. Through my observations I noticed the teacher used strategies that countered the traditional centering of power, authority, and voice in the classroom.

For example, the students had separated into groups to work on math. The older students went into the kitchen area, and the remaining students divided into groups and placed themselves into different areas of the room. The teacher sat in the corner of the room with a group of students who were working on calculating the mass of an object. During their discussion of this concept, many of the students were chiming in freely with suggestions and comments about the task at hand. It seemed to me that the act of sitting on the ground in a small group with their teacher almost made raising their hands to speak irrelevant. However, after observing them for a few minutes, I recognized that the students and teacher seemed to regard each other in such a familiar way that they could anticipate when and how to interact. I can compare it to experiences with my family. There are times when we are all engaged in a particular project, and when conditions are right, the patterns of communication are implicitly noticed and observed. There is less effort and energy spent in guiding communication—it just seems to "happen." This allows us to worry less about how we "do things" and instead allows us to think more about the "thing" itself.

In addition, the teacher also allowed the students the opportunity to choose how they would like to complete the worksheets for calculating mass. The students chose the option of working in a group without the teacher walking them through the process step-by-step. This was another example of how this teacher has negotiated the responsibility of deciding who speaks and who does not in a way that was responsive, dynamic, and shifted the power of communication from the sole domain of the teacher to a shared responsibility by the students. Does this mean that the teacher never asked students to raise their hands? No, but it does suggest that the teacher and her paraprofessionals negotiate the responsibility of voice in the classroom in ways that might differ more regularly than the traditional classroom.

When the students separated into groups, the noise level increased slightly. Most of the noise came from the students quietly discussing the tasks they needed to complete. Occasionally, students would leave their group and walk over to the teacher in an attempt to get her attention. The teacher quickly told them to go back to their group and work with the other students until she could arrive. Competition for the teacher's attention, as well as speaking to the teacher, was high in this setting. This is another example of deciding who can speak and when, as well as the concept of delay (Jackson, 1968). This proved somewhat frustrating for the girls who wanted to complete their project.

However, as the teacher came over to them and looked at their work, it became clear that these students did not complete all of the assignment. The noise in the room jumped dramatically as they protested having to complete the second side of the worksheet. Small outbreaks like this happened occasionally, and the teacher would periodically announce that the room was getting noisy. At these remarks the students would quickly quiet down. It seemed that volume control was an important consideration for the teacher. I found this to be interesting, not only as an observer, but as an observer who is also a teacher. I thought that the room was *pleasantly* noisy and the occasional swelling in volume was simply the way that school should sound. However, I also know that many teachers walk a dangerous line with a "noisy" classroom. In some schools, a "noisy" class is perceived to be a misbehaved class, and a misbehaved class is the sign of a bad teacher.

I wondered if my presence in the room brought those concerns to the attention of the teacher in some small way, and perhaps, her attempts to keep the room quiet as often as she did was a result of my being there, or if it was simply a management strategy—something of a series of preemptive strikes to manage classroom noise before it got out of hand. The teacher never told the students to "be quiet," or to imply that the students could not or should not speak. Rather, she told them to work quietly and respectfully. The students quieted down a bit, and the teacher continued moving from group to group helping the students with their work. I sat near the teacher's desk and heard all of the hushed discussions in the not-so-quiet whispers that kids possess. To my right was a second grade student who had completed her work and was allowed to work on another project. She quietly sang to herself as she fastidiously colored inside the lines of her worksheet with her oversized crayons.

There was only one occasion while I was in the school that the noise in the room became a problem, and that situation was handled by the teacher in much the same way as the other changes in volume. In these instances, the decisions of who can speak, as well as when and how they can speak, were guided by unspoken factors that are shared by all classrooms, but in the one-room school, the teacher understood two important factors: (1) the students must communicate in their groups, and even between their groups; and (2) since those discussions had to occur in a single, small room, they had to be manageable. There were not any walls that separated the first grade, second, and third grades—they were all in this together.

It was apparent to me, as I watched the teacher and her students, that the close-knit relationship they shared was a consequence of living in a small, rural town, and learning and working in the one-room school. As the old saying goes, "Necessity is the mother of invention," and life in this one-room schoolhouse seems to consist of exploring alternatives to certain limitations (i.e., staff, space, and curricular requirements) that requires the teacher and students to develop ways of interacting that foster respect, encourage interaction, and provide opportunities to express their individual voices. This is not a condition that is guaranteed for all one-room schoolhouses (the experiences of Jesse Stuart in his book *The Thread That Runs So True* make that clear) but it does suggest that the nature of the one-room schoolhouse, more so than contemporary multigrade (meaning multiple classrooms and grades) schools, possesses a greater opportunity for students and teachers to transform the dynamics of power, authority, and voice in the classroom.

TEACHER AS SUPPLY SERGEANT

Anyone who has been a teacher can appreciate the role of "supply sergeant." As I sat in the classroom and observed the students, the teacher moved quickly from group to group. At one point, the doorbell to the school rang and the teacher quickly disappeared, leaving her paraprofessionals to work with the students. A few moments later, the teacher reappeared carrying a case of paper. She then slipped through the doorway and returned with one more case. She would repeat this until a tower of five cases of paper was standing in the classroom by the teacher's desk. In addition to receiving deliveries, the teacher was busy managing math manipulatives, pens, glue, and just about every other sort of school supply. As I watched the teacher piling up the cases of paper, I realized that she was much more than a teacher/supply sergeant. She was a teacher/supply sergeant/secretary/purchase officer/nurse/administrator/disciplinarian/librarian/cook and surrogate mother. Although she had the help of two paraprofessionals and the occasional volunteer, the many multiple responsibilities that are taken for granted in a contemporary school are vividly clear to a teacher in a one-room school. Whereas some teachers in traditional schools may feel at times like a ship tossed about on the ocean, this teacher, even with the help of the paraprofessionals, was an island in a sea of potential problems that constantly lapped at the shores, and although there were times when she may have seemed a bit daunted, she was never defeated.

In describing special privileges, Jackson describes the small things that teachers assign to students that help the teacher and provide structure to the classroom without being tied to a specific aspect of the planned curriculum. Examples include cleaning the erasers, safety patrol, and distributing supplies (Jackson, 1968). In this setting, these "special privileges" seem less special and more mundane. It is a reality of this type of environment that students become more active (and willing to be active) so that the teacher can better meet the needs of the students. I am sure there are special privileges that are to be had in this environment, but I did not witness any while I was in the classroom. Perhaps, it may be easier to observe special privileges in traditional schools because so much of what happens in that space is controlled and compartmentalized by the teacher.

At this school, compartmentalization of the curriculum is less noticeable as the teacher is not simply managing a single lesson plan, but is typically executing three (or more) lesson plans simultaneously. Not only are there students of different grades in the classroom, but as in other schools, there are students with certain exceptionalities that must be addressed, as well as students with varying levels of performance within each grade. It should be noted that most of the time, the assigning of special privileges occurs without being specifically brought to the attention of the students or teacher (or in this case, the researcher as well). With this in mind, it is highly likely (if not certain) that the assignment of special privileges was occurring, but that I had not developed the sensitivity to notice this behavior in the classroom.

TIMING AND DELAY

The fourth responsibility that Jackson defines is "time keeper." During my visit to the school, I was convinced that time behaved differently than in any other school. For example, as I was taking notes I suddenly had the realization that I was very tired. It hit me like a ton of bricks. I looked up at the clock. I had only been at the school for an hour and I was already exhausted. The students in the room chatted and worked on their respective projects. The phone rang frequently. The teacher and paraprofessionals were constantly on the move. I thought about my own experience teaching at a high school in Cincinnati. I could last an entire day in my classroom and not feel tired, yet, here I was worn out after an hour. I had no idea how the teacher could do this day in and day out. I watched the teacher also look up at the clock. Her eyes widened a bit and she came over to her desk. "Welcome to organized chaos," she said as she flashed a smile, and with that she started collecting the students for their mid-morning snack.

As it turned out, much of the teacher's thoughts were consumed by a change in schedule. The students were to go to music class in the municipal building next door, but a change in the schedule had altered the normal course of the day. I realized in this situation that such disruptions to the school schedule could be common. In a small school with a small staff, it would not take much to upset the normal flow of events. However, the teacher seemed ever-ready to shoot from the hip and make adjustments whenever necessary. This involved variations of delay that I mentioned earlier. On occasion, the teacher had to delay the recognition of students and their desire to be heard or to express themselves in order to give all of the students what she felt to be a fair and equitable learning experience. This involved having the teacher shape the flow of the classroom into stages. These stages did not seem fixed. Rather, they were pragmatically designed and implemented to make the best of any given situation.

When students were delayed in speaking or gaining the teacher's attention, they were often redirected in a way that kept them actively engaged in some activity. In traditional settings many times the pace of learning in the classroom is affected by different factors including the ability of some students to engage with the concepts that are presented to them. However, in this school, the teacher can mitigate this effect by allowing students to transgress the borders of grade divisions and work with other students closer to their ability level or with a comment interest. In some cases, students who demonstrate a greater understanding of the task at hand can assist in the teaching of their peers. Not only does this assist the teacher in managing the staging of the curriculum, but it also addresses issues of compassion, positive social interaction, and respect. These are values that are held in high regard at this school.

The "staging" of the curriculum in a traditional setting is supported by the structure of the school. Much of what occurs in school, and when it occurs, is dependent upon who is doing the instruction and where. For instance, in a traditional school, the pacing and segmentation of what is learned might be coordinated with other classes that need access to resources such as the gymnasium, music room, or lunchroom. At this school, much of what the students do is located at the school—in their classroom, with the one noted exception being the music lesson which is held for the students at the municipal building next door. Much, if not all, of the staging this teacher provides occurs within the four walls of this room, and much of that staging can be described as whole-class shifts, meaning the entire class stops a task and moves on to the next, or segmented shifts, where groups within the class, for instance, by age or by assignment/topic/project, move from one task to the next.

The ability to manipulate and transgress the artificially imposed boundaries of the curriculum is one of the most significant aspects of the one-room schoolhouse. Granted, "artificially imposed" is a strong term, and I do not mean to belittle or diminish the work curricular theorists and developers have done in understanding how curriculum should be developed and implemented. However, at the same time, we must recognize that the reality of life in classrooms (to borrow Jackson's term) often eludes the most elegant of theories. In these instances, individuals living and learning in these schools must develop their own understanding (through their praxis) of what education means and how they will undertake such an endeavor. I have used the four responsibilities of teaching described by Jackson (1968) above in describing some of the ways in which the curriculum of the one-room schoolhouse helps students, teacher, and even members of the community make meaning out of the experience of school, and although each of these dimensions are important, I believe they are all predicated upon one significant theme.

Concepts of compassion, social interaction, and respect are held in high regard at this school and can be summed up in the word "family"—a term each individual in this study used in discussing the school. This theme serves as the foundation of the educational experience in this one-room school and, although the notion of family may be a prevalent theme found in many classrooms, it acts as a central, differential factor here. As such, it adds a significant dimension to the characteristics of living and learning in a one-room schoolhouse and sets it apart from the learning experiences generally found in contemporary, multigrade schools.

FAMILY, FRIENDS, AND COMMUNITY

There was a stark contrast in the atmosphere of the room once the students left the school to attend music class at the municipal building next door. The room was quiet, still, and empty. The teacher and one of the paraprofessionals sat down with me to talk about the school and life in this little village. We were eventually joined the by a second paraprofessional. Earlier that morning, I had spent some time with a volunteer who had children attending the school. She had given me a lot to think about in terms of what she saw as the value of this one-room school, and I was curious to see if these were values that the teacher and paraprofessionals also recognized. The people who work at the school are an interesting mix of individuals. Both of the paraprofessionals lived in the town. One of them had worked in the school for 6 years and the other for 14. I got the feeling that they were insiders, "townies." The volunteer told me earlier that morning that there were two types of people who lived in this village: (1) those who are not long-time inhabitants or are not as involved in the goings-on in the village; and (2) "townies," long-time residents who have an interest in the village, and most likely, the school.

The teacher lived in a city further up the valley and commuted to work everyday. This was her second year teaching at the school, and I got the distinct impression that even with her apparent love and care for the students and the people with whom she worked, she and the paraprofessionals both felt that she still may be regarded by some as an "outsider." The paraprofessionals were in their mid-to-late 30s and the teacher was in her early 40s. Judging from the way they moved around the room and teased each other, they were comfortable working together and they laughed and joked with one another. They seemed to have a healthy and happy working relationship, although they also let me know that it was not trouble-free. Like any other group of people who work closely together, they have their occasional disagreements.

SERVICE AND THE CURRICULUM OF COMPASSION

As I mentioned earlier, a volunteer had met with me in the morning. She had a child who attended the school. She was friendly and amiable, and seemed genuinely excited to speak with me about the school. I asked her "what is the purpose of education?" and she responded by saying the purpose of education is to prepare students for the workforce and to live in a democracy. She then added, "The kids learn the difference between wrong and right, and then that is reinforced here at the school." I asked her what she meant by that and she responded saying that the students learn what it means to care for each other. "The kids are taught about bullying and about other people's feelings. This school teaches them how to get along with each other and how to accept each other."

She continued, saying that a variety of factors contribute to the ways in which students learn these lessons. She believed having the students together in one-room created a situation where they would need to develop good social skills just to "survive." The constant close proximity caused students to learn how to get along. They had to develop strategies that gave them the ability to accomplish what they needed to accomplish while still considering the wants and needs of those around them. They could not retreat from the reality of the situation by returning to "home room" or to another class.

The volunteer also believes that the older students are "… taught to care for the younger kids because they get the experience of helping them out with their work. They learn to serve each other." These opportunities to serve not only help the younger students in learning the concepts, but also may instill within the older students a larger capacity for compassion and a greater appreciation for finding opportunities to help those who need it. "They really see each other as kind of brothers and sisters in a large family." The volunteer said, "They may understand there are certain differences, but those differences don't matter that much because they're 'all in it together.'"

Not only does the volunteer believes the one-room school helps to develop close-knit relationships founded on concepts of compassion and service, but also believes it opens up social opportunities for students and removes artificial barriers that exist in multigrade schools. For instance, she told me about how her experiences in a multigrade school, and how she felt that the multiple classes and grades made it difficult for the students to "cross grades," meaning that when interacting in or outside of school, the students' social lives were usually kept within their grade-levels. In her experience, the division of students by grade extended to social relationships and interaction outside of school. Here, at this school, the students did not have that division because all of the grades were kept together. The volunteer also mentioned that she felt that in addition to respecting each other, the students also learned to "respect their elders." I asked her to tell me what she meant by that, and I was slightly surprised by her answer. I anticipated the traditional, authoritative view, but instead she said, "...to respect their elders, to think of them later in life. They're our future voters!" I was intrigued by her mention of raising future voters, a discourse that as a teacher I find seriously lacking in public education. I knew there was something behind this, that somewhere there was a story that contributed to this statement, so I decided to dig a little deeper.

DEMOCRACY AND EDUCATION AND THE ONE-ROOM SCHOOLHOUSE

I asked her about the relationship between the community and the school. The volunteer mentioned that it was a fairly positive relationship, but that it had changed over the years. The community was no longer comprised by a majority of long-term, multigenerational residents. Instead, a larger number of newer and part-time residents have come into town. In addition, the population has aged, with fewer families having young students who attend the school. As the population changed, so did attitudes towards the schools. Concerns over the cost of maintaining a one-room school feature prominently in debates regarding the future of the village school. To make matters worse, the current economic downfall has added a sense of urgency and credibility to the arguments posed by those who want to close the school.

At the same time, those who want to maintain the school make their arguments with an understanding that a commitment to this type of schooling experience now comes at an even greater cost. Reminders of the tension regarding the school are ever-present in the village. "There's a guy with a bumper sticker on his truck that says, 'It takes a school to bankrupt a village,'" the volunteer said with a troubled grin on her face. "We may not see the effects of the recession as prominently here," she added, "but we are not recession proof."

Economic tension is felt in the village, particularly when the school is brought into the conversation. As of March, the school was forced to take serious budget cuts. "Everything is done here on a village basis," the volunteer said, "Everyone has his or her own opinion; some want to close the school because they think it will be cheaper and others want to keep it. I want to keep it." The volunteer views the school as an investment. "These are the kids who are going to vote in the future," she adds, and again I am reminded of the importance of individual participation in the democratic process. "We don't do things by ballot here," the volunteer continued, referring to the way citizens vote on things like the school budget. "We take care of everything in the town meetings. If you're not there, you don't get to vote." The volunteer mentioned the last election in March. "We had a full house of about 60 people." She said. This meant that approximately 10% of the residents in this village went to the meeting to vote.

I found democracy to be an important theme in this little school. I thought about John Dewey and his laboratory school in Chicago. Dewey had once written that, "A democracy is more than a form of government: it is primarily a mode of associated living, a conjoint communicated experience" (Dewey, 1916, p. 87). To a degree, I felt that life in this one-room school, and in the village, matched Dewey's description of a democratic community. Like other schools, this learning experience involved members of the community and was intersected by the political struggles of that community. However, themes of community were privileged in this school to a large degree, and the very nature of the curriculum and how it was both planned and enacted seemed to foster respect and a willingness to not only share one's ideas, but to hear the ideas of others as well. The volunteer mentioned that the students' experience a sense of camaraderie and integration. She added that she felt they were more integrated and learned to support each other and work as a group. More important, she felt that although they were often working in groups, the students were also "allowed to be unique," which suggested that there was a certain level of tolerance and acceptance possessed by the students in this little village school. I felt like these were important concepts as I wrestled with the notion of a "great curriculum," and Dewey also recognized these concepts as he defined what he meant by a "good" form of associated living that was:

> ... to be judged good when it contributes positively to free intercourse, to unhampered exchange of ideas, to mutual respect and friendship and love—in short, to those modes of behaving which make life richer and more worth living for everybody concerned; and conversely, any custom or institution which impedes progress toward these goals is judged bad. (Westbrook, 1992, p. 247)

I use this quote from Dewey to describe aspects of this one-room school and its potential to further meet this definition. The volunteer whom I interviewed definitely believed that attending this one-room school made life richer and worth living. She beamed about the care and compassion demonstrated by the students. The teacher and paraprofessionals also echoed this sentiment stating that the students seem to overlook certain issues when working with each other.

They also noted times when problems between students arose. However, they mentioned that these situations were few and far between, and that when they did arise the teacher was able to approach the issues with students in ways that spoke to the relationship they have as students in the school; that somehow their association as classmates was more than simply an association via education, but rather the basis of the association was as members of a community that recognized the individual and his or her humanity. This notion stood in direct conflict with Jackson's observation of students learning to be "alone in a crowd" (Jackson, 1967, p. 16). It was almost as if everyone knew in this school that they were too small to survive if they approached life in their classroom as individuals alone in a crowd. I thought about my own teaching experiences and the large, cosmopolitan schools that my children attend, and wondered how they would hold-up as sites of "associated living" when compared with this one-room school using Dewey's criteria of evaluation.

Family

As the volunteer spoke about the kids, the school and the community, one word kept coming to mind—and then she said it.

"It's like a family."

I smiled at her as we both confirmed that there was definitely something "family-like" about this school. I kept this notion of family in the back of my mind as I sat down to speak with the teacher and the paraprofessionals. Normally, music class allowed the teacher a time to regroup and prepare for the rest of the day, but today she and the paraprofessionals graciously answered my questions about the school. I asked the teacher what it was like teaching in this school. She mentioned that the first year was difficult because she had very little notice before being offered the position and had little time to prepare for the new environment. During her first few weeks in the one-room school, she learned to develop a pragmatic approach to the problems that arose in the classroom. By this she meant that she sought solutions for each individual situation in a thoughtful and analytic way, knowing that there was no guarantee that "what worked" in similar situations during her previous experience as a teacher would work here.

She jokingly described the environment in the school as "controlled chaos." I understood what she was saying because I was there, but I did not know how I would convey that to the reader. The term was oxymoronic, yet, it did describe an essential characteristic of the one-room school. Teaching, as in any classroom with 25 students under the age of 10, requires a certain level of control. However, at the one-room schoolhouse, factors such as the difference in students' ages, space limitations, and the expectations of the planned curriculum, affect the way in which this control is exercised and maintained. Even more important was the emphasis on caring and respect that permeated the entire curriculum. I felt as if there was a broad understanding of "control" as it applied to what happens in the school, and that within this broad framework was a level of flexibility and sensitivity that allowed for this particular type of education.

I am sure the teacher established her "ground rules" at the beginning of the year, and these rules most likely operated in ways similar to those in contemporary multigrade schools. However, ultimately the ground rules had to be flexible. They had to allow for the unexpected interruptions and modifications that often occur, as well as the individual contributions students make to the learning environment. The negotiation of *enacting* a caring curriculum from a *planned*, state-endorsed curriculum, the complexity of teaching across multiple grade-levels and ages, and the monumental task of managing the minutiae of life in the one-room schoolhouse all become manifest in a contained, entropic state. This controlled chaos is governed through the joint recognition that "We are all in this together."

So, to a large degree, the teacher relies on the students and paraprofessionals as much as they rely on her. While there was a structure that governed how school was conducted here, it was a structure that allowed for unplanned and unexpected eruptions in how the students and teachers would learn from, and teach, each other.

An important feature of the education that occurs within this controlled chaos is choice. In describing how teaching in the one-room schoolhouse differs from other environments, the teacher said that she has more choice in regard to what she wants to teach and how she wants to teach it. She feels that choice empowers students and gives them ownership to engage the material in ways that encourage learning. This also speaks to the democratic atmosphere of the school in that students must learn to communicate their choices amongst the voices of the other students and teachers. In regard to the teacher, the freedom to utilize the curriculum of three grades provides her greater choice and maneuverability. However, there are conflicts. The state has mandated the use of a math program that teaches certain concepts by grade, which means she cannot "blur the lines" between grade designations for math, and this is a source of frustration for her considering the nature of this school.

I then asked the teacher and paraprofessionals about the relationship between the community and the school. They mentioned many of the same concerns the volunteer had mentioned earlier that morning. One of the paraprofessionals added that the parents in the community "are concerned about if their kids will be ready to go to the 'other' (traditional school in the town down the road) school." The other paraprofessional responded by saying that the students from this one-room school generally do better socially and academically than the students from other elementary schools. My visit with the superintendent later that afternoon corroborated this claim by mentioning that students from the village school generally are "at the top of their class" by high school and are "almost always" captains of the football team or "recognized as being leaders."

I then asked the teacher about the political atmosphere in the village, particularly as it pertained to the school. The teacher mentioned the recent budget cuts and the normal "growing pains" that are associated with a new teacher in an established school. From their conversation I gathered that, although the teacher was primarily responsible for the education of the students at the village school, many of the community members considered her an "outsider," and instead would approach the paraprofessional who had been with the school for 14 years.

"Can you tell me what this school means to you?" I asked, and the teacher responded by saying that she wanted all of her kids to succeed and excel in what they learn at school. She wanted them to be prepared to move on. She also mentioned the word "family." She mentioned how her relationships with the students who were in first and second grade last year (her first year at the school) are different now one year later. This is a distinct characteristic of this school in that the teacher will remain with students for 3 years of their educational career, and the relationship they develop together is undoubtedly different from those relationships with students and teachers in traditional schools. Both the teacher and students are able to develop a better understanding of each other over the course of the 3 years they spend together living and learning in the one-room schoolhouse.

Both of the paraprofessionals agreed with the teacher regarding the feeling of family at the one-room school. "It's like my home," said the paraprofessional who had been with the school for 14 years. "Sometimes I'll take the kids next door for music lesson, and when it's all over I'll say,

'Alright, let's go back home!'" Her eyes started to water as she spoke. "The kids know I don't mean *home*, I mean the school."

All eyes were on this woman as she spoke passionately about the type of education that happens at this school. She went on to describe how the combination of the history of the school, the small community, and the relationship with the students create a special type of education. While there are challenges in working in this environment, she felt the rewards outweighed the costs. As she described her experiences at the school, it seemed to me that she felt that instilling within the students a desire to learn and helping them develop the ability to respect and care for others, was a task that was undeniably unique to learning in the one-room school. "They don't get that at any other school," she added with emphasis. Unfortunately, this would be her last year at the school, and I felt the weight of that reality as she spoke about her desire to go to school and get her teaching license. At the time, I was happy to hear that she decided to get her licensure. It was obvious she was passionate about teaching, and perhaps some day she could passionately practice her love of teaching at this school. But again, I sensed there was another chapter of this story that was yet to be told.

I thanked the teacher and the paraprofessionals for letting me visit their school. I had enjoyed every minute of it, and to be honest, I did not want to leave just yet. However, I was invited to meet with the district superintendent, who was a principal at the one-room school for several years, and I wanted to hear what she had to say about this one-room school nestled in this quiet, little, New England village. I was curious to see how an administrator, and particularly an administrator who did not spend everyday in the one-room school, would talk about the one-room school. Feeling somewhat conflicted about leaving, I hopped into my car and drove to the district offices that were only a few minutes down the road.

I pulled into town and met with the superintendent who graciously invited me to lunch. We sat at in a booth at a local pub and talked about what I had discovered so far. The superintendent was not surprised. "It's a lovely school." She said, with a smile. I thought about the *untold story* that I felt existed every time I asked about the relationship between the community and the school. The superintendent acknowledged that the relationship had been strained, and that the source of that strain was ultimately due to finances. I asked her about the town meeting, and she corroborated the number of people in attendance. "There were 68 people in that meeting, I believe, but only six of those people voting had students in the school." I was shocked. "Where were the other parents?" I asked, but she didn't have an answer. This was part of the untold story. This is part of the reason why the volunteer was so concerned about raising students who were socially and civically aware and active. The superintendent then revealed the final chapter. The paraprofessionals at the one-room school had both lost their jobs due to the recent budget cuts. What I mistook as a voluntary decision for one of the paraprofessionals to leave the school and earn her teaching license was actually a forced departure. This affected me in a profound way, not only because this woman was losing her livelihood, but also because she was also being forced to leave her "extended family."

I thanked the superintendent for her time and for approving my request to visit the one-room school. As noted earlier, there are precious few one-room schoolhouses in America. The majority of these schools are scattered through the vast, rural expanse of the Midwest, and these schools operate primarily out of necessity rather than choice. Issues such as student transportation to and from school make the contemporary multigrade school model financially unfeasible for many of these districts. I had contacted over half a dozen of these one-room schools for the purposes of this study, and only this district responded to my request. After a careful and extensive waiting period, I was finally granted access, and I am grateful for the opportunity to come to this school. Although I did not have a particular one-room schoolhouse in mind, this school was special in that it did not *have* to exist. The students at this school could very easily attend one of the other elementary schools down the road, but there was something special about this school. With that in mind, I walked to my car and plopped into the driver's seat. A few minutes later, I passed through the sleepy little village and peered out the window at the one-room schoolhouse one last time.

LEAVING THE ONE-ROOM SCHOOLHOUSE BEHIND

As I slowly drove past the one-room schoolhouse I realized it contained (and facilitated) a special approach to education and an educational life-style that was rapidly fading away. For this study, I was not interested in dis-secting methods or evaluating outcomes. Instead, I wanted to experience something that was distinctive and unique, and that challenged my assump-tions of the aims, purposes, and practices of schooling—that is a "great" curriculum. At this tiny school, I experienced a milieu of controlled chaos, political intrigue, and a unique family-like culture that seemed to permeate every aspect of the school. That is what made it great. These characteristics exist to some degree in all public schools, but what differentiates this little schoolhouse from the typical American school is that these features situate it at the heart of this tiny community. The school is as much the community as the village itself. For all intents and purposes, the school serves as the crucible through which the civic discourse and disposition of the commu-nity is smelted, forged, and refined. Here, apart from the teaching of the "official" curriculum, I recognized a commitment to introducing students to a life of democratic engagement and service. I wondered about the members of the community who attended the meeting in March, and more important, about those people who did not. Do the members of that community understand that teaching first, second, and third grades in one room is nothing like the experience of teaching a single grade in a single room? The managing of the curriculum and dealing with children at different developmental stages is a challenge in and of itself, but when those challenges are enlarged through a combination of a one-room learning environment, financial difficulties, and the pressures of politics—it is an almost impossible situation. More important, I wondered if they understood the feelings of family and community that made this school a distinctive learning environment. Here, the teacher and paraprofessionals, along with the volunteers who assist them, continue to work in maintaining a school that appears to be both unique and effective. Apart from serving as an icon of American education, the school struggles with maintaining its own pedagogical orientation while keeping with the demands of a state-mandated curriculum. It is a school that possesses a group of people who are concerned with social and civic development as much as academic achievement, and yet in light of all this, it is a school which stands at the brink of extinction.

As I drove down the winding road that led out of the valley, I thought a lot about this little one-room school and the obscure legacy I was leaving behind. Did this school employ a "great" curriculum? Yes. I believe so, if simply because beneath the academic experiences of schooling in this small town were infused with a concern to democratically address the tensions rising from the interposition of public and private concerns in social life. This caused me to think about schooling in terms of the social relationships that we in education (as parents, teachers and administrators) often take for granted. The curriculum of the one-room schoolhouse has, at its heart, a concern for the development of community. The emphasis on care and respect exhibited by the volunteers, teachers, *and* students contributes directly to the establishment of civic compassion and engagement. At this school, the academic development of the students is complemented by a desire for communal solidarity and responsibility. Ironically, the curriculum of this one-room schoolhouse speaks to communal solidarity, while at the same time the schoolhouse represents the greatest source of discontent in the village.

The circumstances of the school, its finances, and the complicated relationship with the community that it serves reinforces my understanding that education is always at the intersection of political action—whether that is through the political wrangling of elected officials or the negotiations of associated living between teachers and pupils. As the teachers and students in the school engage in their endeavors to learn and promote compassion and solidarity, the reality of villagers campaigning against the school, the apathy of parents in terms of their voting responsibilities, and the difficulties in managing the costs of this extraordinary educational experience, all endanger the future of the one-room schoolhouse.

What is gained if the village closes the school? For starters, the students will be exposed to more students and teachers, which will result in more opportunities to develop social relationships. The opportunity for them to use updated materials and technology while learning will likely increase, and they may be offered more resources in terms of tutoring, special education care, and economic support. However, at the same time, the students will leave their village to go to school at a contemporary multigrade school down the road. They will spend 1 year with a teacher instead of three consecutive years, and chances are members of their community will spend less time serving as volunteers in their school. More important, they will experience a paradigm-shift in terms of how they experience education, as the curriculum of this one-room schoolhouse delivers, to a greater degree than larger, multigrade schools, a contextualized school experience that arises from specialized attempts to meet the students' academic and social needs.

And yet, it is the debate as to what the needs of the community are that threatens the one-room schoolhouse. How can the citizens of the village reconcile the fiscal needs of the village and the existence of this truly distinct educational experience? Will the democratic process that seems to feature so prominently in the lives of the members of the community preserve this great curriculum or eliminate it? Although this little school emerged from the ravages of the revolutionary war, its greatest challenge will be found in the political struggles that will either allow it to survive as a contemporary institution with a living-history, or as an expired relic of a forgotten past.

RESPONSE BY TOM POETTER

I was thrilled that Kevin wanted to take on the study of a one-room schoolhouse. In terms of access, we did not know in the beginning that it would be so hard to gain it. The main issue is the rapid deterioration for support that many of the remaining one-room schoolhouses are feeling so poignantly early in the 21st century. They are nearly extinct now, and I fear that they may be completely extinct by the time the next decade rolls around. The school Kevin studied is distinctly threatened by the economy today and the problem of scale that the one-room schoolhouse poses to the public. Perhaps to be studied, even when calling something "great," constitutes too big a risk for so many in such threatening situations at this time. We therefore extend great gratitude to the Croydon Village School for allowing

Kevin to interact with them, for allowing us to write about them here, and for allowing us to call what they do "great" (Akpan, 2009).

I had known about the incredible power of the one-room schoolhouse concept and practice for a longtime, because my mother attended one in rural Kansas as a child and still speaks reverently and passionately about it, and because I had read about it in iconic books by Stuart (1998) and Jacobs (1997), and as a result of interacting over the years with one of the great proponents of the valuable things that can happen educationally in a one-room schoolhouse, John Goodlad (2004) has written extensively about the one-room schoolhouse, with the power of someone who claims that a long, distinguished career as a teacher, scholar, and voice for public schooling and democracy began with his experiences of teaching in a one-room schoolhouse in Canada. For me, the one-room schoolhouse has always posed the most astounding set of possibilities, because it is small enough for the teacher to honor the developing hearts and minds of each child, while using the presence of students across an age spectrum to develop a working, living community of learners that can act like a microcosm of our social and political democracy.

Of course, the one-room schoolhouse, as the common school made its way across the frontier, could be a violent and threatening place, too, not one conducive to much learning, especially if the schoolmaster or schoolmarm happened to dislike children or the job altogether. There are plenty of stories of early school life in this country—especially when the one-room school-house served a significant portion of our population in rural areas—that would make your toes curl or blood boil, and maybe both all at the same time. But there also exists a certain practical romanticism that comes with the ideal and practices of the one-room schoolhouse that capture notions of "great" and that should be highlighted as they are in Kevin's chapter and here.

For example, the notion of setting up a school in a nongraded manner, not in the sense that formal grades are not given to students (though that might be up for grabs as well in terms of best practice), but in the sense of not dividing students up to receive a school program merely in terms of experiences with age peers only, does have significant appeal and merit, both in terms of helping all students reach significant academic ends as well as social ends.

In terms of the academic ends, nongraded settings in which students learn together in multi-aged groupings often provide the kind of rich cross-age experiences in which older students support the younger and vice versa. Of course, many teachers know that the best way to learn something is to teach it. Learning for older students is often reinforced when supporting the learning of early concepts by younger students. And younger students bring fresh ideas to the table, and often influence the thinking of older students simply by interacting with them around intellectual material.

And in terms of the social ends, a sense of community develops, almost always in the most positive of ways, when students across ages interact with regard to ideas and on significant projects that build a sense of belonging, support, and mutual benefit for all involved. Children have an incredible capacity to honor each other and their gifts when they have a chance to work together on significant projects. And they have the chance to build experiences of working through conflict, interacting with adults and peers to make decisions of import, failing, taking risks, and making a real difference in people's lives on a daily basis based on what they decide to do or not to do. This all contributes to the figurative heartbeat of a person participating in democratic life.

There is no doubt that aspects of progressive education embody the structure and lived experience of the one-room school house, and the remaining progressive schools of a larger scale such as Central Academy Nongraded in Middletown, Ohio, as chronicled in this book. The inspiration that both give lies in the fact that engaging students individually and providing the opportunity for students to build a social life together on purpose are possible in both the small and larger scales. It can be done in schools, and it does not take the isolation and romance of a one-room schoolhouse to do it. The fact remains that the power of the one-room schoolhouse lives on in our culture and in our practice of public education, not only in our collective memories of bygone days spent learning in one-room schools, but also in real one-room schools that live on, as well as in the best progressive schools of the day that work hard to embody the commitments to individual and group education and that help society fulfill the moral purpose of preparing students to function and thrive in the political and social democracies of this great land.

A FINAL WORD BY KEVIN SMITH

I am grateful to Tom for this opportunity to explore the curriculum of a one-room schoolhouse in a contemporary setting, and I agree with his assertion that the power of the one-room school house lives on. For some, the concept of the one-room schoolhouse is relegated to the past. The buildings exist as museums, meeting places for historical societies, or as derelict structures on the outskirts of town. However, for many, the one-room schoolhouse continues to represent the essence of American education. It exists in its iconography. Caricatures of little red buildings with tiny bell towers adorn packages for school supplies. They are found on the Parent Teacher Organization stickers that moms and dads wear when volunteering at their child's school, and they are regularly used by state and federal agencies in the educational materials they produce. Simply put, the one-room schoolhouse is an enduring educational legacy, but conceptually it represents so much more.

In the case of the Croydon Village School, this one-room schoolhouse served to foreshadow the current national debate regarding economy, curriculum, and the aims and goals of public education. Although I visited the school over a year ago, the arguments for and against the one-room school then are now being played-out on a much grander scale in federal and state legislatures, as well as local school districts throughout the country. Although other schools at the time were undoubtedly involved in the same struggles, I find it fitting that I was introduced to these debates here, at the one-room schoolhouse. For me, the greatness of this school not only exists in its distinctive curriculum and culture, but also in its powerful representation of the institution of public education in America. This institution not only creates the possibility of democracy, it is the only institution that can create and maintain democracy as a social reality.

REFERENCES

Akpan, J. (2009). *Zip Codes: 03733—Croydon, NH*. Retrieved from http://www.vnews.com/zipcodes/03733-croydon.html

Barker, B. (1986). One room schools of Nebraska, Montana, South Dakota, California, and Wyoming. Research in Rural Education, 3(3), 127–130.

Clandinin, D., & Connelly, F. (1988). *Teachers as curriculum planners: Narratives of experience*. New York, NY: Teachers College Press.

Dewey, J. (1916). *Democracy and education: An introduction to the philosophy of education*. New York, NY: The Free Press.

Freire, P. (2006). *Pedagogy of the oppressed*. New York, NY: Continuum.

Goodlad, J. (2004). *Romances with schools: A life of education*. New York, NY: McGraw-Hill.

Jacobs, J. (1997). *A Schoolteacher in Old Alaska: The Story of Hannah Breece*. New York: Vintage Books.

Jackson, P. (1968). *Life in classrooms*. New York, NY: Teachers College Press.

Kaestle, C. (1983). *Pillars of the Republic: Common schools and American Society, 1780–1860*. New York, NY: Macmillan.

Krueger, M., Evans, A., Korsmo, J., Stanley, J., & Wilder, J. (2005). *A youth work inquiry. Qualitative inquiry* (Vol. 11 #3, 2005, pp. 369–389). Thousand Oaks, CA: Sage.

Marsh, C., & Willis, G. (2007). *Curriculum: Alternative approaches, ongoing issues* (4th ed.). Upper Saddle River, NJ: Pearson Education.

Pinar, W. (1995). *Understanding curriculum: An introduction to the study of historical and contemporary curriculum discourses*. New York, NY: Peter Lang.

Stuart, J. (1998). *The thread that runs so true: A mountain school teacher tells his story*. New York, NY: Simon & Schuster.

Westbrook, R. (1992). *John Dewey and American democracy*. New York, NY: Cornell University Press.

CHAPTER 2

LITTLE LEAGUE INTERNATIONAL: GROWING UP IN LITTLE LEAGUE

Thomas S. Poetter

AN EARLY START

I suppose that like a lot of other children born at the end of the baby boom in the early 1960s, we spent most of our waking hours—especially in the spring, summer, and fall—outdoors. I know that my parents expected me to be outside playing and not under foot indoors, at least until suppertime, throughout most of my childhood, from age 4 or so until early adolescence. I never minded it, that is just how it was. I filled my days with other neighborhood kids and siblings bike riding and playing sports such as basketball, football, and baseball, and active games of all sorts on vacant lots and in the street (kick the can, hide and seek, etc.). Such were the spoils of growing up in an era when my small, Midwestern town's neighborhood was never thought of as anything but "safe," and the directive by parents to "be home by dark" was meant literally, even in the summer months when the evening seemed to last

10 Great Curricula: Lived Conversations of Progressive, Democratic Curricula in School and Society, pp. 29–50

interminably. It might be nearly 9 pm before I ran into the house just under the summer bedtime curfew. Pure heaven.

It was during those hours spent playing mostly ball sports outdoors that my neighborhood friends, both boys and girls, honed the skills that would make us competitive athletes later in interscholastic, and, in some cases, intercollegiate athletics. My love for playing baseball outdoors led to my first organized athletic experience in Little League in 1971. I was drafted to play as an 8-year-old boy on the Goodyear team representing the local Goodyear Tire Store. The league was considered "minor league" for boys at age 8–9, one step below the "major league" for boys who were at age 10–12. Back then, there were no coach pitch (or machine pitch) minors or t-ball teams organized by our local Little League for children younger than 8. You had to be 8 to play organized baseball, no exceptions.

I remember attending the "tryout" (now usually called an "evaluation" since everyone, in most Little Leagues internationally, makes a team) as an 8-year old, catching grounders and pop flies off a coach's fungo bat and swinging at a few practice pitches at the high school field, then winding up magically on the Goodyear team a short time later for the spring/summer season. Like most of the other teams named after local businesses or community organizations, the Goodyear team's name as it was spoken among participants took a pejorative twist and was usually referred to as "Badyear." And this was not too far off the mark descriptively for the 2 years I played on my first team, since we did not have a very good season either year. In fact, we were pretty bad, so the name stuck. Other teams took on mythically pejorative names, too: St. Marys Hardware was "Hard Underwear" and American Budget & Loan Company was "American Birdsh_t." Hard Underwear was a perennial cellar dweller; American Birdsh_t, perhaps not so ironically after all, usually ran away with the league championship.

In fact, I pitched in one of my first games against American Budget as an 8-year-old boy. I desperately wanted to be a great pitcher, like the 70s gods of pitching Tom Seaver or Bob Gibson in the real major leagues, so I practiced for hours in our driveway throwing rubber balls at our back stoop, treating the stairs as my catcher and working on my control and velocity. All of this practice was great for developing fielding skills, too, since the pitched ball had to be caught on its way back, and it did not always bounce true! Back then in our local Little League minors division, I guess in order to produce more opportunities for players to hit the ball than simply to take a walk, it took six balls instead of four to "earn" a base on balls. Well, it did not matter how many balls it took, because I walked plenty of batters that night as the pitcher of record against American Budget! And most of the pitches I threw for strikes were struck for solid hits that night, too. It was a bloodbath, and we lost big. I doubt that I lasted an inning or two after all the damage was done. And all during it, I stormed around the mound and infield, swore (recall the antics of tiny shortstop Tanner Boyle in the infamous movie *Bad News Bears*), kicked the dirt, and yelled at my teammates. This happened to be one of the games my dad attended that season, probably because he knew how badly I wanted to pitch and that I would pitch that night.

My father was a community leader, a protestant minister in a mainline denomination. He had an athletic career through high school and college, and followed games and sports on tv as an adult. He was probably very proud that I wanted to play baseball and that I was athletic and showed potential as a player. He was relatively soft-spoken, as a father and as a pastor; he was intense, yet mild-mannered. However, he did not like my antics that night and on the ride home in the car with me (he tossed my bike in the trunk so we could have some time together), after I had been warned after the game by my coach about my unsportsmanlike behavior and that it would not be tolerated in further games, dad gave me a choice, intensely expressed just short of an angry tone that might have caused me to fear him if he had taken it up one more notch. He was very clear: I could either pitch and support my teammates and blame myself for the bad things that happened during the game without erupting into the antics I displayed during that night's game, *or* I could stop playing organized baseball. No third chances. It was an either/or, and had to do with personal character and playing team sports. I only got one more chance. If he saw me pull a stunt like that again, I was finished with organized baseball. I knew that he meant it, and I changed my tune. I am not saying I was a choirboy through my playing days, because I was still hot-tempered and fiery (I found out later that we were very much alike in this regard, no doubt part of the reason for his exceptional understanding that night) in games and practices, but I never got thrown out of a game or stomped around and swore out loud or blamed my teammates for poor play. This lesson has served me well, for the most part, my entire life, so far.

As far as I knew, Little League had been around my hometown for a while. My brother, 8 years older, had played Little League, too, for Union Building and Loan in the minors and for the Home Bank Yankees in the majors. I do not have any pictures of him in those uniforms, which he wore over forty years ago. But the image of him in them, of the colors and the embroidered-on team names, are indelibly stamped in my memory, because at the time and even now I remember how proud he was to wear his Little League baseball uniform shirts around the house before and after games. And I was, too, when it came my time to play for the Goodyear team. I do not remember much about watching him play, probably because my parents hardly ever went to his games and took me along, and later they hardly ever came to my games. It is just not something parents always did back then, load up in the car and go to the field for every game, like we do now. I usually rode my bike to the games, dad was working late into most evenings, and my mom stayed home with my sisters. We only had one car. My brother was busy with his friends and activities. Every once in a while the family would show up, but not often. Back then, it truly was a kids' game, and we relished it.

But adults were involved in Little League, and always have been from the beginning, of course, as managers and coaches, and no doubt behind the scenes—as I know so well now as a Little League volunteer manager and member of the board of directors and officer in my sons' local Little League. But the feeling back then in the 1970s, as I hope it still is now to the greatest of degrees, was that it was a kids' game played under safe, real conditions, shepherded by adults who managed and umpired, but run by children who actually played the game. This is the trick to creating opportunities for children to play a sport as great as baseball/softball without being bullied or left out of sandlot games, as they so often did before Carl Stotz (1992) created the first Little League in Williamsport, Pennsylvania, in 1938: provide safe, sound instruction in the game; provide real game experiences for competition and enjoyment; and provide opportunities for character growth for youth as well as control of the game by youth, not adults.

CARL STOTZ, THE FOUNDER'S LEGACY

You could say that Carl Stotz, founder of Little League Baseball, went down swinging when he lost control of Little League in 1956, after spending the better part of 18 years creating and nurturing the fledgling organization, literally from coast-to-coast and beyond. I am terribly conflicted about this aspect of the Little League story, the most recognized and most widely participated in youth sports organization in the world, with more than 2.6 million players participating worldwide today in baseball and softball, all grown up from the beginning of it all in Williamsport. Stotz' legacy *is* the corporate, nonprofit giant that Little League has become, though he fought to keep this from happening when corporate interests moved quickly to commandeer the game away from him in the 1950s. He worried that the interests of big business would be placed ahead of the children's interests, that expansion would happen in a haphazard way and without care, and those tensions still exist today, considering the huge influence of television and the high stakes associated with corporate advertisers and equipment vendors vying for the attention and dollars that come from the consumption of their products through youth participation in sports. When he was driven out of his position with Little League in 1956, he settled out of court with Little League and worked the rest of his life to support the original Little League in Williamsport, but not on the main stage as it became brighter and brighter. Stotz died in 1992 before any final or happy reconciliation occurred between him and the Little League of today ("Carl Stotz," 2011).

But, the progressive and democratic roots of the original Little League movement that still exists in locales today, despite the over-corporatization of the enterprise in the past several decades, still make Little League a desirable entity that allows for local, community control, and wide participation. Over the years that Stotz helped the concept of organized youth baseball grow into a living reality in so many communities across the nation and the world, he built the organization with others so that it would be run democratically in local communities, provide flexibility for local context and nuance in decision making, and provide competitive baseball experiences while also focusing on personal development of the participants.

It all goes back to a promise that Stotz made to his young elementary school-aged nephews in 1938, that he would help them create teams in Williamsport with other youth in order to play an organized season of real baseball games. At that time, youth baseball teams existed in other places, but not as leagues of teams playing each other competitively in one community in any organized way. Over the course of that first summer, after experimenting through several informal games, Stotz hit upon the main aspects of the game for children that would form the foundation of the first Little League in Williamsport, PA, in 1939, and for more than 70 years across the globe:

- Make the dimensions of the field smaller so that youth could play the game without strain.
- Form teams that would be relatively "equal" in skill level to make for competitive games during the regular season.
- Create rules for play that would not change from game to game like they did on the sandlot, and rules that would provide for a better experience for youth as opposed to adult players, including the well-known "no lead off" rule.
- Provide quality equipment for play designed to the players' sizes.
- Focus on the overall personal character development of youth, not just the development of baseball skills (Stotz, 1992).

Stotz knew that financing the new league would be difficult, but getting the three original sponsors needed to form the league on the heels of the great depression was more than challenging. After many queries and rejections over that winter, he finally found three businesses to sponsor the original three teams in Williamsport; these sponsors helped defray the costs for player uniforms, equipment, and fieldwork, making it possible for the league to start-up. Today, many Little Leagues worldwide rely on the contributions of local businesses, who often advertise their services/products at local fields and on the backs of team uniforms, to keep costs of participation low for families and to make the leagues run. This tense marriage between business capital and youth baseball resulted in the ultimate loss of control by Stotz in the 1950s, but was a necessary step for the genesis of Little League. The mix of the corporate and the democratic impulses together, in a way, define the tense relations between them in our current society and world. We have to work together to keep them balanced.

Over time, as the Williamsport league grew and Little League baseball grew beyond the city's borders, Little League Boards of Directors developed and worked together to maintain and develop the strongest qualities of Little League participation, that is focusing on participation in the sport, not excellence in the sport, as the key aspect of the league; coaching excellence all along the way by the all-volunteer legion of managers, coaches, and umpires emerging across the country; and developing personal character, as opposed to merely the development of baseball skills among all participants.

All over the Americas and across the oceans, while the baseball world sleeps following the World Series, Little League Boards of Directors gear up each mid-winter for another season in the spring. They themselves are elected to serve, do the work with the direction of elected officers, and make every effort possible to solicit the support and action for children playing the sport from among citizens in the wider community, businesses, and community organizations. They make the best decisions they can given their pledge to abide by Little League's main principles while also taking into account local context and needs. They make decisions in public meetings, usually by consensus or by majority vote. Finances are public and open to viewing by anyone. Transparency is critical and a hallmark of the work. Everyone who participates is insured against injury. At least, at the beginning, everyone has an equal chance to make it to the world series. We all have Carl Stotz to thank for all of that.

MAKING THE MAJORS

When I turned 10, I aspired to be drafted by a majors team and to move on from the minors and the Goodyear club. Some 10s stayed behind and played minors for another season, or even two if need be. But I felt I was ready to play up, and went to the spring tryouts in 1973 with every intention of making a majors team. The Rotary Club Cubs, in fact, drafted me and I played in every game for the Cubs as a 10-year old, though not in nearly every inning of every game like I did in the minors. I had to learn that year to be patient, to take my turn, and to make the most of my opportunities among the older players.

But things ramped up during my 11 and 12-year-old seasons, as I grew bigger in size and more confident. I became one of the better players in the division, and ultimately got to pitch and play in a district tournament all-star game win in 1975. I still have the newspaper clippings from it. And my parents and family were there to see the game. We did not make it past the second game in the tournament, though. Back then the tournament was single-elimination, so when we lost our second game in the international tournament our dream of playing in the World Series in Williamsport, which was televised every summer on ABC TV, was extinguished. But I still remember walking from the field to the car with my dad after that tournament win, after pitching well and hitting an over-the-fence home run in the game, with his hand on my shoulder pulling me close in congratulations. No temper tantrums to critique, just a great game. This remains one of my most cherished childhood memories of my dad, since he passed away suddenly the next year. He saw me play well, and not curse during the course of the game. That means a lot to me still, even after more than 35 years.

I learned a lot of lessons over those 3 years playing in the Little League majors division. I not only learned to control my temper, but I learned to get along with and to admire boys I did not know from my public elementary school. I got to play with boys who went to the local Catholic grade school, and they would become lifelong friends as a result of those early connections forged in Little League. I also learned that with practice and coaching, a player could improve immensely even in a short season. No one, no matter where he started or how he was perceived as a ball player, could or should be under-estimated as a player or as a person. Do that as an athlete at your own peril. You can strike out the same player nine straight times. That does not mean he will be a pushover the 10th at-bat.

Bill Tolin proved this to me in the last regular season game of 1975, when I was preparing to pitch in that first all-star game just a week later. I was pitching comfortably into the last inning leading the Pirates 5-3, when Bill came up with the bases loaded and hit my best two strike, two out pitch on a line to the right field fence for a bases clearing, game winning triple for the Pirates over my Cubs. Bill had never even touched a pitch I threw him in 2 years.

I also learned a little about politics, about gender equity, and about families. I learned that some of the more deserving boys, for whatever reasons, would not make the all-star teams. I learned that my coach's son, whom I liked as a person but was a terrible baseball player, would get to play every inning of every game at third base and make a million errors and bat second in the order every game and never get a hit. But he never came out of a game. We won a lot of games despite him. Ultimately, we may not have had a coach without his dad volunteering and taking his payment in the form of his son's playing time at third base. And, I learned that girls can play baseball, too. I already knew this well from playing in the neighborhood, but my local league, while not blazing any trails in terms of gender equity before the law stepped in, quickly picked up the flag and created girls softball teams and allowed girls to play baseball in 1975, immediately after Maria Pepe's (2011) ground-breaking challenge to Little League's all-boy participation rules was decided by the courts. I wish the decision to let girls play Little League baseball would have come sooner; we would have had a much better baseball league if girls had been allowed to play before 1975, and of course, my friends would not have been denied an opportunity that should have been extended to them long before that.

TRANSPLANTED, OUT OF THE ASHES

When my wife and I moved to Oxford, Ohio, in the late 1990s with our two very young sons, I had already decided that I would leave coaching youth sports behind. I had made a decision that I could not devote the time necessary to coaching high school sports, which I had done as part of my teaching career for many years. I knew the commitment it took to be good at it, and I had decided to take another career path into higher education anyway. And, considering the kind of coach I had become—successful, but far too intense and self-absorbed with my own advancement as well as with winning—I figured it would probably be better if my sons had other adult role models as coaches rather than me. They did not need me pushing them or—in terms of my best guess in terms of potential outcome if I coached them in any sport—ruining youth sports for them and their new friends.

This all changed by accident when I signed up my oldest son Mitch for Little League when he was just 6 years old in the year 2000. The new Miami Little League that had just been created in Oxford to serve basically all boys and girls within the boundaries of our local school district agreed to let him play machine pitch minors baseball, a division in which 6–8-year olds play a real game but without hitting live pitching. Instead of young players pitching, a pitching machine lays the ball in the strike zone so each player has an equal chance of striking a "pitched" ball solidly. Pitching would come later when they entered "kid pitch" minors at 9 years old.

We got a call from Coach Matson about Mitch being assigned to the Padres machine pitch minors team in Miami Little League. At Mitch's first practice, Coach Matson—a young man in his late 20s—showed up with his own three boys and the Little League equipment bag to run practice.

I learned that one of the boys was his natural son, and the other two were his stepsons. They were not very good baseball players, but neither was anyone else on the team at that age, really. But they all seemed to have fun, and I watched and waited on the sidelines, except during the second meeting when I agreed to throw batting practice when Coach Matson asked me to help out. What could be the harm? I always have been a passable batting practice pitcher.

But at the third practice, on a cold, wet evening in early April, Coach Matson showed up, got out of the car, walked slowly toward me, and handed me the baseball equipment bag. I reached out reluctantly to accept it when he said, tears streaming down his face, "I'm sorry, but I'm moving to New Mexico tomorrow. My boys and I have to go. Our family is breaking up, and I lost my job, and we have no other choice. You're the only person I've met so far who can coach the team. I'm so sorry." He handed me the bag, got in his car, and drove away. None of us ever saw him or his boys again.

He left me there, literally, holding the bag. I didn't quite know how to turn around to face the rest of the team and parents already assembled. Certainly, several of them were no doubt relieved that they were not handed the bag. Of course, I knew what to do. But I didn't really want to do it; after all, I'd told myself that I wouldn't! Sometimes, though, life puts you in circumstances that perhaps are inevitable, maybe serendipitous. At least for that night, I did not see much choice but to run practice. One of the problems that the team would face all season was the loss of those three boys who drove off with their dad in the rain. We made do the best we could with only 10 players. So I ran practice that night, the boys started calling me "Coach," and Mitch was thrilled. No turning back. I became the coach and saw that team through its season, and through the first season of Miami Little League's existence.

That first Padres team was terrible, but I loved those boys and their parents. We got killed most games, but wound up winning two very close and exciting games. And I had the coaching bug again. I tried to keep my distance from the rest of the league leaders, knowing full well that if I let on too much that I knew what I was doing that I would be recruited to run for the board of directors. That did not work, since my team the following year, by the luck of the draw in the designation of players, was loaded with talented boys, and we won nearly every game in the machine pitch division. As I learned more about what was at stake and what needed to be done, I decided to run for the board in 2003. Since then, I have been elected to serve as president, to manage all-star teams, and to serve in almost every capacity possible in Little League baseball/softball on a local and district level. Over time, I learned about the many things that Miami Little League had overcome, and the immense challenges that it would continue to face.

OVERCOMING LONG ODDS TO DO SOMETHING
COMMUNITY-ORIENTED

What I found out about Miami Little League was that it overcame long odds to form. Like-minded, yet very different people created the new league out of several relatively small, area youth baseball organizations. For many of them, they had been similarly tied to small town commitments in the area over the years, working to develop one or two youth teams in an age group and then to piece together the needed equipment, field space, and schedule to have meaningful youth games for their own geographically-bound teams. There were at least five small organizations serving the clientele that became Miami Little League today. It was simply becoming more difficult to fund the small leagues, requiring more and more sweat equity and money from leaders and parents to make things work on a small scale. Throughout the 1990s, the various area youth baseball/softball organizations realized that they needed to consolidate, and that they needed to develop a stronger organization for girls' softball. After all, the players in these different leagues all went to the same schools ultimately, as classmates and teammates in middle and high school. Change needed to happen, and everyone knew it, but what to do?

Little League offered the best option because it has rules for organizing a Board of Directors; for making decisions democratically; for attending to children and their overall development first; for developing teams fairly; for including girls; for taking care of money in open ways; and for running tournament teams for all-stars. Little League won out over other youth baseball/softball programs that were considered and became the new governance/organizational framework for Miami Little League. One thing in particular needs to be clarified for the reader in terms of "other" baseball/softball programs. There is a proliferation of them right now, competing with Little League for a share of the youth market in terms of participation. The problem is that "little league" tends to get used generically, so that when the average citizen talks about youth baseball or softball he or she often refers to it as "little league" when it may or may not actually be a Little League sanctioned organization undertaking the sport.

The distinction lies primarily in the ways that Little League adheres to fundamental principles, many of them outlined here, as critical points of commitment and action. Just because an activity involves youth does not mean that it is "Little League." This is no doubt one of the pitfalls of having a brand that becomes identified with a whole genre of things/phenomena. I suppose it is not a completely negative problem to have, like every soft drink in the South being called "Coke" or every tissue being used or bought being called "Kleenex." But distinctions are important and do hold to identify and place value on certain approaches and procedures.

In the case of our Miami Little League forming in 2000, it had growing pains to undergo. One of the main things to overcome was the leftover set of feelings, both negative and positive, framing individuals' commitments to past organizations and their different values, their different ways of doing things, their different experiences and traditions. The leadership teams of the youth baseball organizations being left behind formed the new Miami Little League Board of Directors, and they brought their own experiences and successes/failures to the new table. And clashes occurred, some that continue to this day. For instance, instead of individual coaches volunteering to manage teams then personally recruiting the best players to play on their teams, with the force of personality and prestige associated with who is on the team and the recruited players' skill level and the coaches' perceived talents, ostensibly creating the most excellent, most competitive team possible as far as the available talent will take you on your own, everyone drafts from the same pool of players so the teams are as even and as competitive as possible in Little League. This structurally places teaching and playing the game for fun ahead of competitiveness and winning. But this set of core Little League values and procedures had a lot of work to do to overcome the ways that were set in the stone of experience for many of the early participants in the league.

THE GREAT MIGRATION

The truth is that after one or two years of playing Little League, even with the prospect of sons and daughters getting to play in one of the most competitive district all star tournaments in the state of Ohio (and in retrospect, maybe even because of that high level of district level competitiveness and the growing acknowledgement that we could not win as a league in our district's tournament no matter how good our players were), significant numbers of talented coaches and players have left our league each year to find "more competitive" teams to play on. To me, this type of decision—while defensible as an individual one made in a "free" country—hurts the community and ultimately shortchanges everyone involved and not involved.

In fact, the irony associated with this most complex of issues of deciding "where to play" continues to plague Little League on a larger scale, despite the high skill level of play displayed on television during the robust World Series games in August: some parents of talented players perceive Little League to be beneath them in terms of competitiveness and skill level, so they opt for starting up or playing for more "select" travel teams and leagues that they think allow for the best chance for skill development and competitive experience. The reality is that while Little League remains the largest youth sports organization in the world with the most participants

(2.6 million players as of this writing) and its numbers are actually rising somewhat after a dip of participation in the early 2000s (Little League Baseball and Softball Online, 2006; McKibben, 2004), many of its best players are leaving to find other playing options.

This has a direct impact on our own Miami Little League. Certain parents have taken their own children out, had them try out for area travel teams, and then left our league to play somewhere else. This is palatable, to a certain degree. We really hate to lose those players, whether they are really as good as they think they are or not, because they are committed to baseball/softball and we would like to have them participate with us. Some parents have said to me, "Let them go, it just opens up more opportunities for my kid in Little League to make an all-star team." Well put, and well taken.

But now, exponentially threatening and damaging actions are taking place including parents taking their sons and daughters out of Little League and forming their own traveling teams and taking other Miami Little League players with them! Now it is not just the occasional player here and there defecting to find a supposedly better "situation," but it is whole groups of players 12 or 15 at a time leaving, usually players and parents with the most skill and commitment. This action decimates an age division in a local Little League.

The founders of these new opportunities claim to offer a more competitive experience for players. That may or may not be the case in certain circumstances. Certainly, I concede, that grouping all the best players together in one place makes for a more competitive and high level of play. But is that what youth sports are all about? There are costs to this approach, some hidden, and some not so much. Actual monetary costs for playing on a "select" or "travel" team often exceed the cost of playing Little League by 10 times or more (our fees to play a Miami Little League season today are $75 per player; many travel teams charge well over $1000 for equipment, uniforms, tournament fees, travel, etc. per player, per season). Boys and girls 12 years and under often play more than 50 games a season on these teams. Fifty games are way too many to play, especially for young bodies with fragile throwing arms. The statistics for injury bear this out (Goodwin, 2010).

And the fact of the matter is that so many players, with well-meaning parents and a love for the game at the beginning, at least, often get burned out playing that much and that long. The sport loses its fun, and becomes a job. This is no way to experience youth sports, at least in my opinion. And sometimes, players leave Little League, do not find that the grass is greener in another location (they do not get to play very much on their new team, for example, or the coaching is no better, or even the level of competition is comparable to what they left behind and not superior, as they had hoped), and drop baseball all together instead of coming back to Little League, for instance, I suppose too prideful or hurt to go on with the sport. That is really sad, at 10 years old?

What's lost? For the families that leave, I believe that they lose a sense of their place as important members of a wider community that depends on everyone to make endeavors like offering a quality opportunity for youth sports participation and competition possible for all. If everyone leaves and forms their own team, we are right back to the drawing board, unable to find the time or the money to keep it going and depriving those who cannot afford it, or who do not aspire to play 50 games in a summer, or who just do not have the skill level to play on a "select" team from the best opportunity for them to grow in the sport and as human beings, that is, by playing with all of the rest of the strong and not so strong players in their community. Little League loses its best players, the chance to offer everyone the highest quality of games, to help each child reach higher and lower to grow together, and to play for a community in games that mean something. It is not necessarily about making it to Williamsport with the region's best 12-year-old majors team, though that would be nice. It is knowing that Little League Baseball/Softball has the best program around if everyone participates in it, that all of the players, the weak and strong, help each other grow not just in baseball/softball skills, but in terms of human skills, in human experience. That is why many of us send our children to public schools, there is something very deep and educational about the growth that occurs when children flower in the diversity of the wider community. The wider community suffers when parochial interests trump the public good.

People have sometimes asked me over the years why I never took my boys out of Little League to find supposedly "better, more competitive" opportunities elsewhere. Anyone that knows us knows that my sons easily could have made travel teams in the region. My answer is very simple: baseball is a game of skill; it can be learned well by playing anywhere, with/against anyone; the best place to play it is at home for your own community or school; it costs a lot less, in both money and time, to do what is right; I get to be more involved (though I was reluctant at first!); my kids have more fun and get to play with all of their friends, not just a select few of them; and if they are good enough, they make an all star team and get a whole extra season, if you will, to play the game and hone their skills. And besides, if I want to, I can start a team and play on the days when Little League is not playing (which I have actually done in the past).

Why would I make a choice as detrimental as leaving Little League all together when I could form another team that plays concurrently in a more competitive situation, and without breaking the bank? That way, everyone wins, without doing the damage of playing 50 games (my limit is 30 games total in a season). After all, my sons are as ready as the next player in terms of skill and experience to compete for playing time in high school as a result. Besides, look at all the friends we have made and the experiences we have had. I would challenge anyone out there who has left Little League to counter with similarly strong stories of growth, experience, goodwill, and community by being involved with some other youth baseball organization. I believe that would be very hard to do. But I am willing to listen. However, if you dared to counter, you would have to listen first to the rich stories of friendship and experience that my sons would tell about playing in Miami Little League.

MATURING GROWTH

As of this writing, Miami Little League surpassed its goal of signing up 400 local children to play in all of our divisions, from ages 4–18, for another season. We set this mark each year, and it gets tougher and tougher to reach it and surpass each year. Besides the tendency for players and teams to migrate from us, there also exist several other very pertinent threats to growth as well, and they have an impact on what we do and how we do it. One is that having a bad experience with baseball or softball causes many children to leave the sport after just sampling it. The main factors are the level of coaching, and competitive balance.

So, a volunteer parent-coach may be knowledgeable about the sport, but not skillful in working with children. Or, a coach may be great with kids, and not know much about the sport. Of course, if it is one or the other, we would prefer that the coach be great with kids! But the key ingredients are coach education and recruitment, making sure that the coaches and managers who do come forward as volunteers know that their work matters, can be improved, and that people are able and willing to help them. More often than not, if a player has fun playing Little League and improves throughout the season, he or she will return the next season. A lot of this depends on the qualities of the coaching volunteers.

Also, providing competitive balance in each division is crucial. A player might improve and be trusting of and learn a lot from the coaches, but if each game is a bloodbath, either in terms of winning or losing, then the experience is not nearly as strong as it is when most games and most teams are as evenly matched in terms of skill level and experience as possible. This means that individual managers and the league itself have to work hard to make sure that each team is balanced and can compete. If not, then the possibility always exists that a number of players will have a terrible experience.

This is especially the case today since so many players enter t-ball or machine pitch divisions not having learned to catch and throw or bat a ball at home, in the neighborhood, or at school before coming to us. It is a fact that fewer players start playing organized baseball/softball with a set of skills today. What they get and what they develop are often due in large part or all together to what they get from their Little League experience. Of course, this is sad, but it is true. Yes, kids should be playing more outdoors and they should be playing more baseball/softball. But they are not playing baseball/softball outdoors as much, necessarily, especially because parents today do not let their kids run the neighborhood or the entire town without supervision before kindergarten, like I did.

And with the rise of faster, supposedly more engaging games/sports in our culture, such as lacrosse, soccer, basketball, and football, other activities compete with baseball/softball in the spring and summer like they never did before (not just swimming and fishing compete anymore!). Participation in these sports is on the rise among a number of demographic groups and on the whole. Baseball/softball has to compete with them by offering a good experience, and making the game fun. If we do not do better each season, these sports and other pastimes of the indoor variety (video games!) could make playing baseball/softball a rarity, as opposed to an important institution and rite of passage, if you will, for both girls and boys in our communities.

For me, the bottom line in sticking with Little League Baseball/Softball has to do with community, and with my value choices as a parent. In terms of community, Little League offers the safest, most structured experience for youth players, and it engages everyone who chooses to participate across the community, always without regard for where you live, or what you do for a living, or how you worship or not, or what gender, sexual orientation, ethnicity, or race you are, or what school you go to. These differences while rich ones and not to be ignored, do not dominate the experience. Instead, because they exist when everyone plays together, they create a rich, more diverse situation, a less homogeneous one, and that is without even mentioning skill level in the sport. These types of experiences with others, on the whole, set the stage for child and family growth. I want my child learning how people live and learn from all walks of life, not just from people they are surrounded with daily because of our station (or not) in life. And the challenge of helping someone to learn to catch and throw is important, not just finding people to play with who can.

One of my best friends in Little League, who has been there from Miami Little League's beginning in 2000, believes that Miami Little League has actually brought people who would be leading completely separate lives in small enclaves in our school district closer together. He even credits Little League with building the bridges for sharing information about the richness of our communities and schools to the point that enough support was generated to pass a large bond issue in 2008 to build a much needed, long overdue new high school. I am not sure if there is a causal link here, but it stands to reason that the more we work together, the more we share, the more we disagree and come ultimately to agreement, the more we will be willing to trust each other and share our resources, even our children. We need healthy, wholesome, challenging activities for all our children. Little League, though not perfect, makes it happen every year. And we all can be involved to make it better. The door is always open, if we step through and do not walk away.

HOME RUNS?

Not every boy or girl hits a home run in a Little League game. Some kids hit big triples, like Bill Tolin did off my best pitch I was sure that he couldn't hit. Some players strike out a lot and never have much success. There is always a possibility, of succeeding or failing. That is why we try at sports and participate. That is why we take the risk of putting ourselves out there, of playing, of competing. It is fun, and challenging. That is why the successes of my sons, which have been wonderful, are accentuated by the successes of so many players we have worked with who have learned the game and have enjoyed Little League so much that they come back every year to play, even when they do not make the high school team in the spring. I will never for-get, and always cherish, the great successes in real baseball games that boys I coached had when they did not have any success in other sports, and sometimes not in any other parts of their lives at the time. I feel like those successes, the little things, the small victories, are wonderful things that stack up to home runs and wins very, very well.

On the subject of home runs: When Mitch was 12 in 2007, our majors team, the Marlins, had to draft an almost entirely new team, except for his brother Sam, who would be 11. That meant that we had 10 new boys, with no playing experience in the majors. At the end of the first month, we had beaten every other team in our division, and were a shocking 5-0 headed into the last game of the season's first half against the favored Dodgers. We had not played them yet, and they did not like the fact that we threat-ened them at the top of the standings.

We played very well against them in that sixth game to keep it close, but were still down 5-3 in the last inning when Mitch came up to bat with two outs and a runner on first. I thought out loud from my position in the coaching box at third base, "Just put your bat on it, Mitch. Make them make a play." But the first-pitch, right down the middle, was struck so sharply to left field that when it left Mitch's bat I knew it was out of the park. My neck almost snapped with surprise and joy to track its trajectory. Just once in your life, perhaps, you will have the feeling of slapping your son or daughter on the back while he or she rounds third with a heroic game-tying home run. We went on to win that game on plays it would take too long to recount. And it would be our last win of the season, the other teams catching up to us and bringing us back to reality. But I will never forget that hit, or that game. And to think that I could have walked away from it?

Last summer, Sam's juniors all-star team, made up of boys aging 13–14 from our league, won the Ohio District 9 tournament and made it to the semi-finals of the Ohio state tournament. The game was played on Miami University's field, a real treat for all the boys in the state who had made it that far in the tournament. When Sam came up to bat in the fourth inning of that game, which we would ultimately lose, the heat was finally taking a toll on us and the odds of us making a comeback seemed grim. But Sam lined a first-pitch, lead-off shot to right centerfield that rolled all the way to the wall. I was thinking triple all the way, even with no outs, and so was Sammy. The beauty of him hitting second base in full stride, picking me up with his excited eyes at third base, and me waving my arms frantically for him to come all the way, and then him with head down all the way churning and hook sliding into third? Safe. Timeout. Hugs at third base…

Describe something more beautiful than that?

Play hard. Try your best. Prepare to win *and* to lose. Respect your teammates and coaches. Never take anything for granted. Pick each other up when someone is down. Everyone gets to play. Make friends you would not have made by just sitting around the house or by traveling long distances or paying lots of money. Win, lose, or draw, no matter, shake hands with each other and the opponent. Recite the Little League Pledge: "I trust in God. I love my country and will respect its laws. I will play fair and strive to win but win or lose, I will always do my best." Recite the Little League Parent/Volunteer pledge: "I will teach all children to play fair and do their best. I will positively support all managers, coaches and players. I will respect the decisions of the umpires. I will praise good effort despite the outcome of the game" (Little League Baseball, 2010).

Little League has come a long way since 1939. You should join us. Speaking from experience, it is great.

RESPONSE BY KEVIN TALBERT

Tom's childhood experience playing baseball could have been my own, though I never played Little League. I, too, spent most of my summer days in Fort Wayne, Indiana, on the baseball field, participating in Wildcat Baseball (http://wildcatbaseball.org/). Ironically, our stories are bound geographically, as well. St. Marys, Ohio, is the origination point of the St. Marys River, which ends in Ft. Wayne. The Wildcat baseball season marked my summer from the time I was about 8 years old until I turned 16. Well before my 16th birthday, I knew I would never be a big leaguer.

I suspect that Tom's narrative is broadly familiar, which amplifies its curricular and pedagogical force. In particular, an implicit "pedagogy of youthful innocence" resonates throughout. Little League is the specific iteration of a national narrative in kids' lives. Especially at a time when other major sports leagues did not have the cultural import of Major League Baseball, Little League became a way for little boys to play out big dreams—their own chance to make their own Field(s) of Dreams.

Clichés about the position of baseball as America's national pastime and its mythology in American culture abound and do not need further reiteration here. Such clichés, however, reveal the effects and implications of a public curriculum embodied through shared narrative. For Tom, Little League engenders a projection of (Deweyian) Progressive ethos. In particular, the hope is that young people, through their participation, would come to develop their unique skills as ballplayers, yes, but more importantly would develop "habits of public life" essential to forming viable community (Dewey, 2007).

While such shared narratives may serve a generative democratic function, we must also resist the easy and perhaps all too common tendency to long for idyllic "days gone by" that, frankly, may never have actually existed (a romanticization of the past). Such narratives may at once provide the context for a shared sense of public life, but may also be limiting discourses. The democratic conundrum is what to do when some people do not share the narrative. What do we do with a narrative that, in its own effect, marginalizes and restricts? Democracy necessitates the complexity of having broad and inclusive narratives that do not marginalize, or limit the possibility of ever creating new ones.

Tom's description of the rise of Little League's competitors and its struggle to maintain its vitality within an increasingly competitive ecology has important pedagogical implications, as well. As he details the rise of competing summer baseball leagues (not to mention all of the other sports leagues and camps now competing for young peoples' attention and money), he laments the impact this competition has on the youths' spirit of fun, a true spirit of "play." But the stakes may actually be greater. The competitive forces that impact Little League increasingly govern American life.

We may take what has happened to Little League as a result of competition as a case example of the impact of the corporatization and commodification of public life. Indeed, as I understand the stakes of this commodification, and an implicit thread through Tom's narrative, the stakes of commodification are the subversion of community life, stakes much greater than merely ruining the pleasure of sports for youth. As the hegemony of neoliberal capitalism increasingly imposes on and governs public life, the result is "adultizing" life for youth—that, increasingly, it seems, as we succumb to ever-more competition, to efforts to get ahead, we actually are eliminating childhood/ adolescence altogether (for an explicit advocacy of eliminating adolescence, see Gingrich, 2008).

The story of Little League baseball is expressive of larger challenges faced in forging vigorous public life. Competition is not all it is cracked up to be—and certainly creates significant challenges to the maintenance of authentically engaged democratic communities as people compete against their neighbors for individual gain rather than work with their neighbors for the collective good. Tom's adult experience working to create and eventually preside over the Miami Little League, and his own decision not to allow his boys to withdraw to another league, evinces the necessity to resist projection of neoliberal values into all areas of life.

THE FINAL WORD

Early on, Little League Founder Carl Stotz thought that playing Little League baseball would keep boys off the street and out of trouble in Williamsport, PA, in the summer time, and help communities who adopted Little League with youth delinquency (Stotz, 1992). Early exploratory studies showed this to be true. From the beginning, Stotz and the other leaders of the fledgling experiment thought that the Little League experience, as an experiment, as an enterprise, was at least as much about the development of character in youth and the wholesome use of time and effort, as it was about learning to play baseball. Learning to play was a vehicle for greater ends, those being productive citizenship, wholesome, healthy living, and respect for self, others, adults, and our institutions of public life.

My initial response to this type of focus in the curriculum would be to judge it as naïve, perhaps even misguided. But my life experience has not born this out, to me. Of course, it is hard to say that baseball/softball participation saves people from crime, or delinquency of any type, or actually helps produce these very positive values and experiences for all participants. But Major League Baseball, for instance, in an effort to draw embattled populations of boys and girls into the types of experiences that suburban children routinely get, has put money, time, and expertise into its relatively new Little League Urban Initiative (Little League Online, 2007) in order to take a swat at the problems urban youth and their families face, especially the challenge of presenting typical, sound activities to fill, transform, and enrich spare time. Maybe this is naïve as well. Maybe it is merely a corporate nod to neglected "others." Maybe it is meaningless, in the end. But I do not think Joe Morgan thinks so, national spokesman for the Initiative.

And I love Joe Morgan, a great second baseman for my beloved world champion Reds in the 1970s, edgy spokesman for equity of opportunity in baseball writ large, and activist for youth all over the country. In the end, we need to see that as a society we care enough to provide and that we act on those idealistic commitments. I think Joe Morgan works toward these ends as an agent of change and as a citizen with enormous capital at hand. I hope there is even more success with this program than has been garnered so far, and that others will follow his lead.

What I do know for sure is that as a society we need to support and use every positive attempt possible to provide opportunities for development and growth for all children, with equity, with opportunity, and with hope in mind. If we do not, we doom ourselves to lives that are merely private, to hoarding resources meant for all, to allowing corporatization and "big" to win out over the best efforts possible at the local level, thereby limiting opportunities that would not get provided without the ingredients of human talent and time. Not a "1000 points of light," but more. Instead, like-minded, generous people making sure that those institutions get the support they need to do the work that is possible, and to adjust and hone it as it takes shape, as a cultural reality in communities, not as a monolith. Not as agents of the state, not as corporate henchmen. But as human agents, agents of goodwill, paying whatever they have or think that is good forward to the betterment of the public good, for community's sake, for children and their families.

I wonder what might have happened if Carl Stotz's dream of providing opportunities for girls to play, which he claims to have had early on, had become an early reality instead of shelved because of the enormity of the work at hand, as too time consuming to take on while founding the fledgling roots of Little League for boys (Stotz, 1992). Perhaps, the public would view Little League differently now, as a beacon of progressivism and change by more than half the population. Perhaps, the negative feelings and the ill will and the mistake of banning girls would sting less 30 years later. No institution is perfect, of course, and certainly Little League has made its share of mistakes, including its ill-fated attempt to ban international teams during the height of their championship runs over American teams in 1975. But one thing it got right in the wake was developing Little League Softball for girls and allowing girls to play baseball in all divisions in 1975. The progress of girls in the sport has been exceptional, and many lives changed for the good because change came. Out of conflict and mistake sometimes come hope and success.

Over the years, Little League has also spawned the negative image of the terrible parent. The parent who screams at umpires and at managers and at their own and other children (which Stotz says in his memoir was a problem from the first games ever played in Williamsport in the 1930s!), or pushes managers to play her child at a certain position, or criticizes volunteers and never volunteers himself all contribute to the negative image that Little League has helped to spawn. Combating this in the face of public pressure and what it knows to be the right place of parents in the sport (on the sidelines, supportive, allowing the children to play their own game) is a constant battle.

In addition, not one person who believes in the enterprise is immune to the fact that thousands of children each year have a miserable experience playing organized baseball or softball for Little League programs. You do not have to go far to find examples of this in the media. One of our family's "favorites" is the comic riff on his negative Little League experiences as told by comedian Brian Regan ("Lousy in Little League" at itunes). The lesson is that the mix of baseball and character development does not work for every participant. In fact, a bad dosage early on can create a gag reflex for baseball/softball that really is damaging. I am torn about this, about what to do. Adults cannot just treat this as collateral damage. It must be addressed, though in the long run it may be something that adults themselves cannot do anything about. After all, it is a kids' game.

Or is it? As I reflect on my body of work in Little League, my nearly life-long participation in its curriculum, I think about how much things have changed since I was a little boy in the 1970s, living an idyllic childhood outdoors, learning and playing freely in my neighborhood. It is a fact that I was ready for Little League because I had played so much ball before even going out for an organized team. There was no chance I would not succeed and have fun with and learn so much about myself and how to "be" in certain ways in certain worlds. But the bottom line for me was that the thrill of the game lay at least as much at the foot of the back stoop I threw a rubber ball against and in the vacant lot down the street as it did on the Little League diamond. Adults did not ruin the game for me, which I already loved; truth be told, they enhanced it. And if I felt threatened by adults ruining baseball for me, I simply retreated to my own world of experience and make-believe as a child in the neighborhood. But the threat of adults ruining the game today is real, maybe more so that it was when the first parents began screaming at kids and umpires in Williamsport in the 1930s. Many people lament the loss of childhood and free play for children. School and playground today tend to be so scripted, and filled with adult voices. How do children learn to solve problems and make great strides with new ideas and creating rules and treating each other fairly if they never have a chance to do it on their own? (Schwarz, 2011) I think everyone involved in Little League needs to work hard to take the adults out of the game as much as possible, and they need to work on putting themselves into it more playfully, more like the child they continue to be.

There is no doubt that writing this chapter points out the difficulties and the limitations of narrative curriculum inquiry for me. I feel so limited in what I told you about myself and about the great curriculum of Little League even after all these pages; I feel so open and prone to judgment. Kevin so skillfully points out the many threats to the story, including, mainly, the fact that it is so easy for us to romanticize past experience, to paint pictures in colors that sing, even when they depict negative experiences, so that they become so openly assailable, victory narratives of the worst sort. What I can do at this time is settle for "unsettlement," that continuously stirring feeling and truth that accompanies inquiry, when question and answer and being stymied all revolve on themselves to create the science and art of scholarship (Lucero, 2010). That is where I am right now, challenged to think of new ways to make a new story tomorrow with Little League, unsettled by all that I have told and experienced and want to be. Perhaps, this is the best path to be on curricularly, and pedagogically, if I hope to make a difference in the world, a little bit at a time, running the course and changing the course of Little League one step at a time. Enough said. Wait... first... let's "Play Ball!"

REFERENCES

Dewey, J. (2007). *Democracy and education.* Teddington, Middlesex, England: The Echo Library.

Gingrich, N. (2008, October 30). Let's end adolescence. *American Enterprise Institute.* Retrieved March 7, 2011 from http://www.aei.org/article/28905.

Goodwin, J. (2010). Youth baseball injuries becoming more common. Retrieved from http://www.medicinenet.com/script/main/art.asp?articlekey=114292

Little League Baseball and Softball Online. (2006). Participation in Little League reaches 3-year high. Retrieved from www.littleleague.org

Little League Baseball and Softball Online. (2007). Major League Baseball presents grant to Little League Urban Initiative. Retrieved from wwwl.littleleague.org

Little League Baseball. (2010). Official regulations and playing rules. Williamsport, PA: Little League Baseball.

Lucero, J. (2010). Roof of the right size. *Journal of Curriculum & Pedagogy, 7*(10), 15–17.

McKibben, D. (2004). Little League losing its grip on kids. *Los Angeles Times*, August 12, 2004. Retrieved from http://articles.latimes.com/2004/aug/12/local/me-baseball12

Pepe, M. (2011). In *Wikipedia.* Retrieved March 1, 2011 from http://en.wikipedia.org/wiki/Maria_Pepe

Schwarz, C. (2011). Leave those kids alone. *The Atlantic, 307*(3), 101–103.

Stotz, C. (1992). *A promise kept: The story of the founding of Little League Baseball (as told to Kenneth D. Loss).* Jersey Shore, PA: Zebrowski Historical Services Publishing.

Stotz, C. (2011). In *Wikipedia.* Retrieved March 2, 2011 from http://en.wikipedia.org/wiki/Carl_Stotz

Wildcat Baseball League history. Retrieved March 7, 2011 from wildcatbaseball.org

CHAPTER 3

EAGLE ROCK SCHOOL: A "MIS-EQUATION" FOR GREATNESS—HOW A CURRICULUM BASED ON 8 + 5 = 10 TEACHES AND TRANSFORMS

Amy Fisher Young

VICTOR'S PRESENTATION OF PERSONAL GROWTH

Victor paced back and forth in front of the room while his fellow students, teachers, and administrators filed in. Smiling, he said, "I never could have done this back when I first got here. I'm so much different now."

The lights were dimmed and his presentation appeared on the screen behind him. He stood tall, took a deep breath, and began.

"Hi everyone. I'm Victor and this is my Presentation of Personal Growth." His first slide flashed up on the screen—a montage of photos, happy people posing arm-in-arm. "This is my family, my brothers, sister, nieces, nephews. We take care of each other. They are the ones supporting me now."

10 Great Curricula: Lived Conversations of Progressive, Democratic Curricula in School and Society, pp. 51–72
Copyright © 2011 by Information Age Publishing

The next slide appeared, three pictures side-by-side. On the right, a photo of a young woman sitting in a chair, legs crossed at the ankles, long black hair falling over her shoulders. She's wearing a white blouse and jeans. She's smiling. On the left is a photo of a young man with thick, black hair, standing up with his hands on his hips. He's wearing a worn t-shirt and cut-off jeans.

Victor pointed to the woman on the right. "That's my mom. This picture was taken a long time ago, before she became homeless. I saw her once on the streets when I went back home and she didn't even say 'hi' to me. Being taken away from her by Children's Services was the best thing that ever happened to me. I was adopted by my older brother when I was fourteen."

He then points to the photo on the left. "And that's my dad. I didn't really know him. He committed suicide a while ago."

In between the two photos is a pencil drawing, the outlines of these two individuals merged together into one picture: the woman in the chair and the man standing right behind her. The two people are depicted as skeletons, frail, soulless figures.

"This drawing is one that my brother did. It is a representation of my parents. Even though in the photos they look like normal people, they are really empty. They did not take care of us; they abandoned us. This is how we feel about them."

"Let me tell you a little about how my life used to be." A new slide flashes on the screen with a list of bullet points.

"I learned a lot growing up in L.A. I learned things like how to steal from department stores using a stroller or my little brother; I learned how to look people in the eyes and lie; I learned to hate people who did not speak Spanish or who were not of my race." He motions for the next slide. "Before I came here, I didn't love myself. I didn't know who I was. I hated school. I started drinking and drugging. I was pressured to join a gang, but I did not want to. Then one night my friends got drunk and beat me up and told me I was a member of the gang. They became my family. I got into a lot of trouble: stealing, doing illegal things, disrespecting girls. I ended up going to jail for 22 years to life. I knew I did not belong there. But being *there* was what got me *here*. So it was meant to be, you know?"

"I was sitting in my jail cell one day and this guy was talking to the kid in the cell next to me. He was telling him about this school in Colorado where he could get his high school diploma and get his life back on track. It sounded like a good place for me, so I got an application and filled it out. They released me from jail for a week to visit the school and I met another student out here who was like me—someone who had been in trouble like me, failed out of school, and that is what convinced me to come here. I was released from jail to go to school here."

"I know I have changed since I started at Eagle Rock. I keep lookin' in the mirror and askin' myself 'Who am I?' I don't dress the same. The things that interested me like drinking do not interest me anymore. I have realized some things about myself. I realized that I do not know how to love, but I am trying. I have realized that I am not the person I thought I was."

"Eagle Rock has taught me a lot about myself: how to respect others; that I deserve respect. That the world doesn't owe me nothin'. I owe the world."

"But one particular experience here has taught me the most about myself." The next slide flashes up. It is a photo of a wooden patio with a blue sleeping bag laid out on it. Victor explains that last week he broke one of the nonnegotiable rules at Eagle Rock—fighting. And since he was only 2 weeks away from graduating and almost 21 years old he was given a choice: either leave Eagle Rock without getting a diploma, or move out of the dorm and sleep outside alone for the rest of the time. He chose the latter.

"I chose to sleep outside because I want to be the first person from my family to graduate with a high school diploma. I did not want to throw everything I have worked for away. It is not worth it."

"It cleared my mind. I had a lot of time to think and reflect about who I am, what I am doing here, my life goals. It was really the best thing that ever happened to me."

So regardless of the two feet of snow that fell or the rumor of a mountain lion on the property, Victor slept outside.

At the end of his presentation, Victor fielded 20 minutes of questions from the crowd, ranging from what his future plans to biggest fears about life after graduation. Victor appeared confident about his next steps. "I'm going to make a difference in the world. I'm going back to L.A. to see my family and I'm going to work."

Victor's presentation concluded with a standing ovation from his peers and many hugs from instructors, staff members, and friends. I was so moved by his maturity, his depth of thought, and his presence that my heart ached for him to succeed. Eagle Rock's impact on Victor was evident, but I found myself wondering how sustainable and lasting it would be. Would Victor be able to return to the community and his family as a man with a high school diploma without being ostracized or Othered? Would gang membership seduce him back on the streets or into drinking and drugs? What resources would he have to support him in his transition from rural life in the mountains to returning to the projects in Los Angeles? Would he continue to feel the sense of agency and power that he projected in this presentation?

Unknowns abounded, but the combination of Victor's self-confidence and unwavering hope for his future seemed to drown out any uncertainty.

This young man, once discarded from public school and released from jail, had been transformed at Eagle Rock into a person with a vision that his life, even with a sordid past and many challenges ahead, was worth living in a purposeful way. I believed in him.

These "Presentations of Personal Growth" are part of the larger school curriculum at Eagle Rock, a small private, residential high school in Estes Park, Colorado. Before a student is able to graduate, he/she must give one of these presentations to the entire learning community as a part of the reflection and growth process at the school. Each student must prepare his/her presentation, detailing personal growth made since arrival at the school. This, however, is not the exit exam; it is just one step in the process of graduation, which includes multiple presentations and demonstration of mastery of established learning standards.

At the end of Victor's presentation, I was left with lots of questions. As a public school teacher for 6 years, I had never before witnessed anything like Victor's presentation, either in content or personal impact, and it incited reflection in me about teaching, schooling, and curriculum. I wondered how many students in the American public education system could give life-changing accounts of their experiences in school. Could they point to moments or classes that were so profoundly influential they could assemble a 30 minutes PowerPoint presentation to illustrate their transformation? Thinking about this certainly made me wonder how such "Presentations of Personal Growth" could be orchestrated in public schools. Would every single student be able to articulate the power of the education he/she had received as eloquently as Victor had done?

I was also left wondering about how and why traditional models of school fail students like Victor and why more progressive places like Eagle Rock are far and few between. Would Victor have experienced similar success if he had attended an Eagle Rock type school located in the Los Angeles Community School District while still living at home, instead of being transplanted miles from his home and family? What policies and practices would not be permissible in public schools, but were practiced freely at Eagle Rock and led to these colossal personal transformations? For example, what about the school's decision to have Victor sleep outside? Was that inhumane? Possibly unsafe? Ethical? Or was it really "the best thing that ever happened to [him]?" Former teachers, like myself, may be cringing at this punishment, but was it better than the alternative— leaving Eagle Rock without a diploma? Was this experience, though not part of the planned curriculum for Victor, essential to his development and path of learning? And, if this experience was so powerful, how can we give other public school students similar transformative experiences without unduly punishing them all or creating detention in the wilderness?

EAGLE ROCK'S TRANSFORMATIVE
SCHOOLING FRAMEWORK

In order to process these questions and what they mean for student learning, it is important to understand the framework from which the school operates, as well as its multilayered approach to education. Eagle Rock School is, literally and figuratively, far from being a rural school in Ohio or an urban Los Angeles public school. It is a special place, situated in a certain environment, context of ideologies, networks, and energies, making it a school unlike almost any other nationwide.

It is not just Eagle Rock's "Presentation of Personal Growth" requirement that sets it apart from other schools. Opened in 1993, Eagle Rock works as an independent, tuition-free, residential high school for students who are not expected to graduate from traditional high schools. Dan Condon, Associate Director of Eagle Rock's Professional Development Center, said, "There are two types of students who attend Eagle Rock. On one end there are brilliant students who have not experienced success in traditional school, and on the other end, there are students here who have faced personal challenges such as addiction or involvement in crime or gangs."

According to Condon these students have come to Eagle Rock for a second (or third) chance to graduate with a high school diploma. Located in the mountains of Colorado, this school admits proportionate numbers of female and male students, between the ages of 15 and 17 years old, from all over the United States to create a diverse learning community.

Getting through this selection process does require some work. First, an interested student must fill out an application for the school and write an essay describing why he/she feels Eagle Rock would be an appropriate fit for him/her. An adult sponsor must also write a letter on the student's behalf. After review of the essays and application, selected students are offered an all-expenses paid 1-week visit to Eagle Rock. During the visit interested students get to participate in the school's activities, observe classes, and talk with current students. Condon noted that, "the selection process is a collective effort—the prospective student, current students, and faculty must all believe this school is a good fit for the student." If all parties agree, then the student is offered one of the 96 potential slots (though the school is rarely operating at capacity). Approximately, 50% of the students come from within Colorado, while the other half comes from elsewhere in the United States.

After acceptance into Eagle Rock High School, the challenges for the student are just beginning. In the first trimester at the school, students enter into an "initiation" type wilderness experience, which helps them transition to the school's very unique culture. During this 25-day experience, students learn to overcome adversity, work cooperatively, reflect on their own challenges, and build self-esteem. Students are also taught the official curriculum of Eagle Rock, $8 + 5 = 10$, which will be discussed later in the chapter. These skills are helpful to them after they enter back into the culture of Eagle Rock, following their wilderness experience, which culminates with a six-mile run back to the school where the students are welcomed by staff and veteran students.

"But Eagle Rock isn't for everyone," says Condon. Instead of the more traditional model of schooling, with several periods of classes back-to-back, this school's schedule includes two-to-three interdisciplinary courses (depending on the student) per 10 week trimester. Classes range from *Environmental Racism*, a look at the way skin color is related to privilege and oppression in terms of environmental opportunities, to *Math4Life*, which delves into personal financial management skills such as how to create a budget, complete taxes, or manage stocks. While I was visiting, students in this class researched the stock market, graphed the progress of stocks, and planned how they were going to pitch their investment ideas to potential investors. Courses typically do not use textbooks and many include project-based learning, such as in the *Make it Market* class, where students create artistic projects such as jewelry or pillows and then sell them at a local co-op store in Estes Park, concomitantly learning how to use their art and business skills to understand profits, markets, and fair trade, while getting real life experience. A focus is placed on authentic assessments with the goal of mastery, rather than competing for a grade.

Each course is headed up by one instructor and one residential fellow, who is employed as an AmeriCorps volunteer. Both the instructor and the AmeriCorps fellow work together to team-teach the curriculum of the course, integrating multiple subject areas, competencies, and assessments. Each course is open to all students, as there are no prerequisite classes (except in the case of foreign language). This open enrollment offering works because there are no grade-level designations (ninth grade, tenth grade, etc.) at Eagle Rock. Each student works at his/ her own pace to complete his/her Individual Learning Plan (ILP), which is equivalent in some ways to a transcript without all the competitive fuss about weighted grades and class rankings. Instead, the ILP documents competencies and mastery of standards, rather than listing traditional courses such as Algebra or English or As, Bs, and Cs to establish passing versus failing.

According to Easton (2007), this process of giving credit for mastery versus credit for seat time is what standards based education should look like. In traditional models of schooling, students are required to attend a set number of days (180 per school year) and must achieve a rating of 60% out of 100% (at least a D) in a course in order to get credit. In this model, students may or may not master all of the standards in the course, but the student is promoted to the next class regardless. Ever heard the term "D's mean 'degrees,'" uttered by public school employees? Unfortu-nately, if this is the motto, and the attitude is "push 'em through," then the focus on learning has been robbed from the student. However, in the standards-based model implemented at Eagle Rock, students are enrolled in courses with the goal of mastering the standards. If the student does not master the standards by the end of the course, then there is no "D" for effort given on the ILP. Consequently, the student will be enrolled in another course, for another opportunity to demonstrate mastery of the missed standards.

In order to graduate from Eagle Rock, a student must demonstrate mas-tery of standards along with completion of a series of activities. These activ-ities include a "Presentation of Personal Growth," like the one Victor gave, as well as a "Presentation of Learning (POL)." For a POL, the student presents his/her learnings to a panel of teachers, outside evaluators, and personal friends/mentors. In this presentation, the student must articulate his/her achievement, educational set-backs, and areas of growth. This artic-ulation and reflection are unique to this school and solidify Eagle Rock's commitment to learning and transformation over grades and transcripts as a part of the entire schooling experience.

What also sets Eagle Rock apart from most other private/ public schools is its relationship with a corporate entity. Fully funded by the American Honda Education Corporation, this school offers students year-round (three trimesters) school in a residential setting. The school was founded after Honda had first developed the Eagle Rock Professional Development Center, a teacher training facility to improve education. Because of the nature of the professional development center, a learning laboratory school was created to practice ideas taught at the Professional Development Center. This partnership between the school and the professional develop-ment center is significant in that each supports the other and works to make the Eagle Rock experience a place of learning for teachers and students alike.

The purpose of the professional development center, according to Condon, "is not to have schools see Eagle Rock and replicate it." Instead, he suggests that "schools can take what will work from Eagle Rock and apply it to their own settings." And each school's situation is different, as is what they take from the professional development experience. "Some schools will focus on building community, while others will work on reimag-ining their schedules. Some even focus on working with staff to see the talents and positives of students, the whole student, rather than looking at students' deficits."

Condon noted that sometimes the professional development program can be overwhelming for some educators. "They look at everything we do and think that we are only successful because of our corporate sponsor or because we are residential. We tell them that we spend about the same amount per student as most public institutions. It is not the resources that make Eagle Rock successful. Strip them away. We would still be effective with students."

THE CURRICULUM OF EAGLE ROCK: PLANNED LEARNINGS WITH A SMALL SCHOOLS APPROACH

It was not just Victor's jaw-dropping presentation that hinted at the greatness of Eagle Rock. At each meal, I talked with students about their experiences prior to this school and what impact this place had been on them. I heard story after story that resonated with the same message that Victor had proudly shared: Eagle Rock is a transformative school where students graduate with relationships, skills, and visions that they never thought possible.

Although I believe there are multifarious reasons why this message prevailed, I contend that one component that makes Eagle Rock so successful is it's thoroughly thought out and planned curriculum. Using Marsh and Willis' (2007) curriculum frameworks, I define *official* school curriculum as all the planned learnings for which the school is responsible. As I understand it, these learnings include the explicitly planned curriculum of each class, as well as the experiences that a student may have in between classes, in study tables, in an administrator's office, or in extracurricular activities. This curriculum, the official curriculum, can be seen through the lesson plans of teachers, the policies of the school, the rules of the school, and educational initiatives (such as wellness programs). However, this curriculum definition does not include the unplanned experiences that a student has throughout his/her day, such as interactions in the library or tangents a class takes instead of following the plans for the class. Though these unplanned curriculums are important, I am selecting to focus on the planned learnings for this section of the chapter.

Though workable for the purposes of this chapter, this definition does come with its own set of problems. For example, the definition states that the official curriculum covers the "planned learnings," which is problematic because it is difficult, potentially impossible, to teach exactly as planned, so much of learning is like spontaneous combustion, leaving teachers baffled all over the country as to reasons why some magnificently planned lessons fizzle and other haphazardly planned lessons go down in school history as legendary. Additionally, this definition assumes that what is planned is actually taught, which we know is not always the case; the planned curriculum is not necessarily the enacted curriculum. In some cases, the planned curriculum is multilayered and complicated and might require superhuman powers to actually integrate all the "plannings" in ways that satisfy all of the educational watchdogs of curriculum. For example, the State of Ohio has standards for what should be taught in an American government class—this is part of the planned curriculum for the course. On top of that the district may have a curriculum/course guide for the same class (which is planned). Depending on when this course guide was created (and by whom), the plans for the course may not be totally in line with the plans made by the State. Lastly, individual teachers may have daily lesson plans (also planned), which may or may not match the district's plans for the course or the State's standards (plans) for the course. All of these planning overlays can make for a complicated curriculum, which can be quite confusing.

Besides complications with the planned curriculum, this definition assumes what is taught is what is actually learned by the student. However, we know that what is taught is not necessarily what is learned (as the enacted curriculum is not necessarily the lived or experienced curriculum). Lastly, this definition of official planned curriculum does not question the nature of the curriculum; it takes the curriculum on face value without interrogating the reasons why the curriculum selects some learnings and leaves out others. Although my working definition of official school curriculum is contestable, it will serve my purposes for this chapter because it is focused on the underlying guides that impact what a student learns in school.

Part of the planned curriculum at Eagle Rock has to do with the school's dedication and commitment to the principals of Ted Sizer's *Coalition of Essential Schools* (Coalition of Essential Schools, 2006). Schools who are members of this network must work to maintain personalized, equitable, and intellectually challenging schools, but do not have to fit a certain mold; they can be in the form of public or private schools, technical or general schools. Most are associated with the small school movement, and all must adhere to the Coalition's essential elements: (1) learning to use one's mind well; (2) less is more, depth over coverage; (3) goals apply to all students; (4) personalization; (5) student-as-worker, teacher-as-coach; (6) demonstration of mastery; (7) a tone of decency and trust; (8) commitment to the entire school; (9) resources dedicated to teaching and learning; and (10) democracy and equity (Coalition of Essential Schools, 2006). Not only does Eagle Rock ascribe to these principles, but also engages them in the constructed environment of the school.

On face value, it would seem like these principles represent "common sense" values all schools should adopt (or ones they should have adopted). However, the Coalition asserts that not all schools are living up to these principles and that it takes an explicitly purposeful commitment to them because they are not inherent in the way most schools work today. For example, it would seem commonplace in schools that "Goals apply to all students." Theoretically, we would hope that this is the case in public and private schools all across America. However, this statement may not explicitly appear in the school or even be theoretically manifested in the planned curriculum. CES contends that goals should apply to all students, but means for achieving goals may be different depending on the student and the context. According to the CES, school practices should be tailor-made for meeting the needs of each class and group of students.

Another specific CES principle, "Resources dedicated to teaching and learning" is important when examining the way the school budget is structured. Alignment with this principle requires that the school must provide teachers with competitive salaries, time for collaboration, and reasonable workloads. Additionally, an ultimate per pupil cost cannot exceed that of traditional schools by more than 10%. This is important to note, as Eagle Rock touts that it is not the corporate sponsorship or finances that make the school so successful; it is the other principles that it adheres to that make it great.

EAGLE ROCK'S 8 + 5 = 10 EQUATION: "BAD MATH" ADDS UP TO A THEORETICAL CURRICULUM

CES principles do not represent the only official curriculum at work on campus. Eagle Rock has developed its own set of principles which it adheres to, some of which overlap with the Coalition's principles. The official school curriculum of Eagle Rock is based on the 8 + 5 = 10 equation. First, the school has identified eight themes that undergird all of the planned learnings experienced by the students, from the creation of courses, to the daily schedule, and in extracurricular activities such as intramural sports. The themes are: (1) intellectual discipline; (2) physical fitness; (3) spiritual development; (4) aesthetic expression; (5) service to others; (6) cross-cultural understanding; (7) democratic governance; and (8) environmental stewardship. Using these general themes, the faculty and students at Eagle Rock can work collectively with a loose mission of sorts that unifies them in ways, but also allows for flexibility. For example, "Spiritual Development" is not defined as worship or religion, which carves out a space in the curriculum for this kind of learning, but does not draw boundaries around what that might look like for individual students.

Part two of the "bad math" equation of Eagle Rock is the "5," which represents the five expectations the school has for all its students. These expectations are: (1) developing an expanding knowledge base; (2) communicating effectively; (3) creating and making healthy life choices; (4) participating as an engaged global citizen; and (5) providing leadership for justice. As seen with the eight themes, these expectations are not prescriptive and work more as scaffolding for planned learnings, a stark contrast to district curriculum maps or even codes of student conduct.

Lastly, this "mis-equation" establishes the "10 Commitments" that the students must make in order to achieve success at Eagle Rock. These commitments are: (1) live in respectful harmony with others; (2) develop mind, body, and spirit; (3) learn to communicate in speech and writing; (4) serve the Eagle Rock and other communities; (5) become a steward of the planet; (6) make healthy personal choices; (7) find, nurture and develop the artist within; (8) increase capacity to exercise leadership for justice;(9) practice citizenship and democratic living; (10) devise an enduring moral and ethical code. These nonnegotiable commitments work to more explicitly communicate to all students and faculty at Eagle Rock what it is the school community stands for (and consequently will not stand for). Using these commitments, instructors can create courses and planned lessons within a loose curricular framework that merges and weaves the themes and expectations. Combined, $8 + 5 = 10$, has become the set of principles that govern the school and result in lived experiences at Eagle Rock that transform students (Easton, 2002, p. 7).

EXAMINING THE 8 + 5 = 10 EQUATION IN PRACTICE

Transitioning this theoretical equation into classroom curriculum and planned learnings happens somewhat seamlessly at Eagle Rock. To illustrate the reality and plausibility of such theory in practice, it is important to examine particular courses and lessons, which really "add up" to the transformation of students from arrival to their exit presentations.

The first part of the equation, the "8 Themes," work as the foundational guidelines for Eagle Rock and can be credited with developing the campus climate and can be seen in varying capacities around campus. Though I will not detail how each theme is integrated into the curriculum of Eagle Rock, I will examine a few of these themes and how they are illuminated in the structure of the school.

The theme of physical fitness is taken seriously at Eagle Rock. The first way this theme is seen in the planned curriculum is through the designation of Wednesdays as intramural sports days, which means that classes halt for students to participate in competitive sports ranging from Frisbee football to volleyball. This commitment to athletics is important because it fosters the lived curriculum of self-esteem, a sense of friendly competition, fairness, and teamwork. But Eagle Rock's commitment to physical fitness does not stop here. Every day, all students are required to get up at 6:45 a.m. to participate in physical fitness exercises or a three mile run. Attendance is not optional. Carla, a veteran student, said, "I used to hate the morning run. I was so bad at it when I first got here. But now it's better. I've improved a lot." This official curriculum is set up so students participate in various physical activities to stay healthy and fit, finding strength in themselves along the way.

Another theme, Service to Others, is fostered in a variety of ways. For example, every student is required to work in the kitchen at least 1 week out of the month. Students help prepare the meals, serve, and clean up afterwards. The curriculum is that everyone is expected to help out and all students should serve others. Cafeteria work also provides students with job experiences, as they are expected to arrive on time, clock in to work, and follow proper safety and health guidelines. Besides working in the dining hall, students are also assigned duties on campus, such as picking up recycling, shoveling snow, or taking out trash. These chores also relate to the theme of serving others through a commitment to keeping the campus a clean and safe place. Aside from these chores, a student could also be assigned a "Sunday Sweat," a disciplinary assignment if the student is caught breaking a minor rule or one of the ten commitments. The curriculum is that service to others should be a part of the daily lives of individuals, as well as a way to give back to others if a disservice has been done.

The theme of cross-cultural understanding can be seen through multiple curricular modes. First, it can be seen in the courses that address issues such as racism, classism, and diversity. Courses such as *The World of Spanish II*, *Study Abroad*, and *Oh God!* give students opportunities to examine multiple perspectives and see the world through different lenses. But encouraging cross-cultural understanding does not stop at the classroom door. When I visited Eagle Rock, students were also participating in a school-wide empathy exercise, which required white students and minority students to segregate themselves for a period of 3 days. Privilege and power was alternating, as during one lunch period, the white students would be served first and allowed to get seconds, while the minority students would be served second with no additional helpings of food. Then the following meal, the minority students would be served first. Students were required to "sit with their own color" during gatherings and anyone breaking the rules was threatened with a "Sunday Sweat." Following the 3-day exercise, students and instructors gathered to discuss the issues at play during the exercise. Though I was unable to observe the discussion following the activity, I was able to talk with students about their experiences with the exercises.

Maria, a veteran student at Eagle Rock, said, "Things really have not changed. People stick to their races anyway. They eat lunch with people like them. This is the way things are." However, other students like Marcos said, "It's weird. I don't like it. I can't sit with my friends. Some people aren't following the rules [of the exercise] because they think it's wrong."

The curriculum of this activity is multilayered. On one hand, it emulates the Jane Elliott's blue eyed/ brown eyed activity of 1960s by segregating students in a simulated exercise based on a characteristic[1]. However, this particular exercise performed at Eagle Rock is more complex. For example, some students like Carlos were torn on where to fit in. "My mom's white and my dad's Hispanic. What does that make me? Am I colored? I just go with the colored kids." The planned curriculum of this exercise is that of cross-cultural understanding, but the lived and learned curriculum for students may turn out to be something different. What about light-skinned minorities or dark-skinned white folks?

What about the ways in which the activity reinforces thinking about race and the binary nature in which it is frequently viewed—in the black-white dynamic? Questions about power are also raised. Even though students of color and white students supposedly alternated privileges, can white students fully examine their power if they continue to be labeled in a category that historically privileges them? Does not being "white" come inherently with power just by nature of the designation? And can an empathy exercise be truly transformative?

Situating these themes in a culture of democratic governance is especially significant as it positions activities such as the empathy exercise in discussion where each student has a voice. According to Easton (2005), Eagle Rock subscribes to the theme of democratic governance through its commitment to allowing for students' voices in a variety of ways, such as through decision making about their schedules, and when they would like to graduate, and how to document their learning in these classes. Student voice is also heard and valued during morning gathering, a routine meeting after breakfast where students and staff meet and students can share things they have learned or present their talents as musicians or artists.

During my visit to Eagle Rock, I observed morning gathering where students and staff participated in the democratic activity of crafting the school's anthem. Their anthem was not a typical ballad referring to the grandeur of the school or fond memories of campus. It also was not made up of lyrics created and handed down from previous generations of students. Instead, it was a harmony of spoken dreams, realities, and challenges faced by the current student body. Students, one-by-one, shared their contributions to the school's spoken song of hope.

> "I will be the first in my family to graduate from high school."
> "I am struggling with myself."
> "I am Mexican."
> "I believe in Eagle Rock School."
> "I will be a strong black woman."
> "I will be a college graduate and a successful individual."

All students' voices and experiences were heard and valued. This anthem, situated in the context of the present, could not be replicated by future groups of students, and that is just fine with Eagle Rock. It was symbolic and representative, a true anthem.

The official planned curriculum and the way it relates to the eight themes is important. But partnered with these themes are the five expectations of students and staff. They merge together what the school staff and students will bring to the table in order to create the type of environment to foster maximum student learning. It would seem like these expectations should be standard for all students in our public educational system. Do we not want students to develop an expanding knowledge base? Make healthy life choices? However, the difference between what we want and what we expect from students comes in the form of these explicit statements, which lay it on the line for students. Because Eagle Rock explicitly states these, students know what to expect.

Lastly, the 10 commitments come into the equation. They represent the 10 commitments that students need to make in order to enroll in school at Eagle Rock. These 10 things represent values much like the 8 themes or 5 expectations and are committed to memory by the students. They range from learning to communicate effectively in speech and writing to developing a moral and ethical code. They connect the planned curriculum of the school with the student. These 10 commitments represent rules of sorts that bind the student to the school's principles. When a student breaks one of the commitments, he/she will face consequences such as a "Sunday Sweat" or if the infraction breaks one of the nonnegotiables, he/she could face expulsion from school.

The curriculum of the nonnegotiables is also one worth examining. The official policy is no drugs, no alcohol, no violence, no tobacco, no sexual relations. If a student breaks one of these rules, he/she might be expelled from the school. Associate Director of the Professional Development Center, Dan Condon, noted that "Just because a student is asked to leave, he/she may still reapply and come back. Sometimes this is what it takes for the student to be ready to make changes in his/her life." There are varying opinions regarding this policy. Many of these students have long histories battling these same issues, some of them are the reasons why they ended up out of public school. Condon also mentioned that the "one strike, you're out" policy is being examined and reconsidered. "We are giving students like Victor, who broke the 'no violence' rule, some alternatives instead of just kicking them out." Imagine if such an explicit policy were applied in public schools. Would violence in schools be curbed? Would bullying cease? Or would many students end up out of school, without a diploma?

The planned and lived curriculum of Eagle Rock is more than what has been presented here, of course. There are so many ways in which it manifests itself in the daily learnings experienced by students. Especially since the school is residential, the planned and lived curriculum actually extends for 24 hours and includes everything from rules in the houses (dormitories) to procedures for calling in "sick" to school. It is the way Eagle Rock integrates these experiences and weaves them into its thematic framework that sets us up for examining the ways in which this school represents a "Great Curriculum."

EAGLE ROCK'S GREATNESS

When defining Eagle Rock as representing a "great curriculum," many questions are posed. How was the school selected? Why was it selected? What makes it "great"? What are the tensions surrounding its greatness? I contend that there are multiple complexities which encircle these questions. I will attempt to address these in the following paragraphs.

Eagle Rock was selected from a list of possible schools that do business outside of traditional models of education. It represents possibility and potential for our educational system, one that often labels and casts out "at-risk" students. Eagle Rock does extraordinary things with students that other schools have given up on, kicked out, or neglected to meet their needs. I hear the objections to that statement already. "But it is the kid's own fault he/she did not make it in public school..." "Schools can only do so much..." "We can't help students who don't want help..." There are tensions surrounding this issue that lead us to question whether or not it is the school's responsibility to "save" or redirect misguided or failing students and at what cost. Do schools have an ethical obligation to educate and help all students, regardless of the choices they make or how difficult they may be to work with? At what point do we let students fail? And when they fail, do we continue to help them or focus efforts toward students who are putting forth effort? At what age is a student mature enough to choose to fail? I do not believe a simple conversation could bring us, as educators, into agreement with answers to these questions. However, when we look at what schools such as Eagle Rock are doing with students labeled "at risk," we must continue to dialogue about what makes them effective and how they are effective. Eagle Rock is making strides with this population. It is helping these students and finding ways for them to be successful. We can continue to study and learn from this model, as it opens the window for us to see the possibilities in students labeled "at-risk" and the commitments to them we may need to consider all over again.

Another way Eagle Rock exemplifies "Greatness" is through its dedication to a thematic vision. Some schools have mission statements or visions, developed by committee, written on letterhead and rarely discussed and revised by the staff and students. At Eagle Rock, the mission is the school's $8 + 5 = 10$ equation, complete with an open invitation by Director Rob Burkhardt to challenge, question, or revise this framework. Not only is it up for debate (if desired), it is integrated into the daily workings of the school in innumerable ways. A commitment to such principles is rarely seen in other educational institutions.

Eagle Rock also represents greatness in curriculum through its explicitly stated expectations for students (in the form of the 10 commitments). In public schools, sometimes educators get lost in the shuffle of preparing kids for state mandated exams or trying to fit in teaching the state standards. What do we expect from students and do we spell this out for them very clearly? Do we have them commit our expectations to memory and use them as they delve into the daily curriculum of coursework? Or do we present them with a laundry list of rules to follow and different expectations for each class? The cohesiveness represented by the thorough integration of these expectations makes it clear for students what is expected, how they should behave, and what the school stands for. There are no grey areas. These principles rule the school.

But Eagle Rock is not a crystal palace. It does have its weak areas, places where it could improve. One of these weaknesses is the fact that the school is residential. It takes students from a variety of communities and displaces them in the mountains, far away from their families and support systems. Time and money is spent educating the Eagle Rock student out of context, out of his/her home environment. The complexities of this issue are multifaceted. On one hand, Eagle Rock acknowledges that the student's home environment might be one of the reasons the student struggles and taking him/her out of this environment could be beneficial. On the other hand, this environment is part of who the student is, it makes up the student's culture and regardless of how dysfunctional that may be, so it should be viewed as an asset rather than a deficit in the education of the student.

If the student's home is viewed as a deficit, an "Othering" takes place, which positions the student as coming from a context lacking in resources (such as support or mentoring). If students are viewed as coming from deficient environments, there is an underlying belief that the school can provide a richer, more suitable environment for the student to find success. In this model, the school is positioned as a "Savior" to the student. According to social theorist, Paulo Freire (1973/2000), this type of deficit thinking is detrimental to the student and will not equate to a transformative education. Instead, this model is set up like the banking model of education, in which students are seen as empty containers, ready to be filled by the school. In this way, students will never fully recognize their power and agency and will not be able to truly transform to find long-term success.

And what about the public schools from which Eagle Rock students have come? Instead of working with these schools to help meet the needs of "at-risk" students, Eagle Rock plucks students out of the system, potentially leaving other needy students in the cycle of failure. Does Eagle Rock have a moral or ethical obligation to these public schools and/or the students at these schools? I believe in some ways Eagle Rock's Professional Development Center works to address this issue and gives back to schools seeking assistance. But what about schools not seeking assistance? What if the Honda Corporation gave its money to help mend public education instead of creating an alternate private school to meet students' needs? Although I do believe that Eagle Rock gives back in some ways through its Professional Development Center, I question whether or not it values and serves the school communities from which its students have come.

Another way Eagle Rock challenges the designation of "greatness," is through the way it defines itself; the school does not claim to be a college prep institution. According to Condon, Eagle Rock is "life prep." This concept elicits a series of questions. What does it mean to be a "college prep" school? What does it mean to be "life prep"? And shouldn't all schools (even college prep schools) be preparing students for life? Is it a disservice to students attending Eagle Rock to not be enrolled in a college prep school? Are Eagle Rock students who attend college prepared for the challenges they face? These questions are not easy to filter. In traditional thinking, college prep elicits associations with a Renaissance-type curriculum, studying the canon, taking core courses. However, thinking of this sort has changed in schools over the years. College prep should be synonymous with critical thinking, challenging coursework, and diversity in experiences. The classes I observed at Eagle Rock did encompass these elements, but they also answered for students when and how this type of thinking will be used in real life. The courses also did not cover traditional offerings such as American government or British literature. Sometimes in schools, students are tracked according to their projected future (i.e., this class is "general education," this class is "college prep"). Do such designations make the whole school a college prep institution or just some classes? And what about Eagle Rock graduates? Is it considered setting the bar too low by not making the school college prep? And if it were to transition to college prep what would that look like? How would it be different?

CONCLUSIONS

Examining Eagle Rock's practices and curriculum can lead us to a better understanding of the potential and possibilities for education. It presents us with a model of schooling outside of the traditional paradigm, and challenges us to think about other ways to imagine education. Although Eagle Rock presents us with this progressive model, its concept is not a new one to educational circles. Its foundational principles and practices are aligned with schooling concepts presented by philosopher John Dewey (2001). Dewey advocated for schools that prepared students for life and addressed the needs of the whole child. Instead of looking at curriculum as a separate entity from the child, he pushed for educators to synthesize concepts of curriculum with education that considers the child's emotional, social, and academic aspects. The curriculum, according to Dewey, should be designed with the learner's needs in mind and should be flexible enough for the student to navigate through the curriculum, adapting, building, and revising it along the way. This concept is realized at Eagle Rock, as teachers create new courses each semester and continue to modify their plans as students engage in the curriculum. This model is very different from what occurs in traditional schools around the country.

Dewey's (2001) progressive model of education also included integrated curriculum, rather than categorized classes such as physics or algebra. He contended that students must learn to navigate the universe and life spaces full of interwoven complexities. In order to prepare students for this layered life experience, he promoted an organic multidisciplinary, cross-curricular model of education. Eagle Rock takes this philosophy and puts it in to practice as it has reconfigured traditional subjects and classes into integrated, relative courses which are not bound by curriculum guides or state standards (though they do loosely reference these). Instead, these courses present real-life issues in complex ways that naturally include a variety of subject areas in traditional and nontraditional ways. For example, a class titled "Eagle Rock Cares" may integrate traditional subjects such as geography and civics with more nontraditional "subjects" such as service learning and environmental studies. A focus is placed on authentic assessment and hands-on learning, rather than inauthentic performance assessments and seatwork. This model steps outside of the boundaries of what is currently done in more traditional schools and illuminates what a great, progressive curriculum could look like.

The Eagle Rock model, though brimming with "great aspects," is not flawless. It is one we need to analyze, question, and reposition as we take from it snippets of wisdom. As noted before, Eagle Rock cannot and should not be replicated. However, it can be used to shed light on what is being done well in education and what needs to be improved. From re-imaging schedules, to creating thematic foundations for learning, Eagle Rock represents a vision of what can be realized with students, regardless of students' backgrounds, struggles, and past experiences in schools. This vision, which encompasses elements of greatness, gives hope and promise to our educational systems for working with students who pose extra challenges in traditional classroom settings.

RESPONSE BY TOM POETTER

One of the most personally influential books I have read about secondary education is Tom Gregory's (1993) *Making High School Work: Lessons from the Open School*. Gregory's effort is one of the best depictions of progressive, alternative education. His study of a public school getting progressive alternative education right while keenly describing and troubling it has always made me wonder "why not here, there, or everywhere?" in terms of a wider implementation of student-centered school programs. Of course, examples are around us, although not abounding, like George Wood's Federal Hocking High School in Ohio (Murray & Wood, 1999) and Deb Meier's Central Park East Secondary School legacy in New York City (Tyner-Mullings, 2008) and some charters that are popping up that are not just small but actually implementing a strong, progressive curriculum and pedagogy, the kind you might find in influential pockets of teaching and learning in the best, most iconic eastern prep schools in the United States. But the approach is not prevalent. We still seek to control and shape adolescents with the traditional high school plan. It works well enough for some, where a strong financial base, talent, and teaching make the traditional high school at least palatable for the upper 30% of students or so. But high school, in general, as a concept, practice, and as a rule, is not working very well for us.

One thing that rankles educationists like me and the ones that are putting this book together is the presumption that big business has the best set of ideas about how to create a 21st century high school, like Bill Gates and friends, or that state education departments know what they are doing when they rely on technical solutions that have not worked in the past that just keep getting recycled not only in practice but in reified public policy for educational practice (Karp, 2011)! Reform du jour usually means intensifying what is already being done, like delivering a supposedly better instructional system, or requiring more content, or making students go to school for more hours/days a year, or focusing on nailing down standards and objectives to be taught in each grade and controlling the delivery through high stakes tests, etc. But these intensification efforts only intensify what is already not working very well for most students. Strong students can handle whatever the education system throws at them; they are in tune enough to do whatever it takes to succeed, knowing that the rewards will come to them for persevering, such as entry into and scholarships for opportunities in higher education. The students at Eagle Rock have been failed by a system that is deep and rich, and sometimes ineffective. So at times, of course, drastic measures are in order.

At Eagle Rock, ironically perhaps, this is where the powerfully corporate structure met education in a unique way: Honda asked Rob Burkhardt nearly 20 years ago to create an alternative school for students with talent who are not succeeding in public schools for a myriad of reasons and it trusted him, gave him the professional freedom, to do it the way he knew best, that is by honoring each student where he or she is at the time of admission, challenging the student to create a better life plan for him or herself, then to create the conditions where freedom and order meet in complex ways in the company of talented, responsible adults and ask the students to navigate, set their course, make a path with help that would lead to high school graduation and a new life.

It takes expertise and know-how to put a complicated, grounded, progressive educational opportunity in place for students with incredible needs in the United States. And Eagle Rock has gotten it right the entire time, both in concept, and along the way, student-by-student. Like many schools, Eagle Rock works to overcome its limitations and mistakes, wondering should we have been that strict or that lenient with that student, or should we have focused more on math and science and less on literature in that course with that student, or should we have extended our wilderness experience or cut it shorter? These are the nuts and bolts of a complex organism that always bears scrutiny. But over time, like the thousands of students and faculty at Eagle Rock, the bottom line becomes, "Am I a better person for having experienced this curriculum? Do I understand the possibilities for my life within and among complex cultures and societies? Can I get along with peers and elders and act responsibly with my life's challenges and gifts? Do I have the skills to navigate my way forward, figure out what I do not know, solve problems, and contribute to society, even if I have been dealt a bad hand initially?"

I think the answers lie in the complex road to the final word, in the journey, something we are valuing less and less along the way in our society because of our worries over purpose and direction and control in our education system. But in the opening of this paper, Victor had the final word in his amazing presentation. Any educational endeavor that is progressive, forward thinking, democratic, responsible, and dynamic, should always come back to the student. Where does he or she stand?

A FINAL WORD, AMY YOUNG

Educational reforms as we currently know them are code for rebranding what is already being done in schools, remixing practices from the past, and requiring that these "modifications" be done with tighter budgets, larger class sizes, and in conjunction with an overload of restrictions. As Tom mentioned in his response, it is important to consider the students that present reforms privilege—students who already find success in the traditional model of school—and those other students who have been marginalized by the current school system. Doing the same things public schools have been doing for decades, within the same structure and framework, but calling them "new" will not lead us to better, different results. Students like Victor, despite mandates and standards, are being "left behind."

Figuring out why this happens is not a matter of pointing fingers or placing blame on students or teachers or even individual schools. This issue is much more complex and cannot be fixed by changing a textbook, firing a teacher, or closing a school. While Victor is one student from one particular school with very specific family dynamics, his story represents a larger silenced narrative of students who have not found the traditional model of schooling or the reformed models to be positive spaces of learning and growth. Victor, fortunately, had the opportunity to tell his story and be a part of a school community that valued him and allowed him to share this message. Many students who have been "left behind," and do not find schools like Eagle Rock, never get to share their experiences. For me, Victor's message was so much more than a personal story, it was a wake up call, reminding me of the potential and talent that current schools cast aside, and compelled me to help him share his story, hoping to make change for all students, especially those who have not experienced success in traditional schools.

If we want to create transformative learning experiences for all students in schools, we can learn a lot from the great curriculum of Eagle Rock. But as Dan Condon mentioned to me on several occasions throughout my visit, no one can or should replicate Eagle Rock. It is a unique place, with circumstances and resources different than any other school. But that does not mean we cannot glean from them and work to reform more traditional schools undergirded with these concepts. I believe looking specifically an Eagle Rock's $8 + 5 = 10$ curriculum can be a positive place to start.

What I love most about Eagle Rock's "mis-equation," which they fondly refer to as "bad math" is that it does not add up in the practical sense; we know $8 + 5$ will never equal 10. In essence, the message they are sending is clear: greatness in schooling is not about a technical, rational kind of equation in which integers can be substituted and the sum remains predictable and stable. Creating school experiences that teach and transform students, leading them to mature reflections like Victor's, are not achieved through formulaic means. The challenge for us is to learn from the *curricular spirit* of Eagle Rock, from the literal and symbolic meaning of the "mis-equation," and for us to re-imagine or renew our current schools with our own "bad math" that is culturally relevant, tied to our official curriculums, and supported by real themes, expectations, and commitments that allow for flexibility and keep all students in mind, not just the ones that enjoy school or excel in their studies. Schools must configure their own mis-equations, baffling the most skilled mathematicians, knowing that the sum of their efforts for students like Victor, will be the greatest gift an education can provide.

NOTE

1. Jane Elliott, a third grade teacher in Iowa, developed an empathy exercise for her students, commonly referred to as the "blue-eyed/brown-eyed" exercise. Over a period of a few days, students with blue eyes were given privileges over students with brown eyes. This activity, which was and is highly controversial, laid the foundation for diversity training.

REFERENCES

Coalition of Essential Schools. (2006). *The CES common principles*. Retrieved May 2, 2009, from http://www.essentialschools.org/pub/ces_docs/about/phil/10cps/10cps.html

Dewey, J. (2001). *The school and society & the child and the curriculum*. Mineola, NY: Dover Publications.

Easton, L. B. (2002). *The other side of curriculum*. Portsmouth, NH: Heinemann.

Easton, L. B. (2005). Democracy in schools: Truly a matter of voice. *English Journal*, *94*(5), 52–56.

Easton, L. B. (2007). Walking our talk about standards. *Phi Delta Kappan*, *88*(5), 391–394.

Freire, P. (2000). *Pedagogy of the oppressed*. (M. B. Ramos, Trans.). New York, NY: Continuum. (Original work published in 1973)

Gregory, T. (1993). *Making high school work: Lessons from the open school*. New York, NY: Teachers College Press.

Karp, S. (2011). Who's bashing teachers and public schools and what can we do about it? Retrieved from www.commondreams.org

Marsh, C. J. & Willis G. (2007). *Curriculum: Alternative approaches, ongoing issues* (4th ed.). New Jersey: Pearson Education.

Murray, S., & Wood, G. (1999). *Creating a democratic learning community: The case study of Federal Hocking High School*. Columbus, OH: Ohio Department of Education.

Tyner-Mullings, A. R. (2008). Central Park East Secondary School and The Alternative School Movement in New York City. Paper presented at the annual meeting of the American Sociological Association Annual Meeting, Boston, MA Online from http://www.allacademic.com/meta/p243091_index.html

CHAPTER 4

MCDONALD'S CORPORATION: MCDONALD'S & YOU—JUST EAST OF EATON

Daniel Ciamarra

INTRODUCTION —A COMMUNITY CENTERED CORPORATION

Upon exiting the highway, my car's "gaslight began to ding and flash. I became keenly aware of the adverse surroundings. Boarded-up buildings with caged windows lined both sides of the street. Landmarks had been tagged by gang-like graffiti. There was an absence of newness and an abundance of dilapidated cars, homes, buildings, and businesses. I thought, "Where would I find fuel and what could survive these conditions?" I continued to drive in search of gas, as well as my final destination, noticing the barbed wire fences and countless companies that had gone out of business. On my left were street vendors selling grilled food and on my right were empty lots filled with people wandering the town. Lo and behold I came across a gas station, but the credit card reader was broken and I was not carrying any cash. I moved onward, driving for several miles and getting closer to my meeting location, when at last I discovered a fully functioning gas

10 Great Curricula: Lived Conversations of Progressive, Democratic Curricula in School and Society, pp. 73–97

station. I filled up and proceeded to my appointment. Suddenly, I came upon the bright and glowing arches of a McDonald's Restaurant, clearly out of the blue; I had reached my final destination.

I embarked on a journey to unearth and analyze the curricular and pedagogical commitments McDonald's makes in order to educate its staff and ensure the success of its stores, on many levels. This particular business location was in a gloomy town in Southwest Ohio, just east of Eaton, Ohio. All around me there were condemned buildings that had been vandalized, even the gas stations, but not the McDonald's store. There is a peculiar ambiance about McDonald's that gives it a sense of belonging in any location. How does this company thrive in such foreboding conditions while other businesses have perished? Reingold (1992) recalled that while the streets of Los Angeles were being torched during the riots in the early 1990s, one company's locations were able to stand tall and remain untouched—McDonald's. Ray Kroc, the founder of the McDonald's corporation was an adamant and ingenious salesman who had many brilliant ideas; one of them was, "If you are going to take money out of a community, give something back" (as cited in Reingold, 1992). Although Kroc believed in this statement, it was the drive by local franchise owners that leveraged the effective use of community relations in McDonald's worldwide business approach.

For instance, it was the operator of a Philadelphia based McDonald's, not corporate officials, who crafted McDonald's most visible charity, The Ronald McDonald House (Love, 1986). For families whose children require extended hospital care, this charitable organization has made room and board affordable, or in many cases, free. Likewise, numerous franchisees jumped aboard this generous concept, and today there are close to 300 Ronald McDonald Houses in 31 countries worldwide (Ronald McDonald House Charities [RMHC], 2008). Each RMHC has become an icon of altruism for the community that it dwells in, where civic groups, corporations, and McDonald's store owners alike chip in to develop and nourish each benevolent house.

This philanthropic notion is one of the founding principles for McDonalds's continued success, and was brought to reality during my recent interview with a store owner in Southwestern Ohio. This particular franchisee had worked within the McDonald's corporation for over 30 years, earning experience along the way as a crewmember, cashier, basic shift manager, swing manager, operations manager, general manager, storeowner, and professor at Hamburger University (McDonald's home for the training of future managers, mid-managers, and store owners). A great deal of this chapter will be devoted to how Hamburger University uses a planned, enacted, and lived curriculum that sets it apart from other "wanna be" fast food chains.

I asked the store owner, "How does this specific McDonald's give back to its community?" His answer was simple, almost rote: "We give money to the Ronald McDonald House and Children's Charities, which is our main focus, and soon we'll see the new $60,000,000 Salvation Army complex that is being built nearby. We do church and civic group sponsorships as well."

McDonald's, under the tutelage of its founder, Ray Kroc, has given and continues to give back to its communities, and for a company that has over 30,000 restaurants worldwide, that is a lot of giving. Take for example, the Ray Kroc Foundation, which was established in order to provide money for research into things like diabetes, multiple sclerosis, and arthritis. In fact, in 1975, Ray Kroc put his money where his mouth was and donated one million dollars to the National Multiple Sclerosis Society, and in return was named the *Outstanding Chicagoan of Today* (Kroc & Anderson, 1987). In more recent times, the McDonald's corporation initiated *World Children's Day* (2002), where participating franchises agreed to give $1 for every specified menu item that was sold. Countries around the world have participated in a number ways, from holding benefit concerts in Taiwan, to selling mittens in Russia, all in hopes to collaboratively raise money for The Ray Kroc Foundation. At present, this organization has raised more than $125 million for RMHC and for children around the world (RMHC, 2008).

In addition to corporately funded organizations, individual store owner/operators—who earn this title because they are required to work in the stores they own (Norren, 1990)—have done their fair share to ensure that they give back to their communities. Like the New York owner/operator who opened the Times Square store with the intention of revitalizing an urban area, or a Texas owner/operator who created "Camp Mickey D's," where school-aged children learn the relations between school and work, or my favorite, the Birmingham, Alabama, owner/operator that proffers scholarship bonuses to her crew members (McDonald's Corporation, 2009). These are just three examples, amid scores of others, where store owners have invested returns into their individual neighborhoods.

I am not blind to the controversies associated with the McDonald's Corporation, nor am I positioning myself as a proponent for or adversary against McDonald's; however, I do attempt in this chapter to speak to the effectiveness of McDonald's vis-à-vis its planned, enacted, and lived curriculum. In particular, I highlight the equitableness associated with the hiring, education, and training of McDonald's employees, as well as its capacity to sustain itself as a business, especially in a topsy-turvy economy, all the while offering benefits and opportunities for workers to advance from within. I understand that this chapter may be highly contested, and I may personally be castigated for speaking to the efficacy of the McDonald's curriculum, but nonetheless, I seek to locate the opportunities associated with this convoluted situation as opposed to following the conventional critiques of exposing its conspicuous flaws (Fishwick, 1978; Love, 1986; Kincheloe, 2002; McSpotlight, 2009).

In essence, I am aiming to view a glass that is often times seen as half empty, as one that is half full. Again, I am not siding with the McDonald's Corporation, but rather attempting to analyze its commitments and successes in an atypical manner. I will begin by highlighting my experiences as a participant in a "fast and friendly" (a crash course training day for new employees) at a McDonald's just east of Eaton, Ohio.

INSIDE THE BELLY OF THE … LITTLE FISH

Right from the start of this project (choosing the 10 great curricula) I knew that I wanted to write about the corporate curriculum of McDonald's. As I left our first class meeting, and began to drive home, I was wondering, how will I get in touch with the people at McDonald's? How would I gain access into such a large and guarded empire? Who would I contact? Where would I go? How many hoops would I have to jump through?

The next day, I hopped online and began to peruse the McDonald's website. I came across several items that would eventually be useful for completing this project, but there was no way to contact the people at the McDonald's Headquarters. Of course I could send a letter, but I only had one semester to complete this project. Then it dawned on me, I could send an email to the "Customer Response Center." So, I sent the email telling them that I was a doctoral student at Miami University and I was interested in writing a chapter about the effectiveness of their "great" curriculum. And, miraculously, I had a response in my inbox the next day. The email encouraged me to track down one of the professors at Hamburger University, in Oakbrook Illinois, and to call him the following Monday, so I did.

The phone was ringing. I was laced with excitement and anxiety. He answered, "Hello, this is Mark, how may I help you?" I explained to him the steps I had taken thus far and that I was really looking forward to touring the university. He said, "We typically don't allow individual tours, but since your project is so intriguing, let me check with some people and get back to you." He thought my project was intriguing! I was filled with hope.

One week had gone by, so I called and left a friendly reminder. He did not call back. I began to grow nervous. Time was of the essence, how long should I wait for him to get back with me? He called back 10 days later telling me that he could not help me. Hope was fleeting. However, he did redirect me to another woman whom he thought may be able to assist me, giving me her phone number and email address. At once, I sent an email and left a voicemail. Again, several days had gone by, and no response. The emotional rollercoaster persisted. I was growing tired of the games and becoming irritated with the all the hoops I was jumping through, only to be let down. Finally, two weeks later and well into this project, she got back with me. "I am sorry sir, but it appears that we will not be able to accommodate your wishes," as if she read it from a teleprompter. Luckily I had "Plan-B" lying in the wings.

Aside from trying to gain access into the central hub of McDonald's, I was also working on visiting some local training grounds. I had been in contact with a local owner/operator, mentioned above, who was stationed just outside of Eaton, Ohio. This man was a McDonald's lifer and had held nearly every position the company has to offer. Thankfully, he had agreed to meet with me and run me through a "fast and friendly," a crash course training with actual employees.

As I participated in the session, I was amazed at how quickly I was immersed into the McDonald's culture. The meeting began. Each worker began to take notes, which seemed strange to me: taking notes in a McDonald's? Without delay, our teacher (the local owner/operator) began to inculcate the mission statement into our minds, "We are committed to excellence" and "There are three conditions of employment ... we always hustle, always smile, and we work as scheduled." Additionally, he added, "We are also committed to the corporate slogan of 'QSV&C,' which stands for 'Quality, Service, Value, and Cleanliness.'" In terms of quality, "the food needs to be delivered hot, neatly dressed, and served with a smile." Also, "keep in mind," he said, "We don't fry our foods in the same oil like other restaurants. The fries, the fish, and the nuggets each have their own fryers." And then, during the next stage of my training, I was blown away.

Finally, "As an employee here, you need to maintain a 'quality life,'" he stressed. This was new to me. In my research, I did not come across any corporate standards that called for a "quality life." Moreover, as an individual bred in the postcritical discourses at Miami University, I was floored that this man, a representative of the McDonald's corporation, attempted to name the elements which constituted a "quality life." On the other hand, as one who unwaveringly maintains his own values and ways of life, I applaud this man for standing up for his beliefs. Nonetheless, the instructor went on to claim, "We seek to hire and employ workers who maintain a good balance between the physical, mental, social, emotional, and spiritual components of life." Pretty much, he was telling us to get plenty of rest, to exercise our minds both in and out of school, to leave our social and emotional problems outside of work, and to find something that morally grounded our lives. These are not the typical facets that come to mind when one pictures McDonald's, especially when thinking of how the employees are trained. However, each trainee took it pretty well in stride.

The service at this McDonald's was a meticulous art. Each order was flawlessly packaged and assembled. Our instructor began to preach, "This is a business, not a playground." That means, "I don't want to see any cell phones out, no flirting, no chitchat, and no profanity," he emphasized. Furthermore, he began, "When you come to work, get situated. Make sure you are physically and mentally ready to begin your shift." He continued to harp on what it means to be a good worker, but myself, as well as the other learners, began to tune him out. It was a lively and poignant presentation, but he was beating a dead horse. Then, we got down to brass tacks. Finally, he started to tell us how to prepare each order.

He began by saying, "The customer is part of our team, so show them that you care about them." Then our teacher informed us of the transactional steps to take for each order. "First, we begin with a personal greeting—be sure to smile and make eye contact," he declared. He was very clear that this greeting was not to be something emotionally detached, but rather something warm and inviting such as "How may I help you today?" Next, we were given a barrage of commands running the gamut of: "take the order"; "make a suggestive sell"; such as, "would you like to try a value meal today?" "collect the money—but do not hand them their drink yet"; "while waiting for the order to be assembled, face the customer"; "open the bag first"; "place sandwiches and boxes in the bag first, then fries and pies on top"; "double check for accuracy"; and "be sure to say thanks and hurry back." Now we were humming. I was actually becoming mentally and physically exhausted.

Yet, the show continued. "When you walked in, whom did you see mopping the floor?" he asked. Upon entering the store, I noticed that he was the one mopping, but I chose to remain silent, hoping that this *fast* and friendly" would live up to its name, especially the fast part. The five seconds of silence felt like an eternity. Then he uttered, "It was me! I was the one cleaning the floor, which means, none of us are above keeping our facilities clean." He went on to say, "If I see a piece a trash on the floor, I pick it up, and you should do the same." If nothing else, it was pleasing to know that the owner/operator was willing to get a little dirty, which was part of Kroc's master plan. Come to think about it, one rarely enters a dirty or messy McDonald's, no matter what time of day or night.

As my training came to a close, I cordially thanked the owner/operator for his time and hospitality. I learned so much that it took me a couple of days to digest the material. As I look back on my training, I am inundated by thoughts, theories, and practical knowledge. Was my experience the embodiment of a "great" curriculum, or was it another taste of corporate efficiency being jammed down my throat? On one hand, I was enthralled by the personal components of the curriculum, such as allowing the workers and customers to feel welcomed and part of the McDonald's experience, while on the other hand, I was turned off by the overly technical step-by-step model that evoked many bad memories of my own days as a student. I was and still am ambivalent. By and large, I was a little frustrated that I did not get to "bark with the big dogs" at Hamburger U., but I did get the next best thing, a live look into the multilayered curriculums of a real-life McDonald's store.

MCDONALD'S THEN & NOW—FROM $.15 HAMBURGERS TO THE DOLLAR MENU

It is a typical morning in the outskirts of Cincinnati, Ohio; I head off on my 40 mile journey to Oxford. As I drive down the busy streets, passing through the clouds of exhaust being emitted by the cars and buses, I pass my first McDonald's, just 1.4 miles from my home. Heading northbound on the same road, I travel another 2.1 miles and the "golden arches" reappear. At the next traffic light I turn left, now moving westbound on yet another busy road, having advanced a shade more than two miles, I encounter my third McDonald's. This seems somewhat unfathomable, though it should be old hat, since more than half of all American's live within three miles of the nearest McDonald's (Love, 1986).

Thinking back to my childhood, I am able to vividly recall the same McDonald's that I had passed on my trip to Miami University, advertising "over 75 billion sold." In those days, Mickey D's—as it was and still is commonly referred to—would keep track of how many burgers they had sold, 5 billion at a time. My brother and I would anxiously await the posting of each seemingly monumental sign change, indicating that yet another 5 billion burgers were consumed worldwide. We actually partook in McDonald's *lived* curriculum! Today, the sign simply reads "billions and billions served," with an advertisement below reading something similar to, "The McRib is back" or "2 Fillet-O-Fish sandwiches for $2.00." However, it was not always this way. At the time of my parents' childhood, there was no such thing as the McDonald's corporation. So, how has it happened that the majority of American's live within three miles of the nearest McDonald's? Where did it all begin? Who is this Mr. McDonald? How did this company become "Super-Sized"?

In order to understand the magnitude and success of the McDonald's corporation, we must first understand the idiosyncrasies of its founder, Ray Kroc.

He (Kroc) searches through his competitors' garbage cans—he scolds his San Diego Padres over the P.A. system—he either enchants or antagonizes everyone he meets. But even his enemies agree there are three things Ray Kroc does damned well: sell hamburgers, make money and tell stories. (Kroc & Anderson, 1987, front matter)

This was not always the case. Ray Kroc was a man who lived by the words he preached. He once stated, "You have to take risks. I don't mean be a daredevil, that's crazy. But you have to take risks, and in some cases go for broke. If you believe in something, you've got to be in it to the ends of your toes. Taking reasonable risks is part of the challenge. It's the fun" (Kroc & Anderson, 1987, p. 59). And that's precisely how McDonald's came to be: Ray Kroc and his supporters were risk takers in it to the ends of their toes.

A BRIEF HISTORY OF MCDONALD'S

Kroc had been working tirelessly at the *Lilly Paper Cup Company*, only to be informed that the recession in the 1920s, which brought about "The Great Depression," was forcing all employees to take a pay cut, even the owners. When Ray Kroc got wind of this, he marched into his boss' office and demanded that he not be forced to take a pay cut because of his impeccable sales records. Even in times of economic despair, this obdurate man was willing to go for broke. Over the next few years, Kroc would continue to move from company to company, playing the piano at bars when he was unemployed, because he believed that all of his dreams could come true by way of hard work and determination (Kroc & Anderson, 1987).

By the late 1930s, Ray Kroc was a salesman for a company that marketed six-spindled milk-shake machines called "Multimixers." Around the year 1940, a great deal of attention was being paid to San Bernardino, California, where two brothers, Richard and Maurice McDonald, had constructed a drive-up restaurant called McDonald's. Kroc had heard that they were selling so many milk-shakes that they needed eight "Multimixers" going at once just to keep up. Without delay he headed to California to witness this phenomenon. When Kroc arrived at the McDonald's restaurant, he was in awe of the simplistic operations. He began to feverishly scribble down what was taking place, giving extra attention to the manner in which the workers efficiently served their customers. Over the next 10 or so years, Kroc had continued to bounce around from job to job, never forgetting what he had observed in San Bernardino. A lot transpired over this time period, especially in terms of political, economic, social, and historical events.

In particular, President Franklin D. Roosevelt had brought the country out of the "Great Depression," World War II had come and gone, family values were reconstructed, the American dream of free enterprise had been fashioned, and one of the most important aspects of McDonald's success was underway, the Interstate Highway Act. Kroc envisioned the magnitude of what the McDonald brothers had started, and in 1953, he decided to strike while the iron was hot. Kroc believed that there could be a McDonald's eatery near every major highway ramp across the U.S. But Dick and

Mac McDonald, two elderly and humble gentlemen, were content with the two restaurants that were already up and running. After countless negotiations, at the age of 52, Ray Kroc finally convinced the McDonald brothers to let him build a store near his hometown of Chicago. History was made, and in 1954 Kroc had borrowed money from everyone he knew to start his very own McDonald's restaurant in Des Plaines, Illinois (McDonald's Corporation, 2009).

Just one year later Kroc had created the "McDonald's System, Inc." and had hired June Martino and Harry Sonneborn, which proved to be instrumental for the successes that are still to this day associated with the company. Later that year, Ray Kroc hired Fred Turner (who later became CEO and Chairman, as well as the founder of Hamburger University) to run one of his stores in Des Plaines. Kroc had an eye for talent, and he just knew that Fred Turner was going to be a perfect match; in fact, Kroc's gut was rarely off target. Early on in the development of "McDonald's System, Inc." (which was renamed the "McDonald's Corporation" in 1960), Ray Kroc possessed the inventive leadership that set him apart from all other fast-food tycoons. For instance, he once asserted, "We give people an opportunity to get into business for themselves without taking the whole risk alone. All we ask is that they follow our way of doing things, *the proven way*" (as cited in Boas & Chain, 1976). This belief gave every dreamer the opportunity to belong to something, while still calling it their own!

Fittingly, the company had accrued over 100 stores and sold more than 100 million hamburgers in its first 5 years of business. Kroc felt that Dick and Mac were holding his business back, so in 1961 he offered them a whopping 2.7 million dollars for the company name and operating system ("Hamburger University: Ensuring the Future," 2005). This would be their last transaction, as the McDonald brothers had balked on the original offer and kept their names on the San Bernardino store. Likewise, Kroc made a handshake arrangement to give them 1% of all sales, which never was upheld, and the relationship ultimately dissolved on bad terms. This acquisition opened the flood gates and allowed the imaginative mind of Kroc to burgeon.

Kroc was a man who did not believe in moving on to the next big thing until he could perfect the little things. Thus, he was a man of integrity when it came to his patrons, opting not to take shortcuts to save a buck, which he felt would jeopardize their happiness. Of course, his shoddy transaction with the McDonald brothers brings to question his integrity as a person, but as an entrepreneur seeking to create a mega corporation, he held true to his word that the customer should come first. Kroc did what he had to do in order to get the job done. However, he refused to drag his customers through the dirty world of business. Some perceived his actions as corrupt while others viewed him as a business mastermind. In effect, Kroc's adversaries considered him an indignant and dishonest man, but his partners would attest that his fascination with perfection, passion for his customers, and conviction to be a winner, made him a man of integrity. Nonetheless, these attributes paved the way for McDonalds' revolutionary curriculum:

> We wanted to build a restaurant system that would be known for food of consistently high quality and uniform methods of preparation. Our aim, of course, was to insure repeat business based on the system's reputation rather than on the quality of a single store or operator. This would require a continuing program of educating and assisting operators and a constant review of their performance. It would require a full-time program of research and development. (Kroc & Anderson, 1987, p. 122)

Hence, the innovation behind the creation of Hamburger University: "It began with 14 students in the basement of a McDonald's restaurant in Elk Grove Village, Illinois, in 1961, and now the university, which has moved twice since then, educates an average of 5,000 students a year" (Williams, 2006, p. 105). Hamburger University is a training facility that turns out uniform owner/operators, but how uniform are they?

Cincinnati, Ohio, was and still is home to many Irish and German Catholics. Since canon law forbade this religious sect from eating meat on Fridays, McDonald's stores in Cincinnati were taking a bath once a week. Therefore, in 1963, Louis Groen approached Mr. Kroc about selling a fish sandwich on Fridays, in order to curb his losses. At first, Kroc told Groen, "Hell no! I don't care if the Pope himself comes to Cincinnati. He can eat hamburgers like everybody else" (Kroc & Anderson, 1987). Then he calmed down and decided to give it a whirl. Turned out, the damn thing was so popular that by 1965 it was marketed as the "Fish That Catches People," and became a popular menu item for all McDonald's stores. This was also the era that Ronald McDonald made his debut, and the company netted its first $1 million, participated in the Macy's Day parade, sponsored the first Superbowl telecast, opened the first McDonald's outside of the U.S. in Richmond, British Columbia, became listed on the New York stock exchange, introduced the Big Mac, opened its 1,000th store, and all during a time when the country was unsettled by the Vietnam War (McSpotlight, 2009).

The next few decades allowed the company to grow quickly, and with each new store, the corporation had to rethink its technical efficiency. The 1970s allowed McDonald's to explode internationally, giving rise to stores in Costa Rica (1970), Japan (1971), Australia (1971), El Salvador (1972), France (1972), Sweden (1973), United Kingdom (1974), Hong Kong (1975), Nicaragua (1975), Switzerland (1976), New Zealand (1976), Ireland (1977), Austria (1977), Belgium (1978), Brazil (1979) and Singapore (1979), among others (McSpotlight, 2009). This decade also unearthed some fundamental transformations, such as new menu items like the Quarter

Pounder (1972), the Egg McMuffin (1973) and the Happy Meal (1979), as well as its first Playland in 1971, and the first drive-thru (1975) in Arizona (McDonald's Corporation, 2009). These vital changes, in my opinion (due to the mobility of Americans at this time), were major contributors to the expansion and popularity of McDonald's.

As you can see, this corporation was on the way up! The 1980s were marked by the death of McDonald's Corporation founder Ray Kroc (1984), becoming the chief sponsors for the 1984 Olympics, and the menu had grown to include the McChicken sandwich (1980) and Chicken McNuggets (1983) (McDonald's Corporation, 2009). In 1989, the Berlin Wall came crashing down and symbolized an age of global progress. In the same way, during the 1990s, the McDonald's Corporation worked to tear down barriers that once stymied peaceful relationships between the east and the west. For instance, the first McDonald's opened in Moscow (1990), which attempted to mend our once tattered associations with the USSR. Likewise, following the end of apartheid, McDonald's opened shop in South Africa in 1996. Additionally, stores were opened in Belarus, in spite of heavy protest, and in India, even though the Hindu religion worshiped the sacred cow (McDonald's Corporation, 2009). This brings us to the dawn of the next generation—generation Y.

Since the new millennium, McDonald's has added new menu items (like the McGriddle, premium salads, chicken selects…), joined the technological craze by adding Wi-Fi (2005) to their stores, and received oodles of negative backlash on a variety of issues, including the chain's contribution to the country's obesity plague. Nonetheless, the company has managed to become "Super Sized." By buying into what Kroc (1987) believed, many women and men, through hard work, common sense, and dedication to the McDonald's principles, had become successful business people. At present, there are more than 31,000 stores in more than 120 countries, which employ over 1.6 million people (McDonald's Corporation, 2009). McDonald's has become a mega conglomerate, and therefore, has left many critics wanting answers to scores of complicated questions.

MCDONALD'S CURRICULUM—FRIEND OR FOE?

Again, I implore you to read this chapter with an open mind as well as dare you to play a part in this lived curriculum, while simultaneously (re)drawing your own conclusions based on my research and *your* prior knowledge. In this section, I am aiming to illuminate the duality of McDonald's, that is, to spotlight an effective company that scads of people across the globe have come to love, while at the same time framing it as a problematic organization. Ultimately, it is your task as a reader (if you choose to accept it) to formulate your own opinion as to whether McDonald's is a friend or a foe, and whether or not it is "great."

With that being said, join me if you will in a walk down memory lane. The year is 1990. My father, brother, and I took a trip to visit my uncle (originally from Pietracupa, Italy) in San Isidro, Costa Rica. One rainy day, on our way from the hilly and subtropical town of San Isidro, we decided to head into town to pick up some groceries. As we approached the capital city of San Jose, I could smell the diesel fumes and sense the hectic pace of what lay ahead. My Spanish was *asi asi*, so I fully embraced this journey. It was nearly lunch time, so my father, typically adventurous and willing to try anything, decided to play it safe—we went to Mickey D's. You may think that I felt right at home, but that was not the case. In terms of what Marsh & Willis (2007) would name the procedural curriculum, I knew exactly what steps to follow, but the language barrier, in addition to the overly crowded, noisy, and high-paced transactions, made me feel like a foreigner, rightfully so.

I proceeded to the counter, and with a trembling voice mustered up the courage to say "*Quisiera una hamburguesa y papas fritas francés.*" I was not sure if I said the right thing, but I was under the impression that I just ordered a hamburger and fries. When my order came up, just as promptly as if I were back home, I did what I would normally do; bit into a delicious, salty, hot french-fry. Only, it lacked the salty and delicious part. It turns out that the fries in Costa Rica are deep-fried in an unfamiliar oil, most likely a recipe common to local culture. But, how is this possible? I was under the impression that every McDonald's had to follow the same unvarying rules. I have also been fortunate enough to sample the McDonald's experience in places like Rotorua, New Zealand; Rome, Italy; Toronto, Canada; Paris, France; and Oranjestad, Aruba, where each followed the procedural curriculum to the letter of the law, but in terms of a lived curriculum, a lived experience, I would have to say that they varied greatly. For example, my European experiences, both in Rome and Paris, left me wondering why they did not serve 44oz sodas, or at the very least—put ice in my drink. Moreover, why were their coffee sizes itty-bitty, tiny, and small? And why did they taste so bad?

GLOBAL FRIEND OR EVIL EMPIRE?

Certain groups would argue that the sprawl of McDonald's global expansion infringed on cultural boundaries, exploiting the people they were invading, and attempting to uniformly Westernize their ways of life. Hunter wrote, "Whether she's Jewish, Italian, Chinese, or whatever, she's the gal the Golden Arches are out to beat" (as cited in Fishwick, p. 387). The article was speaking to the franchiser/franchisee relationship and how it had allowed new stores to pop up like dandelions, a crucial aspect to the success of the McDonald's Corporation. In the same vein, Kincheloe (2002) wrote:

> Outgrowing the borders of the United States, McDonald's has become a truly global enterprise. In this transnational process, the Golden Arches are the symbol of Western economic development—often the first foreign corporation to penetrate a particular nation's market. The Indian social critic Vandana Shiva (1997) found dark humor in the symbol of the Golden Arches. They suggest, she speculated, that when you walk into McDonald's, you are entering heaven, that the corporation wants people around the world to view "the McDonald's experience" as an immersion in celestial bliss—while they are actually eating junk. (p. 30)

The brilliantly constructed critique above brings forth a great deal of information which should not go unnoticed in the discourse about McDonald's. Then again, we as democratic citizens must not mistakenly accept anything at face value, plus, we have to be willing to hear the arguments of both parties before drawing conclusions. So, is McDonald's attempting to Westernize every country they set up shop in? Are the Golden Arches used to suggest a heavenly atmosphere? Are McDonald's customers actually eating junk? These questions, which certainly cannot locate an agreeable response, are for the reader to resolve.

Certainly McDonald's has been blasted, through a variety of media outlets, but what counter stories have been provided to address the former allegations? As for the Golden Arches, they were part of the package-deal that Kroc made with the McDonald brothers in 1954. In fact, Dick McDonald had originally envisioned a building supported by the two arches, but since no one was willing to assemble his concocted structure, he turned to a neon sign maker named George Dexter (Love, 1986). And that is how the prominent, bright yellow arches were birthed. But, what about the allegations that McDonald's has become a global empire?

According to Friedman (1996a), McDonald's stores around the world were not forcing countries to adhere to American customs, but rather embracing their diversity. For instance, the McDonald's in Israel serves Kosher food; the stores in India, where 40% of the population is vegetarian, have a "beefless" menu (with Vegetable McNuggets); and the stores in Saudi Arabia close five times a day in observance of Muslim rituals (Friedman, 1996a). Friedman (1996b) also wrote that McDonald's has avoided much of its negative backlash by becoming a "glocal" company, one which is both global and local at the same time. McDonald's does this "By insisting on a high degree of local ownership and by tailoring its products just enough for local cultures" (Friedman, 1996b, p. A 27). For example, stores in Japan have a "Donald McDonald," since the Japanese language does not have an "R" sound and "Ronald McDonald" would be difficult to pronounce (Friedman,

1996b; N. Reider, personal communication, April 2011). Do international McDonald's stores deprive countries of their cultural values? Are they truly aiming to Westernize every place that they do business in? Does McDonald's devalue its employees?

In an attempt to slow the steamrolling giant (i.e., McDonald's), Helen Steel and Dave Morris created their own website (www.McSpotlight.org) in 1997. These British citizens were infamously linked to the "McLibel" case, where they attempted to prove that McDonald's was misleading children with their advertising, treating animals inhumanely, and failing to pay its workers comparable wages. Since the duo could not prove their allegations, McDonald's turned around and sued them for libeling their name. Hence, the "McLibel" case. It should not go unnoted, this tireless fight put up by Steel and Morris gave rise to much of the Anti-McDonald's campaigning that still goes on today. At present, the website features negative posts about anything from nutrition facts to worker's rights, all of which must be addressed.

WORKERS' RIGHTS OR WORKERS WRONGED?

With regards to workers' rights, some critics would claim that McDonald's training regimen, at Hamburger University, is the reason why many managers force their young workers to be well-groomed and attentive, while neglecting to pay them more than minimum wage (Boas & Chain, 1976). Some feel that this base camp was designed to exploit and manipulate working youth into being a "team player," while forfeiting their individual rights as workers (Boas & Chain, 1976; Love, 1986; Kincheloe, 2002). Kincheloe (2002) added to this argument by claiming that McDonald's *appears* to be kid friendly, ceaselessly promoting fun, and always in the best interests of its workers, but yet they fail to offer any union representation. While on the other hand, McDonald's founder believed that unionization would create a stale company that would fail to embrace individuality and creativity (Kroc & Anderson, 1987). As a result of Ray Kroc's visions, McDonald's has been able to produce unique stores that creatively contribute to the betterment of society.

For instance, a store in Renton, Washington, pays its workers for doing homework an hour before their shifts begin, similar to a Honolulu store's notion of earning an extra hour for doing homework when the shift ends, or in Tulsa where the workers have formed an Algebra study group that meets afterhours, or in states like Colorado, Virginia, and Massachusetts that give bonuses for workers who improve their grades, and in Kansas and New Jersey, reading-improvement classes have been formed (Reingold, 1992). Clearly, one can see that individual store owners, who have some autonomy, have made exemplary efforts to support education, something I feel all companies could and should improve on, especially those who employ teenaged student workers.

Furthermore, the McDonald's family has made great strides to employ elderly persons, as well as persons with disabilities. An owner of multiple stores in Orange County, California, believed that hiring senior citizens and special needs workers created a sense of humanity (Reingold, 1992). Another owner, in Long Island, New York, had employed 26 disabled workers in her 12 stores. It would appear that the company is one that promotes social justice, but of course, it is still repeatedly bashed for appointing conventional store owners and managers.

SOCIALLY JUST OR RACIALLY MISREPRESENTATIVE?

Another facet that makes McDonald's "great," is its ability to staff an organization with a diverse population. I guess that is why its training ground, Hamburger University, delivers its lessons in 28 different languages (Hamburger University: Ensuring the Future, 2005). Or, why it is that close to 60% of the McDonald's personnel are from an ethnic minority group and approximately 58% of them are female (Weinstein, 2008). Better yet, their desire to employ a diverse workforce could explain why "nearly 70% of McDonald's restaurant management and 25% of the company's executives are minorities and women, and so are about *half* its corporate department heads" (Reingold, 1992).

Nonetheless, McDonald's has been attacked throughout the years for being racially insensitive. For instance, in 1972, renowned newscaster Paul Harvey spoke on behalf of the McDonald's Corporation, stating that it took hard work to get things in this world and those too lazy to pursue it should not reap any benefits (Boas & Chain, 1976). As a result, many African Americans were outraged by the speech, and formed a black caucus. Rightfully so, since they had pumped just as much money into the company as any other group. Additionally, Kincheloe (2002) made mention of a TV add, called a "Second Chance," which attempted to rescue a young black man from the street life, and making him a part of the "McFamily." Kincheloe (2002) also claimed that McDonald's irresponsibly designed "Calvin" (the character in the TV add) to signify the dangerousness of black men and portrayed them as needing to be saved by McDonald's. Although this corporation has failed at times to be racially sensitive, they are—in spite of everything—committed to socially just organizations such as the Urban League, N.A.A.C.P., and the U.S. Hispanic Chamber of Commerce (Reingold, 1992). However, the company continues to catch heat.

HEALTH NUT OR NUTTY HEALTH?

McDonald's hit the big screen in 2004 with Morgan Spurlock's controversial documentary film *Super Size Me*. In this movie, Spurlock agreed to eat McDonald's three times a day for 30 days, in an attempt to expose the company's unhealthy food choices. At the end of his 30 days, in which he consumed around 5,000 calories each day, Spurlock had gained nearly 25 pounds, and claimed that he had also experienced mood swings, liver damage, and a lack of sexual desire. It was later revealed that it took him over a year to lose the weight he put on. In an effort to make the food more nutritionally approachable, McDonald's added lighter fares to their menu like the fruit-and-walnut salad, apple slices, and so forth. In order to keep up with the times, McDonald's now offers over eight different healthy salads and dressings, several low fat options, fruit and yogurt desserts, and many other healthy choices. But more important, why would anyone eat anything three times a day for 30 days?

For instance, let us examine the banana. Practically, everyone could agree that bananas are wholesome food items, jam packed with vitamin B6, fiber, vitamin C, and loads of potassium. But, did you know that the average banana contains potassium-40 (K-40), which is a radioactive isotope that emits gamma radiation, one of the most harmful of all types of radiation; it is more powerful than an x-ray. Actually, a banana contains more radiation than your standard basement. Therefore, it may be a nutritious food item, but when consumed outside of moderation (like 3 times a day for 30 days) it too could lead to harmful side effects. So how does McDonald's sustain excellence? How does this company continue to thrive even while being widely attacked?

SO ... WHY MCDONALD'S?

Lunch time in Delhi, Ohio: the drive-thru has an overload of cars stretched out to the street and dozens more customers are dining in. Upon entering the store, I noticed that there was no trash on the ground. Once inside, the place was spotless, in spite of it being the busiest time of the day. I could see that the workers were busy, churning out orders like machines. I approach the counter, order a #1 (Big Mac meal) w/out special sauce, and patiently wait—no more than 30 seconds—for my order to come up. The food was delivered to me, piping hot, with a pleasant smile and a soft voice saying, "Thank you sir. Have a great day!" This allowed me to feel affectionately welcomed. As I was wolfing down my food, I began to hone in on what was taking place all around me. How did this crew manage this large lunch rush, like it was a walk in the park?

Each bag, box, drawer, cup, condiment, and container was neatly positioned, waiting to be used efficiently. The fry guy was reloading his station with an enormous bag of frozen fries. The cashiers were punching buttons faster than a teenager texting her friends on a Friday night. At once, the orders would flash on the strategically placed monitors, alerting the people in their stations to prepare. The burger band began. Wax paper (check), buns (check), ketchup (check), mustard (check), pickles (check), onions (check), beef (check), cheese (check), top bun (check), fold the corners in (check), next! Oh no, "we are out of ice" declared the cashier. She waits for a break in the action, heads off to the backroom—the manager hollers out, "front counter!" There was a customer who had been waiting for no more than 10 seconds. While pushing a massive bin of ice, the cashier is rushing to get to her station. "Can I help you?" asked the young girl—right back on pace. The crew was as efficient as a factory assembly line, hundreds of small jobs, few errors. 1:30 p.m., the manager was assessing their performance, rifling through papers with a calculator. They had endured the hungry horde, only to regroup and wait for the dinner crowd. How did they do it?

This performance was typical of what I learned about in my aforementioned "Fast and Friendly" training. As I was watching the crew, I began recollecting all that was covered in my crash course, asking: Did they smile? Were they hustling? Did the team put their customers first? Were they sincere and enthusiastic? Did the crew perform each task at the highest rate of effectiveness? Did they assemble the orders properly (sandwich, then fries, then desert, finally the drink)? Was the drive-thru staff keeping up? I was amazed! My brief training seminar was coming alive, right before my very eyes. Each position was responsibly managing its assigned area, and ensuring that each customer was at ease. This location, like nearly every other McDonald's that I have frequented, superbly fulfilled the quality, service, cleanliness and value (QSC&V) checklist established by Kroc and his team so long ago and still in place, thriving today. But, how does McDonald's ensure that you will have a pleasurable visit, every time?

TRAINING VERSUS EDUCATING

In Oak Brook, Illinois, there sits a state of the art facility used to train/educate McDonald's workers, managers, and potential store owners about how to achieve success. The place is Hamburger University (HU). Yes, there actually is a place called Hamburger University, and they really do award degrees in "hamburgerology." This campus, which many say feels like you are walking on the grounds of an Ivy League campus, is home to 16 professors who train employees in 28 different languages ("Hamburger University: Ensuring the future," 2005; "The McRecipe for Success, 1995; Weinstein, 2008).

Hamburger University is the hive that (re)produces prototypical drones ready to implement and instill the McDonald's Corporation values. This top secret campus (which I was unable to gain access to) is where the visions are unfolded and the instructions for building one's own empire are bestowed.

However, this is a rather convoluted topic. Does McDonald's educate its workers or do they train them to fulfill an unethical agenda? According to Dewey (1938), education is not the same thing as training, nor is it the same thing as learning, in fact, education is a moral endeavor that leads to growth that is defensible by society. Dewey (1938) would argue that people can learn how to be dysfunctional, how to be a gangster, or even a corrupt politician, but learning is not considered to be educational unless there is evidence of morally defensible growth—a growth that creates conditions for further growth. Do workers get trained by McDonalds to deliver a product that is unhealthy, exploitive, and destructive? Or do they receive an education that helps them do something valuable? Or that might lead to some other defensible ends that are valuable both to the individual and to society? To answer these questions, we must further examine the categories of curricula associated with McDonald's in order to peel back the various layers of this multifaceted corporation.

THE MULTILAYERED CURRICULA

First and foremost is the corporate curriculum of McDonald's. This rich layer represents the heart of this corporate onion, giving way to all structural and procedural operations. The company's curriculum could be defined as follows: a set of values that places the customer experience at the center of its operations; commit to the well-being of their people; ubiquitously believe in the McDonald's system; focus on global environment issues; conduct all business ethically; believe in giving back to their communities; all while striving to continually improve (McDonald's Corporation, 2009). This multifarious curriculum is responsible for sustaining the company as a whole, as well as allowing the company to ward off a declining economy that is currently pulling so many businesses under, except McDonald's. In addition, each individual store must follow these set procedures (with some autonomy already mentioned) in order to ensure system wide success.

In order to implement such a complex and involved curriculum, workers at all levels would need to be educated about the aforementioned subjects and trained on how to best implement them. Ray Kroc said it best, "if we are going to go anywhere, we've got to have talent" (McDonalds, 2009). This proved to be a critical statement, since HU was built in order to guarantee that all McDonald's restaurants were stocked with highly trained/educated folks. This is where we should introduce the second layer of the McDonald's curriculum, the layer responsible for educating workers about how to execute the corporate agenda. The curriculum employed by Hamburger University is delivered using a blend of classroom instruction, goal-based scenarios, hands-on labs activities, and is disseminated in 28 different languages (McDonald's Corporation, 2009). Let us further examine the design, purpose, and implementation of this layer of the McDonald's curriculum.

With respect to educating its employees about the importance of the corporate curriculum, McDonald's heeded the advice of John Dewey (1938), who stated:

> What we want and need is education pure and simple, and we shall make surer and faster progress when we devote ourselves to finding out just what education is and what conditions have to be satisfied in order that education may be a reality and not a name or a slogan. It is for this reason alone that I have emphasized the need for a sound philosophy of experience. (p. 116)

As a result, McDonald's has made experiential learning a top priority. Dewey (1956) believed that the kitchen and home were two places where education could build on prior areas of growth—using experiences from a child's home life to make connections between schooling and the real world applications. Likewise, McDonald's felt that the best way to educate workers was to place them in a simulated version of a real McDonald's kitchen and to allow them to perform daily tasks that would later be applied to their jobs ("Hamburger University: Ensuring the future," 2005; Jones, 2007; "The McRecipe for Success," 1995; Thomas, 2007).

Students at HU are placed into teams of service members, shift leaders, and observers and are given a virtual service lab to experience. Upon completion of the lab, the HU students look at their first results, then they address missing factors and run the virtual shift again, afterward they analyze the results with respect to profits, obviously discovering that little mistakes, oversights, and missing factors would adversely affect their earnings (Jones, 2007). This form of experiential learning allows the students to physically apply what they are being taught, as opposed to learning it from paper–pencil transactions. This is what Dewey (1956) was referring to when he stated "The child can carry over what he learns in the home and utilize it the school; and the things learned in the school he applies at home" (p. 80). Ultimately, through interactive, hands-on, and student-centered labs, HU students are actively taught leadership roles, as well as how to delegate responsibilities, which better groom them for the real-life situations that they will encounter on the job (Galagan, 2006; "Hamburger University: Ensuring the future," 2005; Jones, 2007; "The McRecipe for success," 1995; Thomas, 2007; Weinstein, 2008).

The HU students are immersed into this robust and relevant module for 2 weeks, where they are inundated with job-like simulations and group competitions. The final exam is a cross between *Jeopardy* and *Family Feud*, where the students are placed into teams and are assessed over the material they covered. Not only does this multimedia facility provide experiential education, but also "helps to reduce turnover, increase efficiency and boost morale" (Thomas, 2007, p. 12). With an educational curriculum as rich as that of McDonald's, it is no wonder the company budgets $1 billion for annual training of all of its employees, which reaches all the way up to the top officials (Jones, 2007). More important, a company that is willing and able to spend $1 billion on training genuinely buys into the importance of (re)investing in its employees, which is a staple to the McDonald's corporate curriculum.

This brings us to the construction of the McDonald's store curriculum—derived from the corporate agenda—which was built on three main principles: have a vision, organize your vision into goals, and establish a routine way to monitor it (Thomas, 2007). This sounds stunningly similar to the Tyler (1949) rationale, where objectives are clearly stated, learning experiences are carefully selected and organized, and they are effectively monitored by scientific measurements. In terms of a store-level curriculum, McDonald's begins with well-defined objectives, following Tyler's rational-linear model. These objectives are straightforward: ensure that there are consistent operational procedures; emphasize service, quality, and cleanliness; and develop talented workers from within the organization. Each store then organizes these visions into goals, for the most part; each store sets its goals based on monthly profits. In addition, some stores have individual goals (i.e., improve cleanliness, increase sales of a certain menu item, and so forth). Finally, each vision and goal is scientifically monitored using checklists, computer software, and profit reports which are sent to corporate headquarters. Next comes the final piece, the lived (or experienced) curriculum. How does McDonald's execute its curricula? How is this curriculum brought to life for and by its customers?

What is it about McDonald's that makes us say, "I'm loving it?" Maybe it is their salty french-fries, clean facilities, or friendly service. Perhaps, it is because you *know* what you are going to get every time you go to McDonald's. Possibly it is because McDonald's has become a household term or because they spend $2 billion each year on advertising. Better yet, you choose McDonald's because they offer you comfort, security, or a job during these dismal economic times. Perhaps, you frequent McDonald's because of the value that they repeatedly offer, or because you are underprivileged, or because you are a single mom who has worked all day and is too tired to cook dinner. Regardless of why you choose (or do not choose) McDonald's, one thing is certain; they will continue to bring quality, service, cleanliness, and value to the table because that's what they were built on! By implementing the multilayered curricula that is McDonald's, the customer is able to enjoy the lived curriculum – most of the time. But, why McDonald's?

CONCLUDING THOUGHTS

McDonald's is the first choice of so many consumers and for so many workers because it truly values its customers and does all that is possible to ensure a friendly visit. For the most part the facilities are well-manicured, the food is more than affordable and is delivered with a smile, and the overall experience is one that keeps people coming back. McDonald's is successful because it has an unassailable corporate curriculum that understands that customers are the very reason for the company's existence; because it uses a "three-legged stool" business model that allows the owner/operators, suppliers, and company employees to have ownership without taking risks; because it feels that sound ethics of being individually responsible and collectively reliable make for good business; because it creatively and philanthropically uses resources to help make the world a better place; and because it is constantly evolving through innovative means to meet the needs of customers, employees, and the overall system (McDonald's Corporation, 2009).

McDonald's is also great because it puts its money where it belongs, in the training/educating of employees for the future. "McDonald's promotes continual learning for its employees and expects every worker to go through 40 hours of development each year," (Jones, 2007, p. 48) an expectation that applies to every worker from the CEO to the cashier of a local store. The key phrase is "continual learning." Previously, I posed questions about the efficacy of McDonald's education/training curriculum such as "Do workers get trained by McDonalds to deliver a product that is unhealthy, exploitive, and destructive or do they receive an education that helps them do something valuable?" As already noted, future employees are taught leadership roles, good work ethics, the importance of teamwork, the significance of giving back to the community, as well as how to delegate responsibilities, which in my opinion all lead to a growth that is morally defensible by society. By Dewey's definition of learning, the McDonald's corporation is educating its employees to do something valuable both individually and for the betterment of society.

There is a great deal to be gained from this investigation of McDonald's. For instance, schools in America could stand to learn from the importance of (re)investing in their future prospects. More important, educational facilities at all levels need to grasp and glean the importance of experiential learning both inside and outside the school walls. The multifaceted curriculum used by the McDonald's Corporation has impacted the lives of billions of people. While McDonald's does offer a rich, multipart curriculum that is remarkably effective on so many levels, it also brings with it an ideology that some feel is problematic, exploitative, and inhumane. The two sides may be diametrically opposite to one another, but both ought to agree that the McDonald's curriculum is at the very least effective, if not "great," for what it was intended for. So the better question seems to be, why not McDonald's?

RESPONSE BY TOM POETTER

I am not of the mind that global, multinational companies need defending, necessarily, which is not the point of Danny's chapter. I originally suggested the topic because I thought it would be provocative given all that McDonald's has had to weather in terms of criticism the past 10 years and given its fascinating founding and the practical and conceptual commitments of Ray Kroc to the education of employees, the regulation of the food and service systems for quality, and the extension of opportunities for advancement through the corporation to so many Americans, and now, world citizens. I knew about Hamburger U, and that John Dewey thought one of the greatest labs for learning in life is the kitchen. Where better to find examples of progressive curriculum in action than a famously successful restaurant that boasts about education and opportunity? What would a curriculum inquiry into how this all "works" yield for us to chew on?

We all know that McDonald's has been assailed for its practices, for the marketing it does to segments of the population, for its seemingly low quality and addictive menu, for its cultural insensitivities, that is, bringing the western world and its hamburgers/fries home to the world whether it wants them or not. But the bogeyman is right around the corner, and we are involved with it whether we want to be or not (our relatives and friends are employed there), because the corporation does have a human face and only works because of that and because of us. And bottom line, we continue to make our way to the drive-thrus and dining rooms all over the country and consume the products at hand. My guess is that less than 5% of the people who will ever read this book have made a lifetime commitment to boycotting McDonald's and can actually hold to it. I may be wrong, but I do not think I am.

So, Danny digs deeper into what McDonald's does on the ground with its product and its employees for the reader in order to illuminate its curricular and educational qualities, and as an inquirer to draw us in more deeply to the questions, experiences, and outcomes of the phenomena surrounding the implementation of the curriculum through the McDonald's approach to food and to people. I admit that I have always been fascinated with corporate curriculum, and like the idea of inquiring into it to see how it can illuminate what we think of the intersections of curriculum, learning, experience, and teaching.

For me, the argument for McDonald's surpasses any attempt at showing that it has a corporate agenda for the public good, establishing charities and delivering a portion of its proceeds back to the community through its foundations' endeavors. This is probably good work, but does not cloak McDonald's or get at the heart of the matter. What gets at the heart of the matter for me is the amazing record of extension of opportunity to Americans of all kinds to advance through its structure, learning about hard work and sacrifice and making a living along the way. It is impossible to count the graduates of McDonald's and the record it has for helping to produce responsible citizens. There are lots of factors involved, of course, but the provision of opportunity is one of the main requirements for a democratic republic practicing under the economic watch of capitalism.

And the care McDonald's takes to educate workers, to help them become better citizens, is difficult to take to task. Hamburger U. is a model for excellent educational practice, essentially allowing a real-world lab to show employees the way to success while simultaneously creating the conditions for innovation and change. I am not for the standardization of every thing, or trying to routinize or technicize every aspect of schooling or classrooms as is the case with those who run businesses that depend upon profit and quality control such as McDonald's. What is more important is the fact that McDonald's knows what it is about and is committed to doing what it does best in the most efficient, open manner possible. This is the way to maximize the universe within. We can learn a lot from that no matter what we do for a living or believe in.

THE FINAL WORD BY DANNY CIAMARRA

As practitioners, we are the arbiters of the curriculum. What I like most about the McDonald's Corporation is that it promotes a system where the owners, operators, cashiers, cooks, vendors, patrons, and so forth, become arbiters of both the private and public curriculums. Moreover, the epicenter of this corporate curriculum centers around experiential education, hands-on learning, real-life situations, and is driven by a student-centered approach. Thus, the McDonald's curriculum hinges on many Deweyan concepts, in particular, that of an active and engaging learning environment (such as the kitchen), where new knowledge lends itself to personal and social growth. Therefore, I agree with Tom that McDonald's deserves praise for its capacity to educate workers, to encourage them to become good citizens, and to extend opportunities to Americans of all kinds, but is there more to it than that?

During my observations, interviews, and experiences, both positive and negative, I came to understand the McDonald's curriculum is one that interrupts binary thinking. For instance, this corporate curriculum is able to simultaneously join the individual with the collective group, and vice versa, in order to achieve both similar and disparate goals. Thus, this multinational company exhibits the exceptional ability of pulling everyone together without smothering anyone's individuality. In essence, I witnessed the manifestation of Ray Kroc's (1987) vision, which reads: "In business for yourself, but not by yourself." This radical thought process allows autonomy and dependency to exist side-by-side, which to me is a little more than just giving people an opportunity to advance through a system, but rather giving them the chance to reap some of the benefits without taking all of the risks.

In a similar fashion, I believe that schools have a great deal to glean from this organization. Picture our schools celebrating an authentic and interactive form of learning that bridges school and life. Visualize a place where learning is fun and meaningful. Still yet, imagine a curriculum that invites students from all walks of life to partake in something larger than themselves without fearing that they will be lost or stripped of their individuality. To me, that is what McDonald's is able to accomplish. Whether we choose to explore foreign franchises that allow local practices to coexist amongst McDonald's policies (such as the Israeli stores that serve Kosher foods) or if we examine hometown stores that deviate from the norm, it is safe to say that the McDonald's family welcomes the fusing of separateness and likeness. Imagine if our schools could do the same.

Also, to reiterate Tom's point, this is not to suggest that we ought to take the "routinized" or "technicized" business principles of the McDonald's curriculum and apply them to school processes, since schools are technical enough already. Instead, we ought to focus on the autonomous elements that bring it success. Of course, it would also be easy to jump on the bandwagon and bash this corporation on many levels, but as I have previously stated, I am aiming to view a glass that is often times seen as half empty, as one that is half full. The former allows us to view this project through a critical pair of eyes, while the latter affords us the opportunity to foresee practical solutions. Steinbeck's East of Eden was a portrayal of the battle between good and evil, likewise, so is this chapter—the ending is up to you.

REFERENCES

Boas, M., & Chain, S. (1976). *Big Mac: The unauthorized story of McDonald's*. New York, NY: Dutton.

Dewey, J., 1859–1952. (1938). *Experience and education*. New York, NY: Macmillan.

Dewey, J., 1859–1952. (1956). *The child and the curriculum, and the school and society*. Chicago, IL: University of Chicago Press.

Fishwick, M. W. (1978). *The world of Ronald McDonald*. Bowling Green: Bowling Green University Popular Press.

Friedman, T. (1996a, December 8). Big Mac I. *The New York Times*, E15.

Friedman, T. (1996b, December 11). Big Mac II. *The New York Times*, A27.

Galagan, P. (2006). Old school gets new role. *T+D, 60*(11), 36–39.

Hamburger University: Ensuring the Future. (2005). *Nation's Restaurant News*, 104–107.

Jones, T. (2007). Do you believe in magic? The secret to McDonald's training success. *Chief Learning Officer, 6*(4), 48–48.

Kincheloe, J. (2002). *The sign of the burger: McDonald's and the culture of power*. Philadelphia: Temple University Press.

Kroc, R., & Anderson, R. (1987). *Grinding it out: The making of McDonald's*. New York, NY: St. Martin's Press.

Love, J. F. (1986). *McDonald's: Behind the arches*. New York, NY: Bantom Books.

Marsh, C., & Willis, G. (2007, 4th ed.). *Curriculum: Alternative approaches, ongoing issues*. Upper Saddle River, NJ: Pearson.

McDonald's Corporation Home Page. (2009). – Available from:<mcdonalds.com>.

McSpotlight. (2009). —Available from: *<mcdonalds.com>*.

Noren, D. L. (1990). The economics of the golden arches: A case study of the Mcdonald's system. *American Economist, 34*(2), 60–64.

Reingold, E. M. (1992). America's Hamburger helper. *Time, 139*(26), 66.

Ronald McDonald House Charities. (2008).—Available from: *<http://rmhc.org>*.

The McRecipe for success. (1995). *Industrial & Commercial Training, 27*(10), 25–26.

Thomas, D. (2007). *Path to profits*. Executive Excellence Publishing.

Tyler, R. (1949). *Basic principles of curriculum and instruction*. Chicago, IL: University of Chicago Press.

Weinstein, M. (2008). GETTING McSMART. *Training, 45*(4), 44–47.

Williams, G. (2006). Behind the arches. *Entrepreneur, 34*(1), 104–112.

CHAPTER 5

CENTRAL ACADEMY: LIVING A DEMOCRATIC FRAMEWORK

Susan L. M. Bartow

DEMOCRATIC, PROGRESSIVE PROGENITORS

The long history of the vital connection between public school and a democracy continues to find expression in contemporary progressive schools. Progressive educators believe democracy is more than the process of voting or an individual's right to make choices. Students do not learn to live and participate in a democracy simply by reading about their constitution and legislative processes; they learn about democracy in democratically run schools. At their core, democratic educators believe democracy is an idea of how people live together. Political/social democracies put a premium on the dignity of all people and for caring about the welfare of others, the common good. Everyone has the right to just and equitable treatment, to be able to become fully informed, to pursue personal growth, and to have a say about what matters. Everyone has the obligation to be well informed, to collaborate, and to promote the general welfare of the larger society (Beane, 2005), that is, to develop the intellectual and social capacities to work together for a just and equitable society.

10 Great Curricula: Lived Conversations of Progressive, Democratic Curricula in School and Society, pp. 99–113
Copyright © 2011 by Information Age Publishing
All rights of reproduction in any form reserved.

The curriculums of schools adopting a democratic progressive perspective incorporate the skills, promote the propensities, and provide time for participating in the governance of the classroom and school; involve students to the fullest level in learning through multiple means; are integral to their communities; and offer learning tied to real-life situations. The curriculum must embody living and learning democratically and assumes a core social conscience.

In the pantheon of those who have founded and maintained progressive democratic schools, Deborah Meier is one of the most famous, influential, and successful. She rejects the notion that the most important purpose of education is either to enhance the economic opportunities of future adults or to maintain our position ahead of others in a race of nations to establish and reify power and economic prosperity or military superiority. These notions have been tied to public education since the eighteenth century, captivating and driving school curriculum designers who have responded with technical solutions supporting the status quo at various points in our national history. But Meier (2003) finds the crises in a different place, in "the ebbing strength of our democratic and egalitarian culture" (p. 16).

Meier asks us to look at what we really want schools to accomplish. For Meier, if the democratic project is to thrive it must be available to everyone; its upkeep must be a part of the repertoire of every member of a society. She observes that schools, like democracies, can look different from one another, but finds today's focus on rote learning and easily measured answers problematic because they breed sameness and homogeneity. Schools, according to Meier and other progressives, should focus first on the habits of mind needed to be a rich participant, an active citizen in a democracy. They emphasize productive and inclusive human interaction at all levels, a healthy exchange of ideas, and skillful decision making. Students learn through immersion, apprenticeship, instruction, experimentation, reflection, and discussion, following the behaviors they see modeled by the adults in their school. The curriculum meshes the needs of a democratic society with the needs of children, resulting in an educational experience of vital interest and meaning in children's lives and varied enough to allow many expressions of growth. Reminding us that schools must be aware of their limited reach and of the powerful role of class in America, Meier emphasizes the critical importance of working in close partnership with the families of her students.

CENTRAL ACADEMY, MIDDLETOWN, OHIO

Dianne Suiter, a graduate of Miami's doctoral program in Educational Leadership and the principal of Central Academy in Middletown, Ohio, for the past 8 years has studied Meier as a part of her dissertation, and has kept in close touch with her over the intervening years. Her school, Central Academy, is a progressive public school of choice in the Middletown City School District and was founded in 1991 (Lolli, 1994). The school is described as a nongraded, multiaged school. With Dianne's leadership, it has become a progressive, democratic school.

Middletown is a small Midwestern city that has seen its share of economic difficulties. It has struggled in the decade following the purchase and downsizing of its major employer, a large steel company. The company and community have weathered extreme challenges, such as a contentious, debilitating lockout of workers at the plant that lasted a year. The city and region are still reeling from changes brought on by the 2008–2010 recession. Central Academy has fought against the regional educational and economic tide to be a unique school, part of a great tradition of democratic progressive schools. Significantly for me, Central is the public version of what's somewhat easier to accomplish and more typically seen in private K-12 schools. To me, Dianne, her colleagues, and the school's families rise to face the ethical imperative of providing an outstanding and relevant public education for all citizens. They push the envelope, having a profound impact on not only academic and social learning but also act to foster the growth of a critical and caring citizenry. As Tom notes in the introductory chapter here, one aspect of greatness in the planned and enacted curricula we examine in this book is the measure in which those who lived the curriculum become able and inclined to create more democratic, just opportunities and institutions in their society for themselves and particularly for others.

Surprised and delighted to learn of a progressive public school very much like the private school where I taught and have been Head of School, I first visited Central several years ago, long before my class with Tom and our co-authors. After my early visit, I urged the other teachers at my school to visit, too, as part of their professional development, declaring they would be amazed to find a public school that felt so much like ours. We visited, had a great time, and happily hosted a reciprocal visit when a few Central teachers were able to come to Oxford. Since those initial reciprocating visits, I have continued and deepened my understanding of progressive education.

What I found is that Central is an emphatically and distinctly democratic progressive school, a definitive characteristic in a universe of overlapping notions of what it means to be a progressive school.

DEMOCRATIC FRAMEWORK: VOICE

As a strong proponent of democratic progressive education, Central allies itself with networks of similar schools. Both size and structure are carefully and deliberately established to align with the philosophical dictates of progressive democratic theorists. Schools must be small to be democratic and to work (Meier, 2002); everyone must know everyone else. Teachers must be able to sit in one room in a circle. Enrollment at Central stays below just 300 students and the students enter by lottery. Even though there is an exciting mix of student interns from the local university at each staff meeting, there are only about 20 faculty members. It is a public school of choice. Families choose to send their children to Central for its unique type of education. Over half of the students are economically disadvantaged, a third of them are from a racial minority, and its attendance rate is over 95%. Central has established and maintains structures and procedures it recognizes as inherently and essentially democratic.

In its new location, the school looks strikingly attractive, interesting, and well kept from the outside. When approached, its distinctive character is quickly apparent. On one of my visits, I walked up the main sidewalk as children were arriving. Children of different sizes and races waited for each other along the sidewalk. One small girl waited, smiling, for another; they held hands as they walked into the building. One young boy had his arm around another's shoulder as they shared a story. It is worth noting that these especially kind and comfortable interactions were between children of different races and ages. When I walked through the door, it did not take long to understand what is unique at Central. I was greeted by a "Wall of Dreams" announcing, "With motivation and determination, dreams can come true." Small signs made by everyone in the building, by all students and adults, expressed their dreams. A large handmade sign welcomed me to the Central family. Pictures with captions described who has visited Central recently and what Central has been doing this year.

Children and adults hustled excitedly everywhere, grabbing stacks of newspapers to take to their classes. My school has just grudgingly decided to instigate a more modern visitors policy. Visitors are now required to sign in at the office and wear a badge, a major culture shift for such a tiny and open school. Even though my school has always been very open, I am conditioned by my own school past and many school visits as an adult to report directly to a school's main office. I generally make a beeline for the office, afraid of being intercepted as a rule-breaker or a possible threat. I am surprised, very pleased, and a little bit worried that none of that is in evidence at Central.

In the hallway there were some interesting and puzzling large signs. Conversation and closer observation revealed those large signs to be handwritten proclamations. Almost a dozen of them line the entrance hallway describing what is important and valued at this school. As I read them, I felt the strong sense of community and distinctly elaborated values they expressed. I begin to understand the pervasive democratic system integrated into the daily operations of the school. The proclamations in the hall were created at the start of the year and the values expressed on them are echoed and lived. One of Central's core democratic traditions is the town meeting, an all school meeting. Tradition dictates its structure, that is, until a future group redefines it. Each year starts with a town meeting, the purpose of which is to set the community norms for the year. Classroom groups of students file into the school's gym, one class going clockwise, the next counter clockwise. Students, one at a time, drop off at each large piece of paper stuck to the wall. The result is a multiaged group in front of each paper. The whole group works to develop a list of their values. Ultimately, one value is written at the top of each piece of paper. These values become the norms of this small society.

> "We are a family."
> "We value our education and learning."
> "Everyone has input."
> "We admit when we are wrong and we make it right."
> "We can all speak here."
> "We are a family. We help each other."

How does it look in a classroom where the occupants believe people should admit when they are wrong and make it right? Each mixed age small group works to illustrate the value at the head of its paper, describing what an observer would see, how that value would be enacted in a classroom. According to the list, the observer would see people apologizing, repaying with something, making better choices next time, not yelling at each other, being kind, and, if someone's property was broken, the person responsible would be asking what s/he could do to make amends. This is a far cry from the "character trait of the month" style of character education.

One of the basic tenets of a democratic society is the right of everyone to participate, to be at the table and heard. At Central each person has a voice. Every person in the school is at this town hall meeting. Anyone can speak; anyone can shape the society being constructed. The town hall meeting, which can be called anytime there is a problem or a situation concerning the whole school, can be called by anyone. Everyone, every student and every employee, comes. Members of the school community listen to each other, propose solutions, and discuss resolutions until consensus is reached.

DEMOCRATIC FRAMEWORK: GOVERNANCE

Within district and larger societal parameters, Central is a staff-run school. Staff meetings are consensus meetings. Voting as the means of coming to a solution that a majority supports is not good enough. The group must work until it reaches a consensus that everyone can live with. Just as the whole school does at a town meeting, teachers develop the norms for their meetings and build the agenda each week. Teachers' meetings provide the forum for addressing building concerns and making decisions about site-based procedures and curricular goals and strategies. The jobs involved with running a meeting —facilitator, task keeper, timekeeper, and note taker—rotate among staff members. Anyone, including students, can put a topic on the agenda. The meeting agenda form is kept on a clipboard in the workroom. The person bringing the item to the attention of the group indicates if this item is simply an announcement or is an item that requires consensus and suggests a time allotment. At the meeting, if the group cannot come to a consensus on a topic, the topic is tabled. If a solution cannot be reached, the reasoning and procedure go, the problem must require more thought. Somewhere there is a better solution. It is the responsibility of the group to take the time to find or build it.

The meetings I visited sounded so deliberate and purposeful. I listened to voices around the circle, taking turns, thoughtfully and considerately sharing their views and responding when input is needed. "I'm hearing everyone saying…" "Should we table this?" "But we may need to make a formal decision for next year." Teachers are at their first of two weekly back-to-back meetings that follow a day of teaching. Large chart papers line the wall of the library, ready to record the important elements of their deliberations. Everyone is contributing; their eyes are on the business at hand. They are operating under the norms they agreed upon at the start of the year. They "acknowledge when we have come to an impasse. The task keeper (or anyone else) can then ask if we want to either go around the table to say 'Yes,' 'No,' or 'I can live with it'; or table the discussion for later reflection" (printed agenda, April 1, 2009). Other norms include: "Everyone speaks for themselves"; "Use positive and professional body language, both when speaking and listening"; and "Write clear objectives for conversations on agenda."

After weekly staff meetings, teachers take a few minutes to grab a snack or go to the bathroom and divide into house or team groups for a second meeting. House meetings are set up by dividing the school in half vertically. Each half-sized group contains a range of ages. The houses meet to discuss student concerns, strategies, and recommendations. During the meeting I attended, teachers shared background about a student getting ready to join an older group. Teachers having experience with the child shared intervention strategies and successful techniques for working with both the child and the family. Veteran teachers helped newer teachers. On the alternate week, they have team meetings, meetings of all teachers in a certain age range, a horizontal component of the school's organization. Teachers and administrators also plan two retreats per year. These are two-day meetings at a nearby hotel to work out themes for the year, solve problems, and make use of professional development or learning community opportunities. Retreat topics are impressive, timely, and organic, including sessions on conferencing with parents, the school's writing program, and next year's themes.

The pattern of democratic processes repeats throughout the school. Students young and older call similar meetings in their classrooms whenever there is a need. Dewey and the democratic progressives that claim him as a forerunner hold that democracy, like other instrumentalities and occupations of our society, must be practiced, must be brought into the real life experience of the child. In their classrooms, Central students learn the skills of listening and speaking, gathering information, evaluating ideas, communicating, thinking critically and carefully, sharing, working, compromising, and looking out for the unheard point-of-view. Meetings in a Central classroom can involve a small group of peers with a stake in the situation at hand or the whole class. Students follow the same processes as teachers do to solve problems, to establish guidelines and priorities, and to make choices. Examples of democratic processes in action are found in a few incidents, each representing a different scale. The first involved the entire school, parents, and interested community members. The second involved the two upper grades.

For 2 years, the school has been growing its middle school at its present location. It was not always that way. More than three years ago, teachers, students, and parents sought the blessings of the school board, asking permission to grow from a K-5th grade school to one that went through Grade 8 and to move from their dilapidated building to one that would accommodate their growing size and type of education. After initial rejections and a year's delay, they regrouped and achieved their goal. The school moved to the new building. Fifth graders stayed to become sixth graders, and, this year, seventh graders. Today, sixth and seventh graders have two blocks of classes and a variety of specials. Each group has half a day of science and math followed by lunch and half a day of humanities. When some students found themselves unable to get their assignments done, they met to brainstorm some solutions. They eventually decided to have "working lunches," a period of flexible time scheduled in every day. One option open to students under their plan is using the time and access to teachers and/or each other to get help and finish assignments.

Class meetings can be teacher or student-generated with words such as, "Circle time" or "Everybody to the carpet." Students hold each other accountable for their words and actions. Examples of child-managed mediations appear here and there in the day. It is telling and instructive to see the trademark signs of the more formal meetings in the school, chairs in a circle and chart papers on the wall.

DEMOCRATIC FRAMEWORK: STUDENT LEARNING

In a wider social and political climate typically very unfavorable to a progressive agenda, Central passionately exemplifies the characteristics of a progressive school. Learning in Central classrooms is very active, student-centered, and student-generated. Students seem knowledgeable about their program and are self-directed and independent. Generally, students move about with a sense of purpose and intent. Teachers serve a variety of roles—facilitator, timekeeper, and checker. Meeting the needs of a variety of learners with different learning styles, differentiating the curriculum, is fundamental. Teachers have obviously spent a lot of time planning diverse activities related to a common theme in order to meet the needs of a variety of learners, but students clearly have a significant role in their own learning. Students move around a lot and are in a variety of groupings. Children interact with others as well as with teachers, learning from and teaching each other. In this way, children learn independence and responsibility. They are learning to take care of their own learning.

Primary students in one classroom follow a list of options on an easel—moving in small groups from station-to-station as time passes, reading, completing activities in a math packet, writing sentences on a computer, finishing word puzzles. In another, the whole class is doing math but each student has his or her own supply of math manipulatives and is proceeding through different series of activities. At the other end of the hallway, middle school students work in different sized groups on a dizzying variety of projects such as writing a newspaper, building models, or planning a re-enactment. Some are online; some are discussing plans around a table; some are painting. Students decide the most meaningful way to answer their own questions under the umbrella of the overall theme.

Broad themes and topics were developed earlier in the year. Teachers chose thematic units for each term, with an eye not only on state standards and the district curriculum but also on Central's goals of fostering thinkers and self-directed lifelong learners. Teachers present mini-lessons, short periods of direct instruction on focus skills or content when necessary. Otherwise, students are on their own, either working individually or with a small group of other students on projects of their own design. Collaborative work, re-teaching, and peer tutoring happen under indirect supervision and guidance. Everyone is busy. Learning is hands-on, developmentally appropriate, and cooperative. Because students are grouped in broader age group bands, veteran students often are the experts, helping younger students learn new skills or techniques. They have the chance and responsibility to be leaders in a variety of situations. Next year, rookies have become veterans and pass along their accumulated wisdom to the new younger students. Some teachers are masters at blending individuals into small partner groups to help each other develop strengths. One provides ample and growing use of "big buddies," older student partners, on various projects such as researching reports, visiting in the neighborhood, and sitting together at lunch. Having students stay with a teacher for a second year enables the teacher and student to know each other very well.

Each term, teachers and students work together to develop individualized student goals. As students get older, they are more and more involved with that process and take different paths to achieving their goals. All but the youngest students work from learning contracts, negotiated plans for work to be accomplished on topics in a certain period of time. Parts of the contract are defined by the teacher; parts are generated by the student, leaving room for student preferences and initiative. Students are responsible for the selection and order of the work and often whether they work with others or alone (Strickland and Suiter, 2008). Students are assessed authentically, through reflection, observation, and conversation, and representing and presenting what they have learned in many formats. Every 2 weeks, the school holds a "Celebration of Learning," a school gathering where any individual, group, or class can present something they are proud of learning to the entire school.

DEMOCRATIC FRAMEWORK: ENGAGING
THE WIDER COMMUNITY, TOO

Practicing democratic progressive education means parents and community members have significant roles to play. They are valuable partners and resources for the educational team and provide modeling, mentoring, and apprenticeship in the democratic life of the society (Sleeter & Grant, 1999). Dewey (1902) positioned the child and the school in an integral relationship with the community in which the child and the school live, bringing the child, society, and the curriculum together in the work of a democratic society. Progressive democratic educators posit an active connection between societal skills, the needs of a community, and the curriculum of a school, giving students the skills and attributes a community requires. Central students are committed to playing an active role in their community. In the months prior to the election in 2008, they went door-to-door registering voters. A few other projects tackled include cleaning up the landscaping around their school, participating in a citizen clean up of a nearby pond, and skating to raise money for a town in Africa.

Parents have a significant role to play at the school, too. At the start of the year, they sign a contract indicating they will help at the school in some way and that they will attend four conferences a year for their student. Students lead the conferences with their families, presenting representative work completed during the previous term. Younger students tell their family members about their work. They may share a book they have learned to read, demonstrate the solution to a math problem, and/or share writing samples. Intermediate students write their own narrative summaries of their term and, at conference time, share a portfolio of work they are proudest of and examples of successes and challenges. By the time students reach middle school, they are well-versed in this process and have a deep understanding of themselves as learners. In the sixth grade, they begin a document they will revise and complete over the next 3 years, ultimately presenting their graduation portfolio, *Myself as a Learner,* a composite and up-to-date look at their needs, strengths, and challenges as learners. The ultimate goal of all this refection and analysis is a sense of voice and a sense of power. They have learned, deep in their bones, that when something is happening, they have a right, need, and/or responsibility to say something. They also develop a sense of power; they know what to do and they know how they can do it.

DEMOCRATIC FRAMEWORK: STUDENT ASSESSMENT

As a part of their assessment, teachers write narrative reports of students' progress. Each report begins with the goals that were set at the start of the term. Dianne described the value of a narrative as compared to receiving a letter grade to two prospective parents at a "parent tea" one of the mornings I was there. She explained it with a story. She spoke about a parent coming into a classroom in which there was a different kind of a cookie on each table or desk in the room.

In her story, parents were asked to give each cookie a grade, an A, a B, a C, and so forth. When they were finished, all the cookies were gathered up. Parents attempted to use grades to determine which cookie was which and how good it actually was. Not only could the parents not tell which cookie was being talked about, it was impossible for them to really know anything about the cookie. The second time, parents again came in to a room with a cookie on each table. This time, they were asked to write a careful description of the cookie, describe what they thought about the cookie, and what they could learn from it. When these cookies were removed and returned, the narrative report was very useful. It was easy to tell the cookies apart and to determine which cookie the parent might like the best. Assessment at Central is multifaceted and used by learners and teachers to inform and modify the nature of subsequent learning experiences. Like the descriptive cookie report, the rich and thorough narrative report provides parents with a more complete and useful insight into students' progress than a letter grade would.

DEMOCRATIC FRAMEWORK: MEETING STANDARDIZATION AND DISTRICT PRESSURES HEAD-ON

Being a progressive school in today's educational climate is very challenging; being a progressive, democratic school is even more challenging. The intrusive pressures of standardization and pervasive accountability measures place demands on this school that are in addition and counter to what they choose. The staff at Central is forced to work very hard to meet the demands of both time and energy consuming systems, the one they choose and the one that is imposed. They do not "teach to the tests" but hope that, even though a standardized test is not an accurate or valued measure of the success of their curriculum, their students will do well enough on the tests they are required to take. Since they do not choose their students, the students have struggled on the state-mandated tests at times, as have the seven other elementary schools in their district.

At times, they have had a hard time maintaining their own governance system. The district has called mandatory meetings with almost no warning, scheduled at the same time as the staff's consensus meetings. Dianne is often summoned away from her work with less than 24 hours notice. The teachers and administration have to work hard to preserve their school. Because they present a less-understood alternative and because their school is a school of choice, they must continually educate the community about their type of education, almost in the same way a private school has to advertise and seek applicants.

DEMOCRATIC FRAMEWORK: BUILDING CONNECTIONS WITH ALLIES

The school avails itself of enriching and supportive networks of similar institutions. It is a member of the National Network for Educational Renewal, a network of partnerships between schools and teacher preparation institutions supporting equal access for all students to a challenging and meaningful pedagogy that provides students with the knowledge, skills, and dispositions to become fully engaged participants in a democratic society. Teachers work hard to find the time and resources to attend yearly conferences and visit other schools. Central is also a member of the League of Democratic Schools, which supports small schools with democratic purposes and striving to make a better society, and is in partnership with Miami University. In fact, its state-of-the-art partnership with Miami includes the presence of student interns and other support staff from Miami who make a contribution as equal members of the school community, not just as visitors. At Central, student teachers are active learners, just like students are. Student teachers are called "interns" and are involved in team-teaching early in their tenure at the school. Veteran teachers benefit from exposure to new ideas; interns apprentice with experts. Interns are expected to participate in all of the meetings, professional experiences, and assessments that full-time teachers do in the school each semester. It is a fully immersive internship, with the student treated as a working, contributing professional, not as a novice. This is a very demanding, challenging, and rewarding experience for Miami intern teachers, who typically have early field experiences at Central, fall in love with it, and want to apprentice in a setting that will allow them to experience and define what it means to teach in a progressive school.

SO WHAT'S GREAT ABOUT CENTRAL ACADEMY?

Seeing such a school in action makes both the literature on progressive education and my work at my school come into sharper focus. Never quite in the mainstream, even in the heyday of the open school movement in the 1960s, it is especially inspiring then to explore the relevance of Dewey's impact on 21st century progressives and their work in today's overly standardized and mechanized system of education. Central is great, in part, simply because it exists at all, against great odds and against the typical machinations of power to standardize and disallow anything different that cuts against the grain in large public school systems.

Another aspect of Central's greatness is exemplified in the integrity of the alignment between the expressed theory and practice of democratic progressive education. It is tenaciously and vibrantly cohesive. The vision as articulated in the planned curriculum is evident in the enacted and lived curricula. Students and teachers take responsibility for their own learning and for the circumstances that allow others to learn well, too. Participants intend to create circumstances where the curriculum is responsively negotiated, where the links between the planned, enacted, and lived are not linear but loop back purposefully to revise and re-vision.

Central's power is in its relevance in each student's life, the priority it places on the genuine engagement of everyone involved. Restricting education to a technical focus limits its relevance. Expanding it to include personal, local, contemporary problems and challenges makes it come alive. Greatness lies also in the ethical nature of its commitment; participants are dedicated to the lofty goal of changing lives.

Even as an observer of the enacted curriculum, it has become lived for me. Central forces me to ask what my responsibility as an educator might be in a democratic society and gives me a sense of possibility. Work at Central makes democracy tangible. Rather than being just the effort or responsibility of distant and powerful politicians, democracy happens everyday in the hallways and classrooms of the school. Democracy is a daily, human endeavor there. Despite the messy, time-consuming, and painful nature of democracy, the enthusiasm, care, energy, engagement, ownership, and empowerment of Central students and staff make such a vast undertaking possible. The key is making time in education for practicing the skills and habits of democratic living and believing that the outcomes will bring freedom, liberation, justice, knowledge, and know-how.

RESPONSE BY TOM POETTER

I am sure that most people think that progressive schools like Central are impossible to replicate, and of course they are in terms of taking a framework and implementing it in steps like those found in a factory making automobile engines. Building human beings and structures that support democracy is not like building a machine. Relationships, trust, experience, context, culture, and humanity matter when educating more than they do under current conditions when designing a factory for the completion of highly standardized production ends. These are all highly prized aspects that should matter all the time when we think about schools and creating places for learners to both experience access to knowledge and to participate in a democratic way of life that is both political and social. So a democratically progressive education is not something that you can just create by replicating approaches, since it is a deeply human affair, involving complications beyond belief. But that does not mean it cannot be done, and that doing it is so complicated that it takes geniuses like Meier and Suiter to do it. It does not. It is really not that hard if we allow the better parts of who we are as human beings and the machinations of power and standardization not to dominate how with think and act at every moment. Children and society are depending on that. To wit, it means being more like ourselves than we are when we typically create and deliver schooling today.

Therefore, the curriculum work that is design-oriented, and at hand when thinking about how to create a more democratic and socially just educational environment of any type, is to focus on commitments to key principles; the commitments over time will yield the structures and processes by which the entity can become and act purposefully according to its own cultural and political norms, not someone else's. So what would these great principle democratic commitments be?

It is easy: Everybody has a real say in what is happening. Everybody shares the responsibility for producing and judging learning. The outside community is just as important as the inside community, and they should be meshed together purposefully, if not perfectly. Outside realities that are political, economic, and educational cannot be ignored but must be met head-on. This does not mean giving up on principles; it means fighting for ground and space for doing the work and holding it when necessary. It means believing in something and others bigger than yourself, that is the public good. It is a risky, life-giving thing. Just ask Dianne Suiter, and her school, or Sue Bartow. But do not ask for a how-to recipe to make it happen. The directions are already inside you, or right in front of you, living and breathing.

FINAL WORD BY SUE BARTOW

Central Academy makes concrete the challenge and promise of education that restores the primacy of democratic living and places public education at its heart. It is a spark, a place that makes one say, "Oh. I get it! I can do that!" Seeing how they built a responsive system that fits their community provides not the blueprint but the inspiration, the feeling of trust in ourselves, in each adult and child.

Democracy is not an established list of conditions and procedures but a continually contested space, a way of living rather than the work of a responsible elite. It is *not* efficient. It *is* hopeful, however, and based on the belief in everyone's capacity for creative problem solving and responsible self-government.

When I take education for granted, stories of slaves taking life-threatening chances to learn to read and masters making it illegal to teach them remind me of the connection between education and power, between education and autonomy and dignity. Learning is power. Who else knows it? The children, teachers, staff, and families at Central know it, expressing it in their living commitment to individual capacity and a social whole. Democratic schooling might seem impossible but when I hear of teachers and learners, people full of endless and energetic curiosity, enduring weeks of preparation for tests, held to a tightly uniform schedule, asked to repeat back pre-articulated state indicators, spot-checked with 2-minutes "walk-throughs," operating in fear of missing a specific mark, performing de-contextualized skills and drills, marching from one topic identified by someone somewhere else to the next topic, it does not seem so hard. What seems hard is facing such dispiriting, disabling days.

Where is the democracy in leaving someone behind? Where is the democracy in skirting difficult issues? Where is it in the valuing of only one type of learning? I do not think we can turn away from Central's challenge. Democratic progressive education places faith in the role of education that develops participatory parity (Knight-Abowitz & Karaba, 2010), a working faith in developing everyone's ability to be deeply deliberative. The people at Central Academy make it possible.

REFERENCES

Beane, J. (2005). *A reason to teach: Creating classrooms of dignity and hope*. Portsmouth, NH: Heiemann.

Dewey, J. (1902). *The school and society & the child and the curriculum* details coming when book arrives.

Knight-Abowitz, K., & Karaba, R. (2010). Charter schooling and democratic justice. *Educational Policy, 24*(3), 534–558.

Lolli, E. (1994). *An examination of a nongraded, multiage school from the perspective of the participants: A case study* (Unpublished doctoral dissertation). Miami University, Oxford, OH.

Meier, D. (2002). *The power of their ideas*. Boston, MA: Beacon Press.

Meier, D. (2003). So what does it take to build a school for democracy? *Phi Delta Kappan, 85*(1), 15–21.

Sleeter, C. E., & Grant, C. A. (1999). *Making choices for multicultural education: Five approaches to race, class, and gender*. Upper Saddle River, NJ: Merrill.

Strickland, J., & Suiter, D. (2008). Toward democratic schools. In J. I. Goodlad, R. Soder, & B. McDaniel (Eds.), *Education and the making of a democratic people* (pp. 117–137). Boulder, CO: Paradigm Publishers.

CHAPTER 6

THE INAUGURATION OF BARACK OBAMA, JANUARY 20, 2009: LIVING THE SPECTACLE, LIVING HISTORY

Christopher L. Cox

The coffee aroma poured from the kitchen and lingered into the living room. I had slouched into the sofa with my laptop and the first of many mugs of coffee to begin my daily routine. My early morning ritual consists of checking email, glancing through friends' updates on Facebook, and flipping through the hundreds of feeds delivered in Google Reader since the previous morning. Sunrays beaming through our northern facing window wall suggested that it was a warm January morning even though the outside thermometer claimed the temperature was just barely hovering above 0 degrees. Even though the morning rituals during the first few sips of coffee were typical for a January morning, there was an overwhelming sense of excitement and anticipation for the remainder of January 20, 2009—the inauguration day of Barack Obama as the 44th president of the United States.

10 Great Curricula: Lived Conversations of Progressive, Democratic Curricula in School and Society, pp. 115–137
Copyright © 2011 by Information Age Publishing

I vividly remember the anticipation I had that morning. For past presidential inaugurations, I never had the opportunity to be completely consumed by the events of such a day because of work or school commitments. Fortunately, I was both able and willing to invest the day to absorbing as much political fanfare and as many memorable events as possible.

As history began to unveil itself on that Tuesday morning, I grabbed my second mug of coffee before nestling back onto the couch ready to partake in the traditions, the ceremonies, and the personal stories that would be told on this Inauguration Day. Unlike any other Inauguration Day, this one offered some hopeful evidence that in fact "all men are created equal" with the election and inauguration of the first black American president. Just as compelling, though, were Obama's messages of new beginnings and hope for a brighter future.

As the day progressed from the wee hours in the morning, I found myself completely captivated by the coverage of the inauguration on CNN. Almost to the point of being mesmerized, breaking only for a fresh mug of coffee, I found myself glued to the television watching CNN and also to the laptop interacting with a variety of online sites including CNN.com, BBC.com, Facebook.com, Wikipedia.com, Flickr.com, and a host of other online destinations. Living through such an event with multiple forms of media opened a treasure trove of history, news commentary, and the personal stories of others throughout the world in ways that were not available even during the last inauguration. Accessing sites outside of the United States offered worldly perspectives and insights about the change happening in Washington, D.C., and what that change might mean to our neighbors across the globe.

Since that day it has occurred to me that there is so much educative potential in major world and national events, similar to the inauguration, which is often under-curricularized or not even curricularized in schools today given the weight of a standardized curriculum. How schools negotiate major current events with preplanned curriculum presents a real challenge for schools to navigate. With the aid of faster and cheaper internet connections, tapping into real-time curriculum can happen instantaneously—within schools and within homes. What follows is an attempt to examine my personal experience of Inauguration Day while considering how we might curricularize major events more thoroughly for the advancement and achievement of an even wider population.

After indulging in my third mug of coffee, I found myself entrenched in very richly steeped national traditions and truly felt like I was part of history in the making as I watched the morning activities leading up to Obama's inaugural address. As mentioned previously, as I was watching the CNN broadcast on television I was multitasking on the internet with my laptop. I was able to simultaneously read blog updates and view picture updates from people within the crowds on the National Mall gathering for the inauguration swearing in ceremony. Attending vicariously through their stories and images, I was able to experience a small fraction of the many emotions bubbling through pockets of the crowds. This was not the inauguration of just any president. This was the first election of a black American. He has led a political life thus far that values humanity and respects the numerous cultures and ethnicities that have been woven into the fabric of the United States. He, himself, represents that part of the threadwork that for so many years has only been on the fringe of our nation's woven tapestry. At last, his inauguration is a beacon of hope that all people are, in fact, created equal. Listening and seeing the enthusiasm and excitement of those in the crowds overwhelmed me with senses of empathy, peacefulness, hope, and a momentary feeling of harmony. I was unable to fully imagine the feelings and emotions that were worn on the faces of so many black Americans. Their many tears of joy and happiness momentarily masked the history of tears, which could paint a picture that might include struggle, frustration, discontent, and mistrust.

There have been 11 inaugurations for eight different presidents during my 38-year life span as shown in Table 6.1. As I look back, I do not recall a time where I was as interested in politics as much as I am now. I suspect that my increasing maturity (certainly my age, possibly some wisdom thrown in) has greatly contributed to this rise in interest over the recent years.

I have offered my age for each of the newly inaugurated presidents in Table 6.1. Looking back over the years, Barack Obama is the 4th newly inaugurated president where I was of age to truly grasp all that surrounds Inauguration Day and more important, the changing of a presidential administration.

The events throughout *this* Inauguration Day as well as the changes in administration were screaming *curriculum* in vastly different ways for so many different people in ways unlike inaugurations from the past. Contemplating

Table 6.1.   U.S. Presidential Inaugurations Since 1969

1969	Richard Nixon	I was not born yet	(37)—First Term
1973	Richard Nixon	I was 2 years old	(37)—Second Term
1974	Gerald Ford	I was 3 years old	(38)
1977	Jimmy Carter	I was 6 years old	(39)
1981	Ronald Reagan	I was 10 years old	(40)—First Term
1985	Ronald Reagan		(40)—Second Term
1989	George H. W. Bush	I was 18 years old	(41)
1993	Bill Clinton	I was 22 years old	(42)—First Term
1997	Bill Clinton		(42)—Second Term
2001	George W. Bush	I was 30 years old	(43)—First Term
2005	George W. Bush		(43)—Second Term
2009	Barack Obama	I am 38 years old	(44)

over a fourth mug of coffee, I pondered about the underlying curriculum necessary to flawlessly choreograph the entire day. Anyone who has hosted a gathering similar in scope and size to a wedding knows the amount of specialized detail needed to ensure its success. Imagine magnifying the experience of a wedding to include over 240,000 guests with tickets,[1] 2,000,000–4,000,000 guests in all, and 25,000 security personnel[2] all across Washington, D.C. Consider the thousands of journalists that flocked into the city and all of their preparations such as learning interesting parts of history relevant to an inauguration, the history relevant to the uniqueness of this inauguration, the traditions and protocols, as well as the personal and professional stories of key politicians. Also consider the ways in which journalists plan and enact their news and views in ways that move their audiences. Consider for a moment, the curriculum necessary to coordinate, support and monitor the 25,000 security personnel. Their course of study in preparation for the day's events probably included topics such as timing precision, traffic control for vehicles and pedestrians, crowd control, firearm usage, medical services, communication strategies, to name just a few. Consider the experiences that day of millions of spectators across the world watching the peaceful transition of power in the United States for the first time to a black man. Although these few glimpses of curriculum characterize rare instances of curriculum planning and enactment, I hope that you might ponder other complicated, technical, and philosophical ways in which curriculum is infused into life in ways that we might seldom consider.

Therein lies the big "aha" that I initially had when our class started thinking about writing this book: *Curriculum is everywhere.* Wherever and whenever learning happens, there is curriculum to be studied. The learning that occurs might be intentional, and carefully planned, or unintentional, happening simply by chance. The latter was the case for me with the inauguration of President Barack Obama. Unintentional learning happened. As the events of the day continued to unfold, I was drawn into learning more about American politics, our government, and about the people that help shape the lives of Americans. I found the events surrounding the inauguration absolutely fascinating. I gradually became wrapped up in the many stories of people who were impacted by the historic nature of this inauguration and what it meant to them. Insights were gained from politician interviews, news reporter commentary, and personal tales of ordinary, self-publishing citizens. I read about many of their travels to Washington, D.C., as I perused some of their blogs that were written as they were riding the D.C. Metro. Many personal accounts relayed that they made travel plans immediately after the results of the election by reserving vacation days, reserving hotel rooms, and booking flights. Regardless of the associated costs, especially monetary ones, many were destined to be a part of this day in person. Many shared their personal stories about how important this day was in their own personal pursuits of justice and civil rights. Their perspectives really captivated my interest, and my heart, and before I knew it, a fifth mug of coffee was finished.

More than the inauguration ceremonies that preceded this one, I really looked forward to absorbing the history, traditions, and pageantry of this Inauguration Day. In addition to being enfolded into the many personal stories of folks that traveled to D.C., I also pondered and explored aspects of the inaugural activities, our government, the politics, and our history as a nation. From a curricular perspective, if given the chance, a major event like an inauguration offers enormous opportunities to branch into curricular caveats that might spark students' curiosity. I generated lots of my own questions and curiosities about the inner workings of such a major event. A small collection of topics extracted from those questions and curiosities are listed in Table 6.2. These tangential topics acted

Table 6.2. Partial List of Topics for Learning That Stem from the Inauguration

- Role(s) of Supreme Court in ceremonies
- Upcoming Supreme Court justice selection
- Changes in pomp and circumstance over the years
- Shared stories during morning coffee between Bushs, Cheneys, Obamas, and Bidens
- 2,600 dignitaries and celebrities on the platform where oaths are administered
- Legalities of the oath of office for the president and vice-president
- Population estimates and crowd size predictions
- Individual narratives of many on the National Mall
- Moving in/out for first families
- Transition of the White House Administration
- Security detail around the White House, parade route, Capitol, and the National Mall
- Racial, ethnic, and gender composition of the administration and Congress
- Cultural and political shifts throughout Washington, D.C.
- Ceremonial protocol minutiae, such as seating for the powerful, the appearance of the presidential seal, and the proper use of the label 'Air Force One'
- National climate in which the new president starts term
- First Family and the First Lady—past and present
- Political networking and the connections of those in power
- Impact of race, gender, and class in politics
- Life story of incoming president
- Reactions from those in Washington, D.C., the United States, and from other countries
- Range of security threats that were anticipated and prepared for
- Planning to enact promises during the campaign
- Costs associated with political campaigning leading to and including Inauguration Day
- Responsibilities of the Joint Congressional Committee on Inauguration Ceremonies

as "learning stems" that provided a more personal and deeper look into the inauguration while offering greater opportunities to further elaborate a simple viewing into an educative experience.

This short list offers some of the learning stems that prompted me to drift away from the main inauguration activities. These learning stems offered ways to dissect the spectacular nature of the day. Instead of just viewing the pomp and circumstance of the day, these learning stems helped me extract meaning from the historic day's wonderful nooks and crannies, all accessible with modern, interactive and multiple forms of media technology at most of our fingertips today. Lastly, these learning stems were essential to the formulation of questions that provoked my curiosity. I knew that within a few moments of time I would be able to land on at least one web page that would allow me to follow any one of the learning stems deeper. The day was fertile with personal purposing and experiences that were direct consequences of these learning stems. While guided particularly by personal interests, the educational aims of this curricular experience resemble what Elliot Eisner describes as "expressive educational objectives" (Eisner, 1969), or as he later referred to them, "expressive outcomes" (Eisner, 1985).

The uniqueness of this experience provided the impetus for me to revisit that day in more detail and with some analysis to better understand the curricular undergirding that brought to bear such learning for me. Looking back, there are three particular aspects that seemed to catalyze this experience into an educative and curricular experience for me. I will mention the three curricular catalysts briefly here and use the remainder of the chapter to illuminate each one. First, this was an arousing spectacle. Suffice it to say momentarily that online viewership throughout the day drew an all time record audience[3] validating the inauguration's spectacular nature. Second, the environment in which I had this experience, while it was my living room, had a participatory orientation that allowed for digital interaction with conversations, thoughts, and ideas from around the world. Third, there was this aura of curiosity and question generation that sustained my interest throughout Inauguration Day. There were lots of connections to be explored within the context of the inauguration. The constellation of these three curricular catalysts provided a unique frame in which to pursue a curriculum inquiry. Indeed, the learning that was incidental to Inauguration Day offers a distinctively unique, and perhaps great, curricular experience to investigate.

TO BE OR NOT TO BE GREAT

Late in January, several weeks after the inauguration, when Dr. Poetter proposed the idea for each of us in the class to inquire into a *great* curriculum,

I was drawn to take a closer look at the intersection of curriculum with the context of Barack Obama's inauguration. Perhaps, such an inquiry would lead to some insights for future opportunities to curricularize experiences arising from major events. I was reluctant to propose that my suggestion be considered *great* but as we talked about those characteristics of a curriculum that might be considered *great* it became clearer to me that the events surrounding this Inauguration Day provided some great contexts in which to study curriculum.

A handful of students in the course were able to pin down their selection of an inquiry into a great curriculum in the first few weeks. So I pitched my idea to Dr. Poetter that I was interested in studying the curriculum surrounding the inauguration of Barack Obama. He seemed receptive to the idea although I suspected he hoped that in the weeks to come I might be able to talk about it and articulate some of the curricular aspects in greater detail. With an initial nod of approval, I began my journey.

As with all of the curriculum inquiries throughout this book, I too had to gain "access" to conduct my curriculum study. In part, the access I was looking for would allow me to re-experience what I learned and felt that day. Initially, a first task was to find an archived copy of the CNN television broadcast. This would have been unnecessary had I known on January 20th that I would be deconstructing the day for its curricular components. With some success using the search capabilities of Google and YouTube, I was able to locate a variety of *short* clips that showed the CNN television broadcast as well as the CNN.com online video clips. However, as I began reviewing them I was intrigued by the differences in the actual CNN television broadcast and the CNN.com online video clips. The CNN television broadcast had additional multimedia aspects that included (1) picture-in-picture video, (2) scrolling agendas on the bottom of the screen, (3) periodic flashing factoids, and (4) "call-to-actions" prompting watchers to email pictures or comment on the CNN blog. The addition of these multimedia aspects certainly influenced my participation as a viewer. In part, they also helped grab my attention and pulled me into the broadcast.

The collection of downloads that I had amassed gave me a fragmented look at the day. I really needed a video of the CNN broadcast with lengthier footage. In a moment of desperation, I sent out several updates on Facebook wondering if I might find someone who had recorded the broadcast that day. In the end, I found a copy through a random conversation when a family member revealed he thought he still had a VCR recording from the morning of the inauguration. With a lot of good fortune, the tape did contain nearly 6 hours of continuous CNN television broadcast from which I could continue my curriculum inquiry.

After viewing the video several times, I began to jot down some thoughts and ideas about what aspects of my experience on Inauguration Day led to my consideration of it as a *great* curriculum and as a model from which I might pull some basic ideas for readers about how to go about planning to watch and analyze major events as they unfold. It seemed like a doable task, but as I delved into some of those thoughts and ideas, I found myself lacking the wherewithal to talk about these curriculum aspects floating in my mind in a clear and concise and scholarly way. There were moments when I became rather frustrated with this inability to communicate about my thoughts and ideas. On several occasions, I wished that I had selected one of the other proposed great curricula to study. In my mind, they seemed to have more familiarity and perhaps had more conventional curricular aspects about them.

I persevered and continued to better understand the uniqueness of this experience and its connection to curriculum with no less than a few peeled Post-It pads, half a dozen Word documents each with only a thought or two, and notes scribbled on random sheets of scrap paper constantly surrounding me. As I became better at seeing broad connections to curriculum, I began to struggle with attaching language to my developing thoughts and ideas. In *The Tacit Dimension*, Michael Polayni (1966) writes about this tacit knowledge that we all possess, that is—a knowledge that we have but are unable or unequipped to communicate, suggesting that "we can know more than we can tell." His often quoted line seemed apropos at this juncture of this curriculum inquiry for me. I knew more about the inauguration—about its value as a learning tool in the moment, and about its symbolic, deep meaning for transition of power in a democratic republic, as well as about the transformational and healing power across boundaries of difference in our country—than I could tell at the time. But I was making progress.

As you can see, the setting for this curriculum inquiry was somewhat different than the other curricula presented throughout this book. This curriculum experience was not associated with an established school or program; but instead, it was associated with an intangible relationship with ideas and emotions that were developed through multiple mediums including television and internet broadcasts. Most interesting curricularly was the way in which this very personal curriculum experience evoked emotions of wonder, patriotism, optimism, togetherness, and hope. Schooling experiences have so much to gain by infusing such qualities, if at all possible.

LIVING THE CURRICULUM

Using the context of an inauguration of an American president for a curriculum inquiry propels us to consider potential phases of curriculum described by Marsh and Willis (2007) including the *planned* curriculum and the *enacted* curriculum. However, it is the *experienced* curriculum that best characterizes the curriculum inherent in the viewing of the inauguration as it was lived. Regardless of what was planned or enacted it is the *experienced* curriculum, also referred to as the *lived* curriculum, that considers the absorbed skills, understandings, and attitudes of a learner during and after an educative experience.

As in my experience with the inauguration of Barack Obama, not all educative experiences have curriculums that are planned prior to being lived. Throughout that morning coffee, I was truly unaware of the learning that I was headed towards. Sometimes experiences are evocative rather than prescriptive in the learning that materializes in the inquirer (Eisner, 1969). Such learning feels much more organic and connected to those daily encounters that are potentially enlightening. Learners have the opportunity to "explore, defer, or focus on issues that of peculiar interest or import" (Eisner, 1969, p. 18). The resulting lived curriculum is dynamically contoured around previous skills and understandings as well as the current interests of the learner. As a result of my past life experiences and education, my personal experience with the inauguration as a lived curriculum was contoured in a different way than say someone who lived during the civil rights era throughout the 1960s. In a paper that was written in 1969, Elliot Eisner expands some of these ideas about curriculum that sharply contrasts prevailing thought about objectives, standards and evaluation. His thoughts help frame the uniqueness of this curriculum inquiry.

> The *expressive objective* is intended to serve as a theme around which skills and understandings learned earlier can be brought to bear, but through which those skills and understandings can be expanded, elaborated and made idiosyncratic. With an expressive objective what is desired is not homogeneity of response among students but diversity. In the expressive context the teacher hopes to provide a situation in which meanings become personalized and in which children produce products, both theoretical and qualitative, that are as diverse as themselves. Consequently, the evaluative task in this situation is not one of applying a common standard to the products produced but one of reflecting upon what has been produced in order to reveal its uniqueness and significance. (Eisner, 1969, p. 18)

Eisner's original work in 1969 used the language of instructional and expressive objectives. Later, when his ideas were solidified in *The Educational Imagination* (1979), he referred to expressive *objectives* as expressive *outcomes* in response to connotations that paired *predetermination* with *objectives*. Expressive outcomes therefore have a tendency to focus on the un-predetermined learning as a result of experiencing the lived curriculum. Furthermore, the expansion and reconstruction of those expressive outcomes add vitality to the development of culture (Eisner, 1969). I did not have a set of instructional objectives while I watched and engaged with the events of Inauguration Day; but, looking back, I find myself reflecting on what I gained that day from the lens of expressive outcomes. The learning stems as listed in Table 6.2, originating as deviations from the CNN broadcast, eventually transformed into what Eisner refers to as *expressive outcomes*.

CURRICULUM CATALYSTS

What aspects of my Inauguration Day situation enabled me to *best* experience such a lived curriculum? How might the undergirding of this lived curriculum best be described? The heart of this curriculum inquiry is focused on those questions. In this section, I explore three aspects of the curricularized experience as examples of supporting pillars for the type of learning that Eisner referred to with *expressive outcomes*. Not all of life's experiences can unfold as being educative or transformative. Those that do, as in the case of the inauguration, are worthy of some inquiry in the hopes of provoking future conversations in the field of curriculum studies.

In the last section, I presented the notion of unpredetermined learning and outcomes in order to shed a bit of light on Eisner's idea of expressive outcomes. Although there is not a predetermination of outcomes, Eisner underscores that there initially has to be an "invitation to explore, defer or focus on issues that are of peculiar interest or import to the inquirer" (1969, p. 18). Looking back to Inauguration Day, there are at least three noteworthy catalysts that provoked me to *enfold* myself into the experience before I was able to *unfold* the experience into expressive outcomes.

CURRICULAR CATALYST 1: A SPECTACULAR EVENT

The inauguration of Barack Obama had all the necessary ingredients of a spectacle. Both remarkable and impressive,[4] the inauguration of the nation's first black American indeed was a spectacle for it symbolized a monumental step of a long journey too many years in the making. With outpouring support and interest, the audience of over 1,500,000 spectators[5] crowding the National Mall reinforced that this event was in fact remarkable and impressive. Looking at the CNN commissioned satellite photo[6] of the entire crowd along the National Mall, I was amazed at the spectacular view of historically large swarms of visitors to Washington, D.C., all snuggled around 20 huge JumboTron displays.[7] If the massive audience and the unprecedented election of a black man to the office of President of the United States are not enough evidence to claim a spectacle, then consider that over 130,000,000 voters[8] turned in a ticket to participate in the United States project of democracy in November 2008, constituting the largest voter turnout by gross votes and arguably one of the largest voter turnouts by proportion of eligible voters in the American history.

Throughout our lives, we have experienced an accumulation of spectacles. We have become greatly calloused by some and monumentally transformed by others. In either instance, what is essential to the experience of a spectacle is the social relationship between people that is mediated by imagery associated with it (Debord, 1995). Social relationships influence the magnitude of emotions that are stirred by spectacles. Spectacles offer us opportunities to rally with some and denounce with others. Spectacles can easily catalyze expressive outcomes as they draw us into lived curricular experiences.

In some regards, there are difficulties in thinking of the inauguration itself as a spectacle. Instead, upon further contemplation, it might be more appropriate to consider the entire journey of the political process reaching from Obama's start of his presidential race in the primaries until his oath of office on Inauguration Day as a spectacle. That journey contained many contrasts between the outgoing and incoming administrations that impacted its spectacle. Also consider as well the dramatic stories throughout the race up to and including the inauguration. Here are a few worth mentioning:

- Democratic primaries featuring the first black nominee running against the first seriously contending female candidate.
- Dire state of multiple affairs such as the war on terror and the financial crisis.
- Use of social media such as Facebook, YouTube, MySpace, Wikipedia, and Twitter to amass huge databases of followers.
- Running mate selections of Joe Biden and Sarah Palin along with their outspoken personalities.

Your personal interests and the levels of importance you place on the above will cause you to vary their spectacularity and their respective contributions as curricular catalysts towards expressive outcomes. Adjoining your personal interest and importance values is the influence of mass media in elevating or reducing the spectacularity of an event. New discoveries in technology platforms and data insights on viewer behavior allow media to reach masses in ways not even thought of just a few years ago. Douglas Kellner (2003), a prolific media researcher from UCLA, shared the following insight:

> Entertainment has always been a prime field of the spectacle, but in today's infotainment society, entertainment and spectacle have entered into the domains of the economy, politics, society, and everyday life in important new ways. Building on the traditions of the spectacle, contemporary forms of entertainment from television to the stage are incorporating spectacle culture into their enterprises, transforming film, television, music, drama,

and other domains of culture, as well as producing spectacular new forms of culture, such as cyberspace, multimedia, and virtual reality. (p. 4)

Along this theme, each of us has experienced, albeit to different degrees, spectacles that have captivated our attention. Spectacles might be known in advance, or not. We have known about the inauguration for some time, we could see it coming. Exiting the realm of politics, think back to December 1999 when many conversations called into question what might happen as the world marked time towards January 1, 2000. This, too, was a spectacular topic that captured the attention of many.

For other spectacles, though, we have little to no advance notice. Take for instance, the collapse of the World Trade Center towers in September 2001 or the Space Shuttle Challenger disaster in January 1986. In these cases, we were taken by surprise. Instances like these undermine the typical planned curricular experience in schools; yet, they also offer enormous curricular potential when learning in the moment is readily embraced by skillful and knowledgeable teachers. I think back to the events on the day of September 11, 2001, while I was a middle school mathematics teacher. Students first reacted with lots of questions as details were emerging. Following a mandate shortly before the lunch hour from the superintendent's office to turn off classroom televisions and to diminish classroom conversations, students filled the void with fear, speculation, and rumors. Are schools so monolithic so as to not respond to students' real-time inquires in a responsible and respectful manner?

Thus far, we have looked at the influence of spectacularity as a curricular catalyst. It is possible for spectacles to be planned and unplanned. At this juncture, it seems plausible to inquire into what other aspects of my inauguration experience, in addition to its spectacularity, initiated a curricular experience leading to expressive outcomes. In the next section, we will explore the contributions of infotainment and technology in creating a participatory environment as a curricular catalyst.

CURRICULAR CATALYST 2: A PARTICIPATORY ENVIRONMENT THAT ENGAGES INTEREST

Just as the 2008 elections were influenced by social media available on the internet, so too, were the 2009 Inauguration Day events and ceremonies. In the domain of my living room equipped with a laptop wirelessly connected to the internet and satellite television, I could watch television broadcasts of the inaugural activities from CNN, BBC, MSNBC, ABC, CBS, NBC, and FOX; and at the same time, I could interact with individuals and groups all across the world over the internet. The combination of television and internet offered a multimedia experience similar to the infotainment characterization by Kellner (2003).

Last fall after the election, my wife and I seriously considered traveling to the inauguration in Washington, D.C. In hindsight, had I attended the inaugural ceremonies in D.C., I would have been part of an extraordinary experience standing shoulder-to-shoulder with others on the National Mall; rather, in the internet and television environment I occupied instead, I gained a bird's-eye view enabling me to see and hear numerous national and international perspectives. This human element was made possible by the use of technology. I was able to read and comment on live blog updates from the National Mall that offered windows to human stories that told about the personal significance of this day. Almost simultaneously, I was able to view and comment on live video and photographs updates on YouTube and Flickr. And yet, within a moment I could tune in to a live broadcast from the other side of the world. This unique participatory environment elicited both my interest and emotions. The use of technology was central to this environment in the development of human relationships. According to Debord (1995), these technology-mediated relationships continue to be essential in the creation and nurturing of a spectacle. Moreover, participatory environments that offer a window on humanity while offering immediate, relevant access to text, images, and video can catalyze expressive outcomes as they compel us to interact with the world as we live.

The digital landscape that we find ourselves in now certainly played an important part in the campaigns and certainly influenced the elections, the inauguration, and the future of politics. The internet as we know it today is relatively young when placed in relation to the inaugurations of 44 presidents. Barack Obama joins the company of only two other presidents, George W. Bush and William Clinton, who have held office since the mainstream use of the internet began. Only a slice of the 16 years under these three presidents has the mainstream internet included the use of social media applications such as Facebook, YouTube, Wikipedia, and Twitter. Kellner (2003) notes that that "the internet has generated a seductive cyberspace producing novel forms of information, entertainment, and social interaction" (p. viii).

The rapid growth of these social media applications and other resources on the internet has influenced the latest election and inauguration in ways well beyond the impact that television brought to politics. The adoption rates of new social media far exceed previous technologies from yesteryear. It took Facebook only 5 years, from 2004 to 2009, to reach 150,000,000 users. The following technologies were adopted on a vastly slower pace considering the same quantity of 150,000,000 users (Hempel, 2009):

- Cellphone took 14 years from 1983 until 1997
- Television took 38 years from 1928 until 1966
- Telephone took 89 years from 1876 until 1965

Nearly instant access to vast government information, political conversations, and massive data sets provides more transparency and analysis elevating the possibility for more citizens to participate in the democratic project. Michael Wesch (2008), assistant professor of cultural anthropology and digital ethnography at Kansas State University, comments that "when students recognize their own importance in helping to shape the future of this increasingly global, interconnected society, the significance problem fades away" (p. 7). Well-designed participatory environments can help students locate themselves in learning that aligns with their interests while engaging with others who share the significance.

Many of the applications on the internet have created a legitimized digital public sphere for curricular opportunities including information, entertainment, and social interaction. Lawrence Cremin (1990) suggests that education should succumb and be transformed by updates and improvements in communication (such as television & radio—the internet was still too young in 1990); the structure of families, friends and peers; the working environment; and, many other societal changes. Curricularly, the use of the internet opens possibilities to learning in very broad ways. Easily accessible scholarly information and data are available inside and outside of the walls of schools—virtually blurring the walls of learning. The implications of this are huge, especially when we think about the censorship within schools, overt or not, of major national and world events.

Postman and Weingartner (1969), borrowing from Marshal McLuhan's famous aphorism, "the medium is the message," argue that the environment (or medium) of learning is more important than the content (the message), and therefore teachers should begin paying more attention to the learning environment they help to create. In proverbial similarity to teaching one to fish—*Give a person a news article and you inform them for a day. Provide them with a news oriented participatory environment, and they will learn for a lifetime*—I would argue that my CNN television broadcast viewing of the inauguration in tandem with the ability to access resourceful and communicative applications on the internet offered a unique participatory environment that fueled my interests and need for more, deeper information.

CURRICULAR CATALYST 3: CONTEXT GENERATES NEW QUESTIONS AND STIMULATES INQUIRY

While I watched the Inauguration Day CNN television broadcasts and the subsequent viewings of them, I was inspired to delve deeper into the experience, being led by *questions* that allowed me to dig into the events and activities of the day. Some of the questions were generated in response to journalists' comments, video clips, interviews, or multimedia factoids. The CNN television broadcast offered more that just a typical news story. The multimedia accessories that accompanied the storyline stimulated inquiry. Along the bottom of the screen, CNN cycled factoids that added to the broadcast. Here is a sampling:

- About 10:20 a.m. ET—"Chief Justice John Marshall administered nine presidential oaths between 1801 and 1833, more than anyone else"
- About 10:28 a.m. ET—"The Obamas and Bidens are having coffee with the Bushes at the White House"
- About 10:30 a.m. ET—"The 20th Amendment states that the president and vice-president's term begin at noon on January 20"
- About 10:32 a.m. ET—"The FBI is deploying four times more resources for security than at the last Inauguration"

Each of these factoids introduced small slices of new facts or insights. Some were included in the journalistic commentary and some were not. As a result of these factoids, questions leading to an internet inquiry emerged. Here is another small sample:

- How long does a typical chief justice of the Supreme Court serve?
- What issues of importance could the Obamas, Bidens, Bushes, and Cheneys possibly be talking about over coffee?
- If the term begins promptly at noon, how important is the oath of office?
- What necessitates FBI resources being magnified four times since 4 years ago?

The commentary of CNN journalists/contributors Wolf Blitzer, David Gergan, Soledad O'Brien, and Jeffery Toobin also contributed to the aura of inquiry. They were sharing thoughts about possible upcoming Supreme Court replacements facing President Obama as some of the justices were being seated on the viewing platform outside of the U.S. Capitol about an hour before the oath of office was to be performed. Almost immediately, I found myself using the search capabilities of Google to locate a variety of information about the Supreme Court including information about the justices, their brief biographies, political stances, and possible conflicts with the outgoing/incoming administrations. I sought information that might help me understand which of the justices are most probable to be replaced in this presidential term and how the composition of the Supreme Court might be altered as a result. This constitutes one example of the many situations in which questions were spawned as a response to something seen or heard either during the broadcast or while interacting online. The abilities to generate probing questions and to stimulate an aura of inquiry comprise a third curricular catalyst that provoked new learning towards the expressive outcomes arising from the context of the inauguration.

Perhaps, the propagation of questions helped unfold personal latent misunderstandings I possessed or filled in gaps in my knowledge. Perhaps, the questions that were stimulated were subconsciously examining underlying issues. With the resources on the internet, the pursuit of answers to these questions helped me gain valuable insights that materialized as expressive outcomes. Neil Postman (1992) is known to be very skeptical of what new technologies bring to bear on the learner and society. He suggests that with the emergence of a new technology, something else nearly as valuable is often eliminated at the expense of larger humanitarian and social goals. It comes as no surprise then that Postman and Weingartner (1969) described aspects of a teaching strategy that concentrate on developing an environment of inquiry focused on larger humanity and social goals. These attitude aspects are adapted and listed in Table 6.3.

Postman and Weingartner offered these attitudes for teachers in the hopes of redesigning the structure of a classroom. These teacher attitudes might shift a static classroom atmosphere to a more dynamic, active classroom. Postman and Weingartner's set of attitudes puts the onus on the teacher for ensuring the application of these attitudes.

The nearly immediate internet access that is generally available to an increasing number of students in school and at home causes me to wonder about the ways in which students will follow their inquiries, even in the absence of schooling. Providing them a framework to guide their inquiry might better help them curricularize an event prior to it occurring and during it. Furthermore, knowing that students will follow their interests and own inquiries outside of school suggests that we might want to consider

Table 6.3.   Teaching Attitudes within an Environment of Inquiry

- The teacher rarely tells students what he/she thinks they ought to know.
- His/her basic mode of discourse with students is questioning.
- Generally, he/she does not accept a single statement as an answer to a question.
- He/she encourages student–student interaction as opposed to student-teacher interaction. And generally avoids acting as a mediator or judge of the quality of ideas expressed.
- He/she rarely summarizes the positions taken by students on the learnings that occur.
- His/her lessons develop from the responses of students and not from a previously determined "logical" structure.
- Generally, each of his/her lessons poses a problem for students.
- He/she measures his success in terms of behavioral changes in students.
(Postman & Weingartner, 1969, pp. 34–36)

Table 6.4.   Learning Attitudes for Students within an Environment of Inquiry

- Learners rarely are told what they should know and are encouraged in their own pursuits.
- Learners are generally engaged in discourse involving questioning.
- Questions should be answered with in-depth responses beyond just a sentence.
- Learners interact primarily with other learners holding themselves accountable for the quality of expressed ideas.
- Final summaries of learning are discouraged in that they stymie subsequent thinking.
- Learners' future outcomes are dependent on current learning.
- Problems are the basis for learning.
- Success in learning can be measured in terms of behavioral changes.

a set of learning attitudes also aimed towards students outside of the classroom. With these in mind, let us reconsider the teaching attitudes from Table 6.3 reframing them as attitudes for the learner instead of the teacher. I posit that part of the work of schools ought to be to consider ways in which these proposed attitudes in Table 6.4 might become part of their approved, formal curriculum and therefore, over time, embedded in the experienced/lived curricula of students in and out of school.

The list of *learning* attitudes above can help the curricularization of educative experiences, particularly those without an educative authority where learners are pursuing their own interests—as in my situation throughout Inauguration Day. My own personal pursuit mapped the learning I experienced allowing the launch of an inquiry that branched from many of the learning stems previously mentioned in Table 6.2. This inquiry catalyst infused with the spectacularity of the event as well as the participatory environment nurtured the evolution of expressive outcomes related to this experience.

THINKING FORWARD

The intent of this chapter was to use the viewing of the inauguration via television and internet as a context for curriculum inquiry and to also examine the differing curriculum catalysts that helped the inauguration event realize its curricular potential. Before being able to examine this as a curriculum inquiry, I needed to experience the inauguration as a learner. Prior to the *unfolding* the curricular outcomes of this context required a full engagement of *enfolding* into the experience (Bowman & Haggerson, 1990). The terms *enfold* and *unfold* help us think about the way in which curriculum ultimately becomes personalized. By *enfolding*, a learner immerses himself/herself into a given topic. By *unfolding*, a learner is constantly reflecting upon the ways in which he/she changes throughout the learning. This recursive process of enfolding and unfolding offers an individual a way to live an experience that resembles the learning that Eisner (1985) imagined as he talked about the creation and acknowledgment of expressive outcomes.

We typically only have every fourth year to experience an inauguration. The context of the inauguration offered a rich example of a major event to be curricularized. Unstated at the onset of Inauguration Day, my learning outcomes were driven by my own interests that emerged throughout the day as they were being catalyzed by its spectacularity, participatory environment, and an aura that inspired curiosity. As such, nearly twice a decade there is a provocative opportunity to explore the current status of the project of a democratic republic as it peacefully transitions the power of its executive branch of government with reflections from the past and visions of the journey ahead. In tandem, the three curricular catalysts identified in this chapter magnified learning in unspecified and unprepared ways which are characteristic of expressive outcomes. The context of the inauguration provides one instance to have been analyzed, yet many more national and international events also are worthy of such a curriculum inquiry. In the face of standardized curriculums based solely on state designated or nationally designated instructional outcomes, we would be remiss as educators not to insist on including a standardization of curricular catalysts that would help our students focus on learning in inquiry oriented environments, using participatory technologies, and analyzing their own and society's real-time learning focused as they are embodied in spectacular events.

RESPONSE BY TOM POETTER

When Chris pitched his idea for a chapter on an inquiry into a curriculum that had expressive outcomes for him that were tangible and transformational, the Obama Inauguration, I felt like the chapter would bring a very fresh, pertinent event into play educationally and perhaps cause those who read about it to think about how to create structures within school settings and throughout society for using spectacular events for learning. For many years, back through my doctoral program under Norm Overly's tutelage at Indiana University, and throughout my time teaching curriculum in the field, I encouraged myself, internally, and challenged students, externally, to look at how educational activities in the world are curricular, from the mundane to the amazing. I put it this way: Look for the structures that resonate or not with participants in activities outside of school; watch for opportunities to tap interest and inspiration that take shape in phenomena all around you, especially those outside of school; note and reproduce, if applicable, curricular structures or commitments and pedagogies that make a difference for people in the world when they are engaged in deep learning outside of school. So this leads me to several questions that Chris' inquiry has raised again for me that cut to the core of several curriculum leadership questions I pose for myself and for educational practitioners of all kinds.

First, how can we tap the fact—as it is playing out for our children and most citizens today personally, socially, educationally —that many people are multitasking, especially by using many media at one time for learning and entertainment and that they enjoy it, learn deeply when engaged in it, and are constantly innovating, trying new things, breaking new ground? How can teachers and curricularists, school leaders and bosses, community activists and citizens all grasp the power that is embedded in the experiences people have when they use multiple platforms to engage an issue or a topic or an interest? I think that one answer that we must consider deeply, and challenge ourselves to take on, is to put our fears and trepidations of technology's quick advances aside and join in. I do not see any point in resistance. I know that I have been slow to move in my own pedagogy in terms of the incorporation of advanced technologies. But what I am learning is that setting up the conditions for learning through technology is the most important commitment to make as a teacher. Once I remove the need to control everyone's every move, or to know everything about a technology or an application before using it, I set students up for learning and for teaching me next steps. This is extremely empowering for all involved.

The need for me to make a significant move in this area became apparent to me in a teacher leadership seminar for undergraduates last semester. My interest in transforming the teaching portfolio for the course to an online project from a project with hard copies in a binder (completely unusable in today's job search culture for teachers) made me rely on the students to figure out how to get their materials into a digital format that could be used not only to house materials that they created in their program for potential use later professionally, but also to show where they are and what they can do to potential employers. The project was a huge success. My biggest contribution was setting things up in terms of broad parameters for the project, then getting out of the way! Realizing where students are and what they can do, can free us up to allow students to use technology to explore, experience, and interpret the world more deeply. When they are in school, the teacher's guidance can help harness and deepen the potential of technology to enhance student learning. Most good teachers know this already.

In the case of Chris' experience, the potential for creating a rolling set of new questions and insights was embodied in the educational media of tv and internet as they manifest themselves in Obama's inauguration. I remember feeling much the same way myself as I dipped into coverage of the inauguration events that day. The event was so spectacular—so rooted in traditions and joy and commitments and ideals—that I found myself wondering many of the things that Chris did and that he reported here in his inquiry. I wondered how many people had attended other inaugurations. I wondered how long ago people decided that the new White House tenants would meet the departing ones. Was that a tradition or just a nice thing to do in 2009? How many secret service agents did it take to protect the president and everyone else there or not there? Etc. Like events of a similar nature, they pose wonderful opportunities for people to inquire, to learn, to participate.

Second, how can educational leaders tap more productively and with more purpose spectacular events? How can we develop means or systems to deal with the ones that we know about, like scheduled events such as inaugurations or space launches, and the ones we do not know about ahead of time, like 9–11, and the Fall of Mubarek and the Rise of a new Egypt? I would propose that schools and other places where people gather or do business develop an agreed upon approach for allowing citizens who are in settings of endeavor like schools or offices to suspend their usual activities for educational activities that focus on inquiry and citizenship. What I mean is that schools, for instance, should have a plan for dealing with a day or days like the ones that followed 9–11. Because of the trauma, because of the uncertainty, because of the way schools simply "are," many places of learning continued on a path of engagement that was disengaged from the most important matters at hand. I would say that they basically "shutdown," incapable of engaging students in ways that they should have been engaged. Where better than at school with teachers, especially in our public schools, for students to talk about issues, express fears and concerns, and deal in a constructive way with amazing, unbelievable, traumatic, or spectacular events? What if the school's plan was to break students down into homeroom teams to decide how best to proceed, to determine what learning tools to engage to understand the event better, and what outcomes they would share with others? What if students and teachers, together, expressed how they thought it best to proceed and in an environment of mutual respect and goodwill decided together how best to be citizens in the moment?

What if on inauguration day every 4 years student in the United States in a public school with multiple media spent the day with their teachers and the technology at hand engaging the deep questions about the peaceful transition of power in a democratic republic? Would not that make for better citizens? Would not that lead to freer, more thoughtful inquiries into how government and politics work? Would not it highlight the similarities we share, and not the differences, and tip the balance of power in our lives toward the "unum," in ways that acknowledge our differences and celebrate the fabric of a 21st century society that going forward depends for its life on creating community, goodwill, and commitment to our most deeply held values at every turn, no matter who gets elected?

A FINAL WORD BY CHRIS COX

Some time has passed since my inauguration experience served to frame a conversation about catalytic learning. At the time, the experience was a profound example of how the conjunction of a spectacle, a participatory environment, and a spirit of inquiry create opportunities for typical observers to become curricularists. At the time of my first draft of this chapter, it was important to document what was happening both in terms of this particular inaugural spectacle, but also in terms of the emergence of my own personal curriculum. In retrospect, while the inauguration of Barack Obama served as a potent context that helped me continuously redefine what I wanted to learn, I find myself now dwelling on *how* the process of the event and accompanying technologies shaped my own personal and continuous refining of curricular goals.

More so than ever, important newsworthy events similar to the magnitude of the inauguration can be instantaneously published thereby sparking spectacles that are able to drive powerfully *great* curriculum opportunities for students of public education. The enabling technologies continue to advance in ways that integrate with our lives in a manner unimaginable even just a few years ago. When I wrote the original chapter in 2009, there were 150 million active Facebook users. In just 2 years there are now over half a billion active Facebook users each of whom are connected on average to an audience of 130 other users and each, on average, generates 90 pieces of content each month (Source: www.facebook.com/press/info.php). This phenomenal growth in content, connections, and users is replicated across many other online applications such as YouTube, Wikipedia, Flickr, and Twitter.

I have come to believe that the process-based approach of catalytic learning described in this chapter is a way for students to write, access, and rewrite their own un-standardized curriculum experiences. We are entering an era where much of our public school curriculum may very well be guided in part by a standardized curriculum framework built upon the Common Core States Initiative which posits an outcomes-based approach to learning. A combination of outcomes-based and process-based curricula offers greater latitude for curriculum leadership to better conceive curriculum guidance likened to Eisner's (1985) view of curriculum as a series of educative activities that are intentionally planned with some of the benefits known prior to the activities and other benefits revealed subsequent to the activities.

Moreover, what continues to resonate with me are the digital conversations, posted pictures, and shared stories with individuals whom I never met who were equally subsumed by both the explicit and implicit events of Inauguration Day. Learning is social. I am forever grateful for the seemingly random people who shared their lived experiences in ways that allowed me and others far from Washington, D.C. to virtually co-experience many moments throughout that day. Those virtual social co-experiences inspired a unique setting and path of teaching and learning, which I believe, is worthy of being alongside the many examples of great curricula featured throughout this book.

NOTES

1. From http://www.cnn.com/2009/POLITICS/01/16/inaugural.preparations/index.html on May 1, 2009
2. From http://www.msnbc.msn.com/id/28733652/ on May 1, 2009
3. From http://www.cnn.com/2009/TECH/01/21/inauguration.online.video/index.html on May 4, 2009
4. The definition of spectacle includes remarkable and impressive as qualifiers. From http://www.thefreedictionary.com/spectacle on May 3, 2009.
5. From http://www.cnn.com/2009/POLITICS/01/20/obama.inauguration/index.html on May 3, 2009
6. From http://www.cnn.com/SPECIALS/2009/44.president/inauguration/mall.satellite on May 3, 2009
7. From http://voices.washingtonpost.com/inauguration-watch/2009/01/jumbotron_locations_revealed_o.html on May 3, 2009
8. From www.fec.gov/pubrec/fe2008/2008presgeresults.pdf on May 3, 2009

REFERENCES

Bowman, A., & Haggerson, N. (1990). Empowering educators through the processes of enfolding and unfolding curriculum. In J. T. Sears & J. D. Marshall (Eds.), *Teaching and thinking about curriculum: Critical inquiries* (pp. 48–60). New York, NY: Teachers College Press.

Cremin, L. A. (1990). *Popular education and its discontents*. New York, NY: Harper & Row.

Debord, G. (1995). *The society of the spectacle*. New York, NY: Zone Books.

Eisner, E. (1985). *The educational imagination: On the design and evaluation of school programs*. New York, NY: Macmillan.

Eisner, E. (1969). Instructional and expressive educational objectives: Their formulation and use in curriculum. In W. J. Popham's *Instructional objectives: An analysis of emerging issues* (pp. 13–18). Chicago, IL: Rand McNally.

Hempel, J. (2009, February 19). How Facebook is taking over our lives. *Fortune-Technology and Tech News*. Retrieved February 25, 2009, from http://money.cnn.com/2009/02/16/technology/hempel_facebook.fortune/index.htm.

Kellner, D. (2003). *Media spectacle*. New York, NY: Routledge.

Marsh, C. J., & Willis, G. (2007). *Curriculum: Alternative approaches, ongoing issues*. Upper Saddle River, NJ: Merrill.

Polanyi, M. (1966). *The tacit dimension*. Garden City, NY: Doubleday & Company.

Postman, N. (1992). *Technopoly: The surrender of culture to technology*. New York, NY: Alfred A. Knopf, Inc.

Postman, N., & Weingartner, C. (1969). *Teaching as a subversive activity*. New York, NY: Delacorte Press.

Wesch, M. (2008). Anti-teaching: Confronting the crisis of significance. *Education Canada, 48*(2), 4–7.

CHAPTER 7

THE ALGEBRA PROJECT: BREAKING THE ALGEBRA CODE

Mary A. Webb

INTRODUCTION

I chose to depict the Algebra Project as a Great Curriculum in order to illuminate its ability to transform the lives of the students who participate in it.
And not only that students' lives changed as a result of participating in the
curriculum in the classroom, but also that their lives are also changed beyond
the classroom as well. Here I describe the Algebra Project; its implications
for changing the lives of underrepresented ethnic minorities through mathematics achievement; and how it has the ability to prepare disadvantaged
youth to become active members of a society that values democracy as a way
of life. While researching the Algebra Project, I visited Lanier High School
located in Jackson, Mississippi, where I met its founder and chief practi-
tioner, Robert Moses. Lanier was the first high school to implement the
project, providing students who graduate from its Algebra Project middle
school cohort experience with a different approach to mathematics as well as

*10 Great Curricula: Lived Conversations of Progressive, Democratic
Curricula in School and Society,* pp. 139–155
Copyright © 2011 by Information Age Publishing
All rights of reproduction in any form reserved.

the life-changing direction provided by experiences inside and outside of the classroom.

FOUNDER DR. ROBERT MOSES

The seed for the Algebra Project was planted over two decades ago when its founder Dr. Robert Moses decided to redirect his struggle for change from the civil rights movement to the right of every child to receive a high quality public education. He developed the concept for the Algebra Project after having taught his daughter's math class in Cambridge, Massachusetts, in 1982. Years later, he took the framework for his project back to Mississippi, the place where he was instrumental as a student activist in the 1960s in helping disenfranchised African Americans secure one of the basic rights guaranteed by the Constitution of the United States, that is the right to vote. In this technology age, Moses equates the need for civil rights during the 1960s with the need for math literacy today: "The underrepresentation of women and minorities in core IT occupations stems partly from their underrepresentation in the educational technical education pipeline that leads to employment in the field" (Department of Commerce, 1999, p. 94).

Bob Moses grew up poor in Harlem. He attended Hamilton College and then went on to earn a master's degree in philosophy from Harvard. Dr. Moses began his work with the civil rights movement in the 1960s. He was a field secretary for the Student Nonviolent Coordinating Committee (SNCC) and later became a Co-Director of the Council of Federated Organizations (COFO) which was an umbrella organization for major civil rights groups then working in Mississippi. In 1964, he became the main organizer of COFO's Freedom Summer Project, which was intended to end racial disenfranchisement (Robert Paris Moses Wikipedia, 2009; see Kevin Talbert's treatment of Freedom Summer at the end of this book).

After completing his Ph.D. at Harvard, Dr. Moses received a MacArthur Fellowship in 1982 and he used the money to create the Algebra Project, a national nonprofit organization that uses mathematics as an organizing tool to ensure quality public school education for every child in America. He has spent over a quarter of a century pursuing the idea that math literacy, particularly in algebra, is necessary for everyone. He argues that math literacy is as important today in this global technological society as the civil rights movement of the 1960s was in its day. "I believe that the absence of math literacy in urban and rural communities throughout this country is an issue as urgent the lack of registered Black voters in Mississippi was in 1961" (Moses & Cobb, 2001, p. 5). Dr. Moses believes that it is this lack of math literacy that closes the door to economic access for many disadvantaged youth, and I would add, the ones that do not fit the mold of traditional schooling.

CONNECTIONS TO MY STORY

Like many of the students who are Algebra Project participants today, my middle and high school teachers wrote me off as someone who would never go to college. Therefore, in their eyes, I did not need to take Algebra. During those school years, I felt disconnected from the mathematics being taught; it had no relevance to my life or what I thought I might be interested in doing in the future. As a result, I quit high school after only one semester and pursed getting a G.E.D. Many years later, after being given a second chance by the United States Army to develop my math skills on the road to becoming a Frequency Manager, I learned the value of understanding mathematics and grew fond of the subject. That experience led me down a path I never dreamed of taking. I became part of a program call "Troops to Teachers." That opportunity opened the door for me to utilize what I had learned about mathematics in the Army and later through college courses to become a middle school mathematics teacher.

Over the last 12 years, I have taught both middle and high school Elementary Mathematics, Pre-Algebra, and Algebra I in grades 5–11. Many of the students I teach and/or have taught come from similar backgrounds as those selected to participate in the Algebra Project. It was while transitioning from teaching in Baltimore, Maryland, to teaching in Cincinnati, Ohio, that I discovered a book written by Dr. Moses called *Radical Equations*. I had never considered the idea of a linear connection between civil rights and math literacy. As I read the book, it just really seemed to make sense and resonate in my soul. As an African American educator who grew up in a family of nine with parents having only a middle school education, I understand that education is the key to ending generational poverty and disenfranchisement. A quality education has the power to change lives as well as attitudes about life. I wondered why this powerful, life-changing curriculum is not being utilized in all schools serving disadvantaged youth, particularly when the achievement gap is widening and many young people leave high school with an eighth grade education unable to find employment.

WHY A RADICAL CURRICULUM?

In his book *Dare the School Build a New Social Order?* Counts (1932) addresses the issue of the purpose of education when he says that "I believe firmly that democratic sentiments should be cultivated and that a better and richer life should be the outcome of education" (p. 17). If we consider education from the perspectives of purpose and function, then perhaps our purpose for education is what we want the end product to be and the function would represent the things that we do in educative settings with intention. For example, in our pursuit of democracy through education we intend for students to graduate with a level of reading and math literacy that supports their choice of attending college or joining the workforce. As a result of the pursuit of and the obtaining of these literacies, students would learn how to live, learn how to care for others and the environment, learn how to think critically, learn how to be concerned about issues outside of oneself (the larger issues of society), learn how to be willing to speak up when one sees an injustice, and learn how to be excited about the possibilities and ultimately what their own personal role as an individual is in the collaborative project of building a democracy.

> Thus, one of the most important responsibilities of educators in a democracy is to enable youngsters to differentiate between constructive and destructive views and beliefs. In a sense, democracy prepares individuals to make decisions and choices that benefit not only the self, but the community as well. (Goodlad et al., 2004, p. 83)

Sirotnik (2002) extends this view, stating:

> Moreover, what goes on after school is equally important, including what happens to students after they graduate from high school. Do they become decent people, good parents, good community members? Do they participate constructively in civic deliberation and democratic practice? Are they economically productive citizens? (p. 666)

Democracy is an idea that I understand has many meanings. I suggest that we view democracy not only as political agency given to all citizens promised by the constitution but also as a social construct (social democracy) where we agree that morality is an important component. As Dewey (1989) puts it, "a moral standard for personal conduct" means to extend a democratic outlook to one's daily living. Are we willing to educate all children so that they might reach this potential by any means necessary? Does not everyone benefit when students are able to participate in democracy on an equal playing field? The Algebra Project affords its students the opportunity to not only participate in political democracy but also social democracy by allowing students greater access to a quality mathematics education, which in turn promotes economic access and a fuller participation in the social life of a democratic society.

But today our current system fails to ensure every student has equal access to a quality education that empowers him or her to be able to fully participate in our democratic society. Our current system values predictive assessment based on race, class, and gender, which in my opinion violates the civil rights of many underserved students. This system simply eliminates those who do not perform well as part of our traditional system.

> Instruction and curriculum should be developmentally appropriate, and should actively engage students in exploring their world. Curricula should be relevant and of high interest to young people, and delve deeply into the conflicting claims inherent in democracy itself. Instruction should engage students in actively working on ideas and concepts as they learn skills and content. (The Forum for Education and Democracy, 2009)

I do not understand why with all the research available and the advent of the NCLB Act that we—the stakeholders, the educators, the parents, the community members, and politicians—have not figured out that what works for some students will not work for everyone. Why do we continue to force a square peg into a round hole?

ALGEBRA IS KEY

At root for math teachers is that the traditional way we teach Algebra does not work for everyone. Algebra is the gatekeeper to upper level mathematics. It serves to open doors for some and closes doors for others. Thus, the lack of math literacy prevents some from realizing their potential and/or their dream of a productive school and work career. An American College Testing study reported that, "whether planning to enter college or workforce training programs after graduation, high school students need to be educated to a comparable level of readiness in reading and mathematics. Graduates need this level of readiness if they are to succeed in college-level courses without remediation and to enter workforce training programs ready to learn job-specific skills" (ACT, 2006).

In the study, ACT looked at the types of occupations that offer a wage sufficient to support a family of four, as well as potential for career advancement, but do not require a 4-year college degree. These occupations—which include electricians, construction workers, upholsterers, plumbers, etc.—typically require some combination of vocational training and on-the-job experience or an associate's degree (ACT, 2006). All require math literacy, namely Algebra. This speaks to the issue of why it is important that we ensure that everyone is given an opportunity to learn Algebra and that we teach it in a way that promotes mastery based upon the needs of the students and not what works for the district, the schools, and/or the teacher. The primary focus in education should be the student.

Nationwide, nearly one in three U.S. high school students fails to graduate with a diploma. In total, approximately 1.2 million students drop out each year—averaging 7,000 every school day or one every 26 seconds.

Among minority students, the problem is even more severe with nearly 50% of African American and Hispanic students not completing high school on time. According to the National Assessment of Educational Progress (NAEP), by twelfth grade, African Americans are typically 4 years behind White and Asian students, while Hispanics are doing only a tad better than Black students. These students are finishing high school with a junior high education (Thernstrom, 2003, p. 13). Also, many of those students who do graduate are not prepared to take college-level courses or to enter the workforce with requisite foundational skills. In the year 2000, data from the Early Mathematics Placement Testing Program suggested that 30% of Ohio high school graduates required remedial math courses prior to taking college-level courses. That number increased to 33% in 2005.

Moses & Cobb (2001) add:

> In today's world, economic access and full citizenship depend crucially on math and science literacy. And in the culture itself—our culture— illiteracy in math is acceptable the way illiteracy in reading and writing is unacceptable. Failure is tolerated in math but not in English. (p. 9)

During my career as an educator, I have seen and participated in numerous mathematics programs that are touted as the quick fix for low-achieving students. These programs generally promise to fill the gaps in student learning but never address the relevance issue in a way that makes sense to the students. Never have I seen a program like the Algebra Project that engages the students on so many levels. The Algebra Project is more than just the formal curriculum of Algebra. Instead, it addresses student's needs beyond the classroom and provides a relevance that makes it a life saving program.

THE ALGEBRA PROJECT CURRICULUM

The Algebra Project is intended for students who come from under represented ethnic minority groups. The goal of the Algebra Project is to help close the gap between universal free public education and universal completion of a college preparatory math sequence in high school (Moses & Cobb, 2001, p. 93). It is founded on the belief that all students can learn algebra if given the proper instructional context, and it utilizes a five-step Transitional Curriculum which Dr. Moses developed to help students make the conceptual leap from arithmetic to algebra. Experiential strategies, social construction of knowledge, teacher education, and community empowerment are the vehicles utilized to accomplishing this monumental task.

Like many progressive educators today, Dr. Moses believes that Algebra is the gateway to upper level mathematics courses required for entry and success in college for those who choose to go, as well as for those who intend to be productive members of our democratic society by joining the workforce. Math literacy and economic access are the Algebra Project's foci for giving hope to the young (Moses & Cobb, 2001, p. 16). Goodlad et al. (2004) states that

> Democracy exists in large part because of a persistent and widespread belief that everyone should be given access to the good life regardless of individual circumstances of birth, religion, race, or socioeconomic class.... For those who are not, by virtue of wealth and status, born into the good life, education is our best hope for providing opportunities to them that otherwise might not exist. (p. 46)

Christine Sleeter (1997) advocates that Multicultural Education is an important product of the civil rights movement. Rooted in activism and in a strong belief in the ideals of equity, justice, and freedom, multicultural education represents a vision of a better society for all Americans, for better schools for all children, and encourages the development of practical strategies, supported by research, for attaining such a vision. The Young People's Project is an outgrowth of the Algebra Project and was established to develop youth leaders and organizers to become social activists as well as change agents for not only our educational system but for their communities. Through Math Literacy Worker trainings and development, workshops and community events, the Young People's Project promotes math literacy as a tool for the young to demand of themselves, communities, and school systems, an education commensurate with the requirements for citizenship in today's technology-based economy. Each established site employs from 30 to 100 high school and college age students on a part-time basis, and serves up to 1000 elementary and middle school students through a variety of on and off-site programs.

Dr. Moses has continued his work to press toward securing quality education for all children. The Algebra Project is often thought of as curriculum for African American students. I suspect that is why it has not received the wide acclaim that other mathematics programs have. The Algebra Project breaks from the tradition of teaching students merely using a textbook, focusing on rote memory skill development, providing numerous practice problems, and following with homework. Instead, the curriculum requires students to be active participants in their learning, to move, to explore, to explain in a language common to the student as opposed to the traditional lecture style in which the students simply receive what the teacher transmits. It seeks to facilitate the ongoing learning of Algebra through creating relevant experiences for the students.

What Dr. Moses has done through the Algebra Project has been described in the *Journal for Research in Mathematics Education* by Sleeter (1997) as what a "good multicultural mathematics teacher knows about how to help students from historically low-achieving sociocultural groups to achieve well in mathematics by using their cultural backgrounds as a pedagogical resource" (p. 682). Like Bob Moses, Sleeter touts multicultural education as a means to resist the hegemonic models of school. She advocates for an approach to education that is Multicultural and Social Reconstructionist, teaches directly about political and economic oppression and discrimination, and prepares young people to use social action skills.

Tyler (1976a) observed,

> The critical task.... is not one of sorting but rather one of educating all or almost all young people to meet the needs of modern society (p. 19).... Hence schools should establish ways of connecting learning experiences to "out of school activities" (p. 63).... If something is learned in school is not utilized by the student in relevant situations outside of school, most of the value of learning is lost. (p. 64)

The planned curriculum of the Algebra Project consists of four components:

- a curriculum which addresses the conceptual leap between arithmetic and Algebra;
- experiential processes which link concrete physical events to abstract mathematical concepts;
- an expectation of achievement that is shared by a community of students, parents, teachers, and administrators;
- an effective teacher education program. (Silva et al., 1990, p. 375)

Offering a new and innovative math curriculum with regard to both content and instructional methods, the Algebra Project also teaches students how to set goals, motivates them to achieve, and mobilizes parents and the community to become active, supportive participants. In the classroom, you will see students interacting with the curriculum. The students call it hands on learning, yet it is much more than that. It is an "experience."

According to Eisner (2002), the "intended curriculum" refers to a body of material that is planned in advance of classroom use and that is designed to help "students learn some content, acquire some skills, develop some beliefs or have some valued type of experience" (p. 34). The planned, intended curriculum for the Algebra Project was developed by mathematics educators from the K-12 classroom and the collegiate level. It is a collaboration between actual classroom teachers who implement the curriculum, critique it, and provide feedback based their experiences with the students. The Algebra I concepts presented in this curriculum are the result of a national consensus about high school mathematics reform and typically go beyond the requirements of many state standards. The planned method of delivery is one in which the teacher facilitates the learning process. Cohort members are required to take 90 minutes of math daily for 4 years.

The planned curriculum includes:

1. mathematically rich physical experiences
2. pictorial representations/modeling of events
3. intuitive language about the events, i.e., People Talk
4. Structured language about the events, i.e., Feature Talk
5. symbolic representation of the events

The relationship between one's experiences and learning can be traced back to Dewey. He believed that student's should learn by doing and that this sort of hands-on learning would allow students to experience the curriculum beyond the traditional way of schooling. It is this kind of experiential learning that moves the students from the experience to the abstract which is described as a bridge, a transition from real life to mathematical language and operations.

In addition to a rich classroom experience, students attend summer institutes to enhance their learning of not only mathematics, but of English and writing skills as well. One of the essential components of Algebra Project that I believe is critical not only to the success of the program but also to the success of the students, is the mental health counseling, which I like to think of as wellness support. We can close the achievement gap for many students, but if we fail to provide the psychological support necessary to help them become productive, functioning members of society, we are again dooming them for failure.

Algebra Project students are isolated from many of their friends as a result of taking this math class at Lanier. They form a cohort in which they are expected to take Algebra I, Geometry, Algebra II, Trigonometry, and Intro to Engineering whereas their peers (non-Algebra Project students) only need three math units to fulfill Mississippi graduation requirements. One of those credits can be earned in eighth grade by taking Algebra I, this leaves many high school students with only two units left to obtain. Essentially students could have met their math graduation requirements by the end of their sophomore year. At Lanier High School (historically the lowest performing of Jackson's high schools), where I visited a classroom, when asked what others thought about their participation in the Algebra Project the response was overwhelming that they are often thought of as special education students as a result of the physical location of their classroom. Many of these students come from dysfunctional, under-educated families that have experienced generational poverty. This program puts them in a unique position in many cases to have taken more mathematics than both their peers and/or family members. Through weekly counseling the students are given tools for dealing with this peer pressure and other life issues through both group and individual counseling with a psychologist.

Tyler (1949) acknowledged that the broad needs of students could be broken down into phases:

1. Health
2. Social Relationships
3. Social civic relationships
4. The consumer aspect of life
5. Occupational life
6. Recreational (p. 9)

Tyler (1949) realized that these were not all the needs of students and schools that they would in fact differ depending on the schools and the groups within the school. He recommended studying the needs of students through observations, student interviews, parent interviews, and questionnaires in addition to standardized test scores. "Once the data had been gathered, it was the schools' role to distinguish between the needs that are met by education and the needs that are met through other social agencies" (p. 15). When asked about the counseling they receive, overwhelmingly each student felt that they benefited from having someone to discuss their problems with. Both the girls and the boys felt like the psychologist genuinely cared about what happened to them. That knowledge seems to have helped many of them change their attitude about life, certainly about math, the number of courses they are expected to take, and what their future would hold.

All of the students I spoke with had plans to attend college and saw themselves as successful, contributing members of society. This is remarkable since we know that youth today deal with crises such as violence, death, parental divorce and remarriage, child abuse, substance abuse, and developmental and educational transitions.

TRANSFORMATIONS

One female student stated that when she was in a traditional math class she felt "dumb" and they were placed in ability groups. The Algebra Project has changed how she feels about herself, about math, and about her abilities to learn. She said that she is now smarter than her friends who are in "regular math class" because she has taken more math. This component of the program seems to reduce mental health barriers to learning while allowing the students to heal and grow from issues of the past as well as strengthening healthy youth development.

The experienced curriculum for these students varies, of course, from student to student. While looking, I found out that 91% of the current Lanier cohort had passed the state required Algebra I test. This was significant to most of them because some of their friends in regular math classes had yet to pass the test. Additionally, in preparation for the test, the Algebra Project students were sent to a regular Algebra I class to study for the test. As the students reviewed various concepts, they found that in many cases they had a better understanding of the concepts and were able to share their knowledge with the non-Algebra Project students. Being able to share their unique strategies with the non-Algebra Project students greatly reinforced their feeling of confidence. During my visit some of the students had received their ACT test scores. One student was extremely excited about achieving a composite score of 20 and a college math readiness score of 22.

The Mississippi Classes of both 2008 and 2007 scored an average ACT score of 18.9. Students who graduated from middle schools where a majority of the students participated in the Algebra Project enrolled in (and passed) college preparatory math courses in high school at about twice the rate of their peers from non-Algebra Project middle schools in the same district. http://www.math.cornell.edu/~dwh/AP/DRK-12-description.pdf

I asked a sophomore who was in her second year with the Algebra Project to describe the Algebra Project and she said "it is math, not abstract, but fun." She was referring to the physical experiences and being able to connect what she was learning to real-life applications. She goes on to tell how as a result of her being in the Algebra Project and the knowledge she had gained, she now felt respected by her non-Algebra Project peers.

Although each Algebra Project site implements the program in a slightly different manner based upon the site's needs, the formal curriculum utilized is the same for all sites. Other site variations include the number of teachers per classroom, implementation of the after school activities for youth, and the level of community and university support and involvement. Each cohort school must commit to reduce the class size to 20 students for the 4 years, provide 90 min of math daily, and provide a common planning period for Algebra Project teachers. At Lanier high school there are two teachers assigned to teach 22 students.

Students participate in community activities. Youth-led community math workshops benefit the students in two ways: (1) students are given the opportunity to showcase their skills, talents, and leadership ability, and (2) students receive a stipend for their work. Receiving a stipend for their work is a significant component to this program as many of these students must work to support themselves and/or their families. Through these activities students lead the community in games as well as teach Algebra concepts to younger students. Perry (2003) found in her research that schools that produce high achieving African American students engage in public demonstrations that communicate and celebrate high achievement.

The results of intensive National Algebra Project research have revealed the following about the Algebra Project cohort graduates as compared with the general population:

- They enroll in eighth and tenth grade mathematics courses at a significantly higher rate.
- They enroll in college preparatory courses at twice the rate.
- They pass state required mathematics exams at significantly higher rates.

Of the 40 Lanier high school 2006 Algebra Project graduates, 34 were known to have attended college for more than one semester. One had left college after one semester, was working, but planned to return to college. Of the three students known not to attend college, two had children. Seventeen were at Hinds Community College in Jackson, three at Jackson State, three were at Mary Holmes College in West Point, MS, and three were at Paul Quinn College in Dallas. Two were at Mississippi State in Starkville, MS, one at Ole Miss, in Oxford, MS; one at Rust College in Holly Springs, MS. At this point, we do not have extensive or definitive data about the students' personal growth and/or how their attitudes have changed as a result of their participation in the Algebra Project.

CONCLUSION

Dr. Moses has used his experience from the civil rights movement to organize the students, their parents, and the community into action for social change. He has created a life-changing program that will transform the lives of students involved. He has found a way to include students who are too often excluded, in schools and ultimately in the democratic process. Why have not more school districts made a commitment as well as a financial investment to the Algebra Project? Certainly, there are school districts across our nation that struggle with how to educate groups of low achievers regardless of ethnic background. What price are we willing to pay to continue our democratic way of life so that everyone is truly given the opportunities to pursue the unalienable rights framed by the founders—to life, liberty, and the pursuit of happiness?

Our failure to provide all students with a quality education has lead to many of our youth feeling hopeless and unable to secure meaningful employment to care for themselves, much less care for an entire family. This has often led to them becoming a statistic in our judicial system.

On average, the cost today to incarcerate an inmate is $24,655.75 per year. According to the U.S. Census Bureau "Facts Release" dated June 14, 2007, the national average per pupil expenditure was $8,701 on public elementary and secondary education in 2005. It cost us, as a nation on average nearly three times as much to incarcerate a young person than it does to provide a quality education.

Even with the passing of NCLB, the United States has yet to close the achievement gap for disadvantaged youth. We as a nation benefit when young people graduate from high school and are able to participate in the democratic way of life. Those who do not graduate are more likely to be incarcerated, suffer from poor health, are less likely to earn enough money to support themselves or a family, and are more likely to require some form of government assistance. Research has shown that the Algebra Project is one way to close this gap, although, its potential for being transformative has gone unrecognized on a national level for many years.

Many school districts have begun to invest the time and resources to give more than lip service to the old adage of "closing the achievement gap." For 2008–2009, the South Bronx School District made a commitment to implement the Algebra Project in all of its schools. It will also be implemented in Mansfield, Ohio. In addition to its curriculum that addresses the relevance issue, it creates an unforgettable life-changing experience for students that are grounded in a vision of democracy, social justice, and equality principals our country holds so dear. Therefore, the Algebra Project gets my vote for being a "great curriculum." In addition, Dr. Moses is a man of extraordinary vision. His passion for service coupled with his lifelong commitment to promoting the idea of "liberty and justice for all" is second to none. I believe the strong curricular commitments include defining the importance of math literacy and its ability to transform not only the lives of the students but our place in this global society, reexamining the purpose and function of education, changing the way we think about schools and what works, and providing alternatives to the traditional route and integrating social democracy in schools. Perhaps, if math literacy were viewed as a larger issue of democracy, then we would consider it immoral not to use all of the resources available to educate everyone.

"We just must not; we just cannot afford the great waste that comes from the neglect of a single child." (Lyndon Baines Johnson)

RESPONSE BY TOM POETTER

Mary and I have discussed the difficulty of implementing wide-scale math reforms that work and are defensible educationally and socially, especially when considering P-12 students of color as the targets for change. For me the issues coalesce around the tensions encountered when I have taught advanced seminars on curriculum and discussed the matter of progressive curriculum reform for students of color with people of color, educators of all sorts, in the classes. The response is always heated, and mixed. Meaning, school teachers and school/community leaders of color in my classes have often rejected the notion of a progressive response like the one Dr. Moses makes through his implementation locally and on a wider scale with the Algebra Project. As a middle class White male, I am often flabbergasted by the response. I should not be.

The truth of the matter is that progressive responses are not often trusted, they do not feel reliable to some, and they look like they will take a long time to implement with no guarantee of measurable "success." They seem like they would take a great deal of expertise to put in place, a large amount of teacher re-education would be required, and the view of students as the center of the educative act, and not the teacher or the school program, run counter to widely held community and cultural values. My counter-arguments are always aggressive, and hinge on my understanding of theorist/practitioners such as Hilliard and Moses (Perry, 2003; Hilliard, 1995) and the fallacies surrounding the high stakes accountability/testing movements.

First, a test-based, standards-oriented curriculum is almost always impoverished in and of itself. The mere fact that the stated end is improved test scores so limits the scope of the endeavor that it cannot help but bore students. While it might raise test scores in the short term, it will not do anything to advance or inspire students in the long term nor will it take into account what is really important about individual students and the communities that raise them. Second, the ends justify the means with a traditional approach, which almost always does not start with students and what they want to know about the subject at hand in terms of its ability to be at work for them in the real world. And third, if we stand any hope of reaching students, it will never happen under traditional conditions, even if we have ultra-skilled teachers intensifying the doing of what we know all ready does not work! There is no reason in it especially when we know what works, like Dr. Moses' approaches to curriculum and pedagogy for students of color in the area of mathematics.

So, one of the things that makes the Algebra Project great is that it takes a head-on view of the problem, addressing students and their needs as they pertain to math and to citizenship directly. The starting point is the students. The math pertains to the real world around them. Skillful teachers help all students excel on a daily basis for the benefit of the student and the class at that moment, not for some extremely distant, futuristic end. And the larger view of the project at-hand extends the classroom reach of the student beyond the classroom and into the community. The continuum between classroom and community is traversed not just by the teacher, but by each student as well. The proof of success is in the student achievement that follows, both in and out of school, through important rates such as attendance and post-secondary school matriculation, but what is more, in the impact that each student has on others in the wider community through their service in the moment, let alone their preparedness for the good life beyond schooling.

For me, the leadership example of Dr. Moses—who led one of the world's greatest, most effective nonviolent social transformation movements for U.S. civil rights in the 1950s and 1960s that the history of the world has ever known—proves to be even more amazing as the life of the great patriot plays out, especially as he uses his talents on a local level to impact individuals, all of whom deserve the attention and the opportunities that follow. Would that we all could dedicate ourselves, like Bob and Mary do, to the transformation of society one child at a time.

MARY WEBB'S FINAL WORD

In this era of No Child Left Behind test driven accountability teachers are under extreme pressure to make the focus of instruction the learning of skills that are tested on the standardized state tests. Almost nonexistent is the relevance that is necessary in the use of mathematics to promote the notion of equity and justice for all. There is little encouragement from administration for teachers to step outside of their comfort zone into what may be uncharted territory for the teacher, the school, as well as the district. Our current system fails to ensure every student has equal access to a quality education that empowers them to be able to fully participate in our democratic society. Our current system values predictive assessment based on race, class, and gender to violate the civil rights of many underserved students. This system simply eliminates those who do not perform well as part of our traditional system.

The ideal that education is a vehicle for social mobility for those historically marginalized and a way in which to eliminate from society inequities based upon race, class, gender, sexual orientation, and/or disability continues to elude our nation. However, the field of mathematics is gaining recognition as being a tool for teaching political and social activism.

Through mathematics I want to change not only the world from which my students operate but the world at large as a result of their seeing themselves as agents of change. This strategy for teaching mathematics is also an opportunity for me to make math culturally relevant based upon their experiences and their reality. It is an attempt to empower underrepresented and undereducated students, their parents and other adults who have a vested interest in their success through their discourse as a result of their experiences in class. Students begin to understand their power and their role as citizens of a democracy and as consumers. As a result, students recognize the relevance of math in their lives, and are eager to share their realities and the connections between their math knowledge and issues of social justice.

The benefits of a rich, relevant, rigorous, engaging, and hands-on experience will have a lasting, indelible impact not only on their lives but on those of others. Twenty first century curriculum must address not only mathematical concepts but real-life problems and issues of social justice.

REFERENCES

ACT. (2006). Ready for college or ready for work: Same or different. Iowa City, IA: ACT. Retrieved from http://www.act.org/research/policymakers/pdf/Readiness Brief.pdf

Counts, G. (1932). Dare to build a new social order? New York, NY: John Day Publishers.

Department of Commerce, Office of Technology Policy. (1999, June). The Digital Workforce: Building the infotech skills at the speed of innovation, p. 94.

Dewey, J. (1989). Freedom and culture. Buffalo, NY: Prometheus. (Original work published 1939)

Eisner, E. (2002). The educational imagination: On the design and evaluation of schools programs. Upper Saddle River, NJ: Pearson.

Goodlad, J., Goodlad, S., Mantle-Bromley, C. (2004). Education for everyone: agenda for education in a democracy. San Francisco, CA: Jossey-Bass.

Hillard, A. (1995). The Maroon within us: selected essays on African American community socialization. Baltimore, MD: Black Classic Press.

Johnson, Lyndon Baines. Retrieved quote from http:educationanddemocracy.net/

Moses, R., & Cobb, C. (2001). Radical equations: civil rights from Mississippi to the algebra project. Boston, MA: Beacon Press.

Perry, T. (2003). Up from the parched earth: Toward a theory of African American achievement. In P. C. Steele & A. Hilliard (Eds.), Young, gifted and Black: Promoting high achievement among African American students (pp. 1–108). Boston, MA: Beacon Press.

Silva, C. M., Moses, R. P., Rivers, J., & Johnson, P. (1990). The algebra project: Making middle school mathematics count. Journal of Negro Education, 59(3), 375–391.

Sirotnik, K. A. (2002). Promoting responsible accountability in schools and education. Phi Delta Kappan, 83(9), 662–673.

Sleeter, C. (1997). Mathematics, multiculutral education, and professional development. Journal for Research in Mathematics Education, 28(6), 680–696.

Thernstrom, A. &. (2003). No excuses: Closing the racial gap in learning. New York, NY: Simon & Schuster.

Tyler, R. (1949). *Basic principles of curriculum and instruction.* Chicago, IL: University of Chicago Press.

Tyler, R. (1976a). *Perspectives on American education: Reflections on the past...challenges for the future.* Chicago, IL: Science Research Associates.

Tyler, R. (1976b). Two new emphases in curriculum development. *Educational Leadership, 34*(1), 61–71.

(n.d). Retrieved from (Robert Parris Moses- Wikipedia, 2009).

(n.d). Retrived from http://thinkprogress.org/2008/08/19/power-of-progress/

(n.d). Retrieved from http://www.forumforeducation.org/our-issues/learning-teaching

(n.d). Retrieved from http://www.act.org/research/policymakers/pdf/Readiness Brief .pdf

(n.d). Retrieved from http://educationanddemocracy.net/

CHAPTER 8

THE UNITED STATES HOLOCAUST MEMORIAL MUSEUM: YOU ARE MY WITNESSES

Dawn Mann

PERSONAL BEGINNINGS

I decided to study the United States Holocaust Memorial Museum in Washington, D.C., for many reasons. A main reason for this choice was because my sister recently converted to Judaism; she wanted to raise her child in the Jewish faith to remain consistent with my brother-in-law's upbringing. We have shared many conversations about their faith and why she felt that it was important to convert. The foundation of their faith is of utmost importance to my sister and her husband. Through our conversations I began to discover the history within my brother-in-law's family.

He had lost many family members in the Holocaust. The Holocaust was the systematic, bureaucratic, state-sponsored persecution and murder of approximately six million Jews (representing two thirds of the Jewish population in prewar Europe) by the Nazi regime and its collaborators.

10 Great Curricula: Lived Conversations of Progressive, Democratic Curricula in School and Society, pp. 157–172
Copyright © 2011 by Information Age Publishing
All rights of reproduction in any form reserved.

An estimated 1.5 million of those persecuted were children. "Holocaust" is a word of Greek origin meaning "sacrifice by fire." The Nazis, who came to power in Germany in January 1933, believed that Germans were "racially superior" and that the Jews, deemed "inferior," were an alien threat to the so-called German racial community.

So this has all become very personal for me. The words, "You are my witnesses" (Isaiah 43:10) jump out at the visitor to the Holocaust Museum; and they resonated with me as I sat in the synagogue waiting for the naming of my niece, my sister's first child. Not only was I about to become the witness to a momentous occasion in my niece's life and in the life of the family, but I also found myself a witness to a faith that was once unknown to me.

German authorities also targeted other groups during the Holocaust era because of their perceived "racial inferiority." These groups consisted of Gypsies, the disabled, and some Poles, Russians, and others. Other groups were persecuted on political, ideological, and behavioral grounds, among them Communists, Socialists, Jehovah's Witnesses, blacks, and homosexuals. My brother-in-law's grandfather played a role in the resistance efforts following World War II as Israel became a Jewish state. Never had I heard these stories about his family until I began to share my curiosity of the Jewish faith and most important the historical repression that came along with this faith. Not only was it personal because of my sister and her family but also because of Jewish friends that I had grown up with, close friends of mine now, some of whom were silenced in my classroom. Jewish students constitute a minority population in my school. The invisible lines of domination silence them.

Throughout my schooling, I was introduced to the atrocities towards the Jews during World War II but never the depth of repression the Jews experienced prior to the Holocaust during World War II as well as after the war. Why did not I know about this? Is it because the teachers that I had throughout my schooling felt that it was inappropriate to share and/or discuss such atrocities? Is it because some people believed that it never happened? Was it because of the anti-Semitic attitudes still prevalent in our culture? Or is it because the teachers themselves really did not understand what happened? These questions have surfaced just recently, yet, I firmly believe that they have been within me as long as I can remember. As I studied the museum, I wondered, "What was it about this museum that roused such a deep curiosity within? What was the 'hook' that inspired me to explore the deep meanings within the museum? What has allowed me to reflect on my past as a human learner as well as directing me to reflect on future learning?"

WHAT IS THE HOLOCAUST MUSEUM?

The United States Holocaust Memorial Museum (USHMM) is located near the National Mall in Washington, D.C., and opened to the general public in 1993. This space is a living memorial to the Holocaust. A public–private partnership, along with some federal support, guarantees the Museum's permanent existence. Nationwide donors make its educational activities and global outreach possible. Today, 90% of the Museum's visitors are not Jewish, and its Web site, the world's leading online authority on the Holocaust, had 15 million visits in 2006 on a daily basis from an average of 100 different countries. Since its dedication in 1993, nearly 30 million visitors have been welcomed into the museum, including more than 8 million school children. A breakdown of this number includes 34% school-aged children, 12% international visitors, and more than 3,500 officials from 132 countries, including 88 heads of state/government.

The conception of the Museum was not immediate. As posted on the Museum website, on November 1, 1978, President Carter established the President's Commission on the Holocaust and charged it with issuing a report on the state of Holocaust remembrance and education in the United States. Almost a year later, on September 27, 1979, the President's Commission presented their results and made four main recommendations:

- That a living memorial be established to honor the victims and survivors of the Holocaust and to ensure that the lessons of the Holocaust will be taught in perpetuity.
- That an educational foundation be established to stimulate and support research in the teaching of the Holocaust.
- That a Committee on Conscience be established that would collect information on and alert the national conscience regarding reports of actual or potential outbreaks of genocide throughout the world.
- That a national Day of Remembrance of Victims of the Holocaust be established in perpetuity and be held annually.

In 1980, Congress unanimously passed legislation to establish the United States Holocaust Memorial Council. The Council, which succeeded the President's Commission on the Holocaust, was charged with carrying out the above recommendations. Elie Wiesel was named the first Chairman of the Council and Mark E. Talisman the first Vice Chairman (website citation, 2009).

Not until 1983, was the land for the museum transferred from the government to the council. The building of the Museum did not begin until July 1989. The Museum building was finally completed in April 1993. The overall cost to build the space of remembrance was approximately $168 million ($90 million for the building's construction and $78 million for the exhibits) (website, 2009). The Museum is the product of a strong partnership between private philanthropy and the government; it is built on land donated from the federal government and funded by more than 200,000 private donations. All funds for planning, constructing, and equipping the Museum were raised exclusively from private, tax deductible contributions, as required by law.

THE PLANNED & LIVED CURRICULUM OF THE MUSEUM

"The museum will touch the life of everyone who enters and leave everyone forever changed—a place of deep sadness and a sanctuary of bright hope; an ally of education against ignorance, of humility against arrogance, an investment in a secure future against whatever insanity lurks ahead. If this museum can mobilize morality, then those who have perished will thereby gain a measure of immortality." — William J. Clinton, 42nd President of the United States at the Dedication Ceremonies for the United States Holocaust Memorial Museum, April 22, 1993

The museum website claims that the Holocaust has become a central theme in the culture of many countries. This theme is reflected in media representation and popular culture. Holocaust education can offer students historical knowledge and skills needed to understand/evaluate these cultural manifestations. Why is the term Holocaust used? What exactly does it mean? Are there differences among the meanings translated by the various cultures? What is the curriculum that the Museum provides to allow one to explore this problematic term Holocaust?

In my description of the curriculum of the museum, I am using Marsh and Willis' (2007) definition of curriculum as "an interrelated set of plans and experiences." In the Introduction, Poetter gives a brief overview of the notions of planned and lived curriculum which I will be using as a framework in the sharing of my experience of the Holocaust Museum. The planned curriculum of the Museum was well thought out and supported by many individuals. I would like to define the planned curriculum more specifically as the design of the museum which would include the physical layout, the content within the building space, as well as the aesthetics of the Museum space. As I take you through the layout of the museum, I will be interweaving the notion of the lived curriculum by sharing my personal account of my experiences as I moved through the permanent exhibit. The layout of the museum consists of permanent and temporary exhibition spaces, a memorial space, areas for meetings and discussion, a research library and archives, two theaters, an interactive computer learning center, and classrooms.

The structure of the building: Architect James Ingo Freed was the individual chosen to design of the Museum. He successfully created a distinct relationship between the Museum building itself and the exhibitions within. Freed visited numerous Holocaust sites, including both camps and ghettos, examining the materials and structures of the various spaces. The architecture was created and drawn upon from memory by Freed, which provides a representation of the history being captured within the Museum. In Freed's words, "There are no literal references to particular places or occurrences from the historic event. Instead, the architectural form is open-ended so the Museum becomes a resonator of memory" (website, 2009).

As I approached the external structure of the Museum, it clearly stood out to me from the surrounding structures. The building has very unique rounded appearance which was being observed by hundreds of museum goers standing outside waiting in line to gain access to this space of remembrance. My attention was drawn immediately to the poster on a small space within the structure to the right of the entrance: "Think the next time you see injustice; About the next time you witness hatred; About the next time you hear about genocide; About what you saw at the Holocaust Museum." This modern structure clearly stood as a metaphor for change and resistance once I read those words.

As I entered into the Museum, the outside atmosphere of the warm sun quickly changed to a cooler and darker atmosphere, almost dampening. I found myself standing in an open lobby area that seemed to take on the appearance of the middle of space in which you became entrapped by dingy brick walls, metal post lights hanging from the side of the walls, and staring at you was a large, dark grey marble wall with the words "You are my witnesses." (Isaiah 43:10) engraved within. Looking down upon me was a ceiling of sky lights with steel girders criss-crossed in fashion, connected from one end of the building to another. It was constructed in such a way that made you feel as if you were outside in an open space yet trapped by these strong steel beams above you. It intrigued me that even though there was this place for natural light to enter, it did not give the feel of a warm and bright environment. What was it that was creating this feeling within me? The aesthetics of the structure were successful in gripping my mind and emotions. I felt myself become more quiet and respectful in the way I moved about the lobby, exploring the space around me. Instantaneous inquisitiveness took over—I wanted to explore it all. What was this building of remembrance about to share with me?

Each permanent exhibit tour began every 15 minutes. The permanent exhibit is a self-guided exhibition that consists of three floors that take you through a comprehensive historical narrative of the Holocaust. As I waited for my time slot, I decided to visit the *Remember the Children: Daniel's Story* exhibit which did not require timed passes. This exhibit was recommended for visitors 8 years or older. I was curious to see how the history of the Holocaust was going to be told through the perspective of a young boy growing up in Nazi Germany, especially since I had children of my own. As I entered the exhibit, I found myself in a makeshift town. Surrounding me were the storefronts of local businesses, including Daniel's father's shop. I felt that I had been transported back in time to a small town in preoccupied Nazi Germany.

As I moved through the exhibit within Daniel's home, through his bedroom, there were various texts illustrating the feeling and emotions of Daniel. He was telling the story of his family and how things began to change around him. These changes led me to a room in which the store front of his father's shop was shattered and racial slurs written across the walls—NO JEWS ALLOWED! The noise around me began to get louder. What was changing around me? Where had I been transported to? It was a place of chaos, confusion and unrest. These were the voices of people, Jews who found themselves being thrown together in the ghetto. The lighting around me became very dark and I could almost smell the odor of dirt, mildew, and sewage. I began to feel closed in; I began to feel as if I was in the ghetto with Daniel and his family. I found myself wanting to pick up my pace to try and leave this dark, depressing area. As I moved through the twist and turns of the exhibit, I found myself in the last room before heading out, where many other museum goers were standing. All of our attention was drawn to a video that was being played on a monitor in a room in which the back drop was that of a concentration camp. The video was of "Daniel" telling his story of how he believed that he was just going to another place to live with the rest of his friends like him, Jews. He had no idea that his mother and sister would be taken away from him, and eventually killed. The innocence of this young boy's voice, along with the powerful images of his family and friends began to stir the deepest emotions within me. And this was only the children's exhibit. What could possibly stir more emotion than to hear about the Holocaust from a young child's perspective? I was anxious to begin the permanent exhibition.

THE PERMANENT EXHIBITION

The museum staff lined all of us up that had 2:00 p.m. passes. I felt that we were being herded into the area in front of the elevators like cattle. Were we being herded like the Jews were as they were being moved from one area to another? There was hardly any room to move as the museum staff was explaining the rules/instructions of the museum. The staff handed each of us a 'passport' which contained the personal information of a person who had been killed in the Holocaust. This immediately made it personal. I now had the name of someone who had not survived. The name given to me was that of a young girl. Once the card was handed to me, it was as if

I had been transported back in time. It was as if I were standing back in the *Daniel's Story* exhibit, surrounded by the voices of young, innocent children playing in the streets of the ghetto, unknowingly waiting to be transported to extermination camps. This passport was more than just a piece of paper with the information of a young girl that had once lived as an innocent Jew. This small card represented a life, a life that was once a vibrant, hopeful member of the human race. The curators of the museum were deliberate in their decision to present each visitor with a passport. This planned curriculum of written words describing the history of an individual in the Holocaust would be translated into a living memory of the individual. As I held the card in my hand, I was about to experience the lived curriculum that the curators of the museum had hoped for. I now had an identity to carry through the exhibits besides my own.

I boarded the elevator, card in hand, with about 30 other people. There was literally no space to even turn around, and the temperature began to rise. We were told that as soon as the elevator doors closed, there would be a short video that would play on the monitor above our heads. I could not even turn to see it but I will never forget hearing the voice that began to fill the elevator. It was the voice of an American GI that had been part of one of the first concentration camp liberations at Dachau. He was describing what they had found which immediately took my breath away; I began to feel sick to my stomach. The last words I heard before the elevators door opened were, "Things like that just do not happen" (American GI, video in elevator).

The elevator doors opened into a very dark room with dim lights shining from above. The individuals ahead of me were looking at something on the wall but I could not see beyond them to tell what exactly they were seeing. As the crowd slowly started to move, my eyes became fixed on one of the most horrific photographs that I had ever seen. From floor to ceiling, wall to wall was a picture of American soldiers peering down on piles of dead bodies in striped clothing. This image was taken by U.S. Army soldiers in 1945 at Dachau concentration camp. Emaciated bodies, faces, bald heads, bones protruding, you could not even tell if they were male or female bodies. Some bodies were lumped together like a pile of rag dolls where others were contorted individually beyond belief. I felt as if I was in the photograph itself, standing there with the American soldiers. I began to notice that there was chanting or some type of singing going on around me. Every one of my senses became heightened. As I began to proceed through the opening floor of the permanent exhibit, I discovered the origin of the noise.

The opening floor of the exhibit explores the *Nazi Assault 1933–1939*. The lighting remained dim which allowed for the photographic images to stand out even more. Surrounding the photographs was text describing the various tools employed by the Nazi party to gain what they hoped for, a totalitarian state. My attention was drawn to the videos being played on the monitors placed every three to five feet as you moved through the exhibit. The exhibit was packed yet all you could hear was the sound of the videos being played and whispered conversations. There are four major themes that were illustrated by the various types of media on this opening floor: (1) the creation of a police state once Adolf Hitler was appointed chancellor of Germany; (2) the implementation of Nazi policies that transformed the German Jews from citizens to outcasts; (3) the movement of the entire nation against groups deemed to be "enemies of state"; and (4) the refugee crisis of the Jews.

The detail of historical perspective of the themes mentioned was incredible. There were examples of how the Nazis used propaganda, through books, posters, photographs, etc. The tools used by physicians and scientists were displayed clearly next to the volumes of photographs catalogued as they worked toward their quest for the "master race." The Nazis wanted to cleanse Germany of those who did not fit their racial ideal. These were things that I had heard of but this made it real! I was trying to take in everything around me but I was so overwhelmed by the content. I was curious to learn more yet so disturbed by what I was experiencing. Who could have done such a thing? These were human lives. These people looked and acted like any other person from the human race. I kept thinking of my niece—a blonde haired, blue-eyed baby girl. She physically met the criteria of the perfect race according to Hitler but would have been executed immediately as an infant because of her faith. How? Why? Even though I was seeing firsthand the propaganda of the Nazi party, reading their by-laws, etc., who could have done such a thing? What was it that made so many people fall in line with Hitler's beliefs and policies? Where did all of this come from? Will anyone truly understand the WHY behind these hatred-driven atrocities?

The last room I came to on the opening floor was dedicated to *Kristall-nacht* ("The Night of Broken Glass"). On November 9–10, 1938, the Nazis began a wave of riots against Jewish businesses and synagogues. Many ornate arks containing the torah in synagogues were destroyed. This part of the exhibit affected me in a different way because it was showing the spiritual aspect of the Jewish people. As I stood there in the middle of the exhibit, I began to reflect upon my own spiritual upbringing. I had transported myself back to the small Lutheran church I was raised in as a child. What if one evening when I had been at our church a group of soldiers came barging in destroying everything around me, just because of my faith? I could not comprehend the pain and emotion that the Jews must have felt. I even tried putting myself in the Nazi's shoes: What could make me so angry and hate so much to want to destroy something of someone else's that I did not even understand? What was it that this exhibit was doing to appeal to every emotion and thought within me? I had never experienced anything like this before in my life. I wanted to continue on to learn more yet I felt as if I could not move beyond the room I was in because I felt I had not learned enough yet.

The middle floor of the exhibit was *The "Final Solution" 1940–1945*. This part of the exhibit examines the evolution of the wartime Nazi policy towards Jews, leading from persecution to the mass murdering of them. The atmosphere of this part of the exhibit became more life-like in the sense that I felt as if I was walking through a makeshift ghetto. Ghettos were places established for Jews to live in major cities after being forced from their homes by the Nazis and before deportation to work/death camps. As I proceeded through the exhibit, I began to think of the ghettos as "glorified concentration camps." I found myself looking at an actual railcar that had transported Jews to the various ghettos, concentration camps, and killing centers. As I stepped foot into the car, my senses began to play games with me. I was visualizing 1500 Jews piled in around me, the smell of near death and despair. I had to get out of there. What was it like next for these prisoners? Did they really believe that they were going to a better place?

I found myself clenching the passport that had been given to me at the start of the exhibit. My emotions were turning from disbelief to anger. Here in the palm of my hand were the details of the identity of one of the many victims of the Holocaust. I realized that I was trying to imagine the emotions and feelings that these victims had experienced. Some of the displays shared that the Jews in the ghettos ran their own schools, continuing to work with the hope of getting out of these living conditions. Family members were being taken from them, innocent lives never returning, headed to killing centers. The surrounding texts in the exhibit told the stories of uprisings in the ghettos, which clearly exemplified the strength and persistence of the individuals held in these savage-like places against their wills. What was it that was creating this fight of hope within them? Was it human survival instincts? There seemed to be some hidden curriculum within the texts, images, and photographs of the exhibit that gave the message to me that because of their faith they were able to persevere. This was amazing to me! I wanted to know! I wanted to read more, talk to people more.

As I proceeded through the exhibit I reached *The Final Solution*. I could tell that I had reached some of the most horrific images and thoughts imaginable by looking at the other museum goers faces. One woman had tears streaming down her face as she peered over this concrete wall, watching a video monitor. There was no sound coming from this exhibit; however, many people were gathered around watching something beyond the wall. As I approached the area slowly, I began to see why this woman was crying. There were videos playing of the examples of torture and scientific experiments being conducted by the Nazis on the "racially inferior" Jews. Handicapped individuals, children, and women were being manipulated and physically destroyed by Nazi physicians. Who had taken these videos? No wonder that these monitors had been placed two feet within a concrete barrier viewing area. Unless you chose to explore what was behind these barriers you would never know what was there. Was this done on purpose by the museum creators? Why? Other horrific images were posted from wall to wall, ceiling to floor within a replicated barrack of a concentration camp. There were bunks surrounding us that had been re-created by actual wood on loan from the State Museum of Auschwitz-Birkenau in Poland. These bunks would sleep five or six across on a single bunk. The barracks themselves would frequently hold hundreds of prisoners at a time. All of the museum patrons were filing in with curiosity as I am sure the Jews did at one time. Did they realize what they were about to find? Did they know what was ahead of them?

Beyond the replicated bunks within the barracks was a scale model of the specially constructed gas chambers at Auschwitz-Birkenau. It was clear from the model that the Nazis had developed a systematic, industrialized form of mass murder. I could not believe my eyes. Yet, again, this was something that I had heard about, had talked about in school. But I had never witnessed an image as powerful as the scale model in front of me. Included in the model were the detailed bodies and faces of many Jews illustrating the path taken to their demise. There were males and females, and small children following parents fully clothed down steps into an area in which they had been told to shower after stripping their clothes. I felt as if I was a witness to them standing there hopelessly. I followed their path into the gas chamber as I watched the Nazi guards open up the hatches above them, controlling their last few breaths to be taken. I felt my skin become clammy as I saw how the Nazi soldiers would pile the dead bodies onto a lift which would take them to ground level, then be dumped into the burning ovens. I could only imagine what it smelled like, the many ashes falling through the sky. What were the other Jews in the camp thinking? How were they surviving? How DID the ones that were eventually liberated survive?

The last room before heading to the final floor of the exhibit was the "shoe room." I had heard from others prior to my visit about this display. No one would go into detail about the display, they just kept telling me, "Wait until you are standing in the room with all of the shoes." I had no idea what I was going to experience. As I turned the corner, I saw heaping piles of old shoes on both sides of me. The shoes were piled so high that I could not see beyond them. The room was filled with a very musty smell that immediately filled my nose. What I was seeing were thousands of pairs of shoes that had once belonged to the Jews in the concentration camps. Once the Jews had been transported to the concentration camps they were forced to give up all of their belongings, including all clothing and shoes. I quickly recalled all of the photographs throughout the exhibit that showed train cars and wagons full of personal items belonging to the Jews. These shoes had been recovered from the various camps. These were the shoes that had been represented in the various pictures. The shoes had now come to life. I found my eyes searching the piles, examining each of the shoes. All sizes, types, men's, women's, children's, some hardly worn and some that were so worn it looked as if those particular shoes had been the only pair that the individuals owned. As I clutched the passport, I wondered if any of these shoes had belonged to the young girl whose translated memory I was carrying around in my hand. I felt as if I was looking at the last tangible items in which these innocent people had literally worn the last moments of their lives. Now I knew why people had talked about the "room of shoes." How does something as simple as a pile of shoes hold such a strong message? The power of representation is difficult to translate. The curators were more than effective in representing the innocent lives of the people lost. The many representations that this display holds remain unspeakable.

I was emotionally exhausted as I reached the final floor of the exhibit, *The Last Chapter*. This part of the exhibit addresses the Allies' victory over the Nazis in 1945, the liberation of the Nazi camps, and the aftermath of the Holocaust. I felt as if I had been a hopeless witness to the persecution of Jews as I made my way through the museum. I thought I was finished feeling bothered by horrific images and well on my way to focusing on what I could do as a responsible individual in the world today. This was not the case. I was overwhelmed with the stories and images addressing the issue of individual responsibility. It is as if the creators of the museum felt as if I had not gotten the message of this recurring theme. The texts, photographs, videos, and personal stories being illustrated around me in this final part of the exhibit showed me that one cannot begin to understand the amount of damage done by these horrific acts of violence and hatred. These images will forever be embedded within my mind; they will constantly be recalled and reflected upon.

GREAT?

Did the creators of the Museum intend for the curriculum of the museum to be "great"? How did they define their curriculum? What did each person involved bring to the table personally that would allow them to achieve this representation of "great" curricula? Let me define "great" in light of my experience of the exhibit as described here. The Museum successfully engaged me in every detail of the remembrance space. The displays including the written texts, graphic photographs, video clips, and the various objects representing items of the Holocaust all spoke to me. The incredible detail behind the planning of the exhibit, structurally, aesthetically, and the actual content, captured my every emotion and thought. The historical perspectives presented throughout created a sense of curiosity and reflectivity within me.

As Marla Morris (2001) states in her book *Curriculum and the Holocaust: Competing Sites of Memory and Representation,* "Of course, historical accounts are not the most authoritative representations; historians are not the only keepers of memory" (p. 5). She also discusses how interpretive work around historical representations of the Holocaust does not allow for one to get a complete picture of this event. A curriculum of such power, that invokes images and representations of history that personalize it and make it real, provides an experience that allows one to walk away without merely so-called answers or merely facts about something, but allows them to walk away asking, "What more is there out there to explore? What can we now do with this information?" The power is in making the things learned about in the historical past so real that they have life in the present.

Morris (2001) argues that historical information is not just a form of memory but expressions of memory (p. 8). The creators of the Museum presented their expressions of memory through the lived curriculum of the remembrance space. Each museum patron that visits walks away with his or her own unique experience. Kincheloe and Pinar (1991) states that "The curricular task becomes to recover memory and history in ways that psychologically allow individuals to reenter politically the public sphere" (pp. 173–174). They will have come from many different types of situated knowledge which plays to the notion of the politics of translation. They will translate the various representations of the curricula according to their own truth and memories.

The Museum creators took on an incredible challenge of presenting truths of the Holocaust to patrons and to the world. Elizabeth Ellsworth (1997) discusses the politics of memory in her book entitled *Teaching Positions: Difference, Pedagogy and the Power of Address* arguing that the notions of dialogue, representation, and understanding cannot help us to understand what is beyond representation. She discusses the responsibility of each person to become a continuous, active member in the ongoing construction of the historical representations of such horrific events. The "great" curriculum of the Holocaust Museum nurtures this responsibility.

FINAL THOUGHTS

This experience has been unlike any I have ever had in my educational career both as a student and educator. As I mentioned earlier, I chose this space to research because of its personal connection to me. But I never fathomed the gripping impact that visiting the Museum would have on my personal life. This should speak volumes to you as to how it can potentially impact so many lives, those that once existed, those that exist, as well as those that will exist in the future. Prior to my trip to Washington, D.C., I began to research as much as possible on the Museum. The Museum website (www.ushmm.org) provided quite a bit of information. As I wrote this piece, all that I had explored within the mission statement of the museum, the Holocaust Task Force guidelines, etc. became more evident to me in terms of personal meaning and lived experience.

The collaborators that came together in the creation of the Museum along with those that still play an active role in this remembrance space argue that there are important reasons to teach the Holocaust. It should be taught to preserve the memory of those who suffered during the Holocaust era. Not only should we expose people to the memory of this horrific event but we should also engage people through intellectual curiosity in order to inspire critical thinking.

One should consider all historical perspectives, victims, perpetrators, collaborators, bystanders, and rescuers when discussing or reflecting upon the Holocaust era. All people should question different interpretations and representations of events, whether there are horrific atrocities or not, personal or not. It is critical to be precise in the language and representation of the events, as were the creators of the Museum. Room for interpretation and translation was given as the various representations of texts and images appealed to the many senses of the observer. Once I walked away from the Museum, I quickly realized that I was still very much experiencing the curriculum that had been presented to me both planned and lived. I was also now enacting this "great" curriculum as I made my way back to my worlds of endeavor, my life.

RESPONSE BY TOM POETTER

One challenge of progressive curriculum is to approach social justice, honoring the student and where he or she is while putting him or her in touch with the social reality that clings to the nature of personal and corporate existence at every turn. The Holocaust Memorial Museum does not have any problem with this issue, since it embodies social justice as its core for existing. That is, that those who enter through its doors have the opportunity, by experiencing the museum, of being inspired to understand and act upon the truths that humanity can be cruel and that we should guard the memory of those who were sacrificed in the 1930s and 1940s as well as the lives of those who live on who may in the future also be subject to discrimination, even genocide. The chief end, beyond the deeply rooted call to help visitors and the wider public to understand the personal and corporate nature of human suffering, is a call to moral commitment: knowing what we know now, and what the possibilities and impossibilities are, then never again. Never again can genocide happen in our society or in the wider world as we know it. We each have a responsibility to recognize it and stop it.

I had hoped that the person who studied the museum and wrote about it here would be transformed, perhaps even in ways similar to the ways I felt I had been transformed on my first visit there. After reading her account, there is no doubt that Dawn Mann was transformed. And I think her lived experience of transformation mirrors the transformation that progressive educators have for students.

First, of great import is the notion of personal growth, the transformation of the "I" that we carry with us as individuals making our way in life. Rugg (1947) calls this "The Person As 'I'" in light of the great goal of progressive education: Developing the Person (p. 203–204). Each of us is on a path in life toward understanding ourselves more completely, judging our talents and mistakes, commitments and ideas, possibilities and limitations— sifting our life experiences through the filters we create at home and in our communities of endeavor. In light of extreme information—the kind that takes us out of our comfort zone of safety and knowledge, perhaps even the set of values and past experiences that makes us feel like we understand what should be happening and what should come next all things being equal—we feel challenge, perhaps despair, disequilibrium. This is when the test of self begins, searching for how to re-ground ourselves given new information, or information that creates other, different, perhaps alternate realities.

In Dawn's case, and in mine, like most people alive today occupying a world nearly 70 years distant from the liberation of Nazi death camps at the end of WWII, we learned about the Holocaust in school. We read Anne Frank's *The Diary of a Young Girl* and Elie Wiesel's *Night* and got it intellectually, perhaps. The Holocaust happened, it was unconscionable, the world can never let this happen again, and if genocide appears, it should be stomped out with the same fervor and moral commitment as the liberation of the Jews in the final days of Hitler's Germany. But the museum creates a different level of personal involvement beyond this level of learning. The use of text and images makes the patron take stock, take a step back, wonder with awe at the depth of violence and sacrifice involved in state-sanctioned genocide. The exhibits draw the viewer into a different level of knowledge, that includes emotion and personal connection and puts aside the distance one can get from mere study. In the end, the museum transforms the visitor. It is impossible not to feel an impact after visiting, and the difference is in the self. The person understands more clearly his or her responsibility for the world, for real people who suffer, and for protecting those who are different, maligned, endangered, violated.

Second, and related closely to the transformation of "The Person As I" is Rugg's notion of the transformation of "The Person-as-part-of-'We.'" Meaning, the "I" is not complete as merely an "I," but only when the self is seen by the individual as part of a broader society, as part of other cultural groups, the "We" we find in community. Persons grow as selves when they have an internal and external sense of the Self as responsible, connected, mutually benefited by the companionship, company, and solidarity of others who are different, but who ultimately occupy the same living space that each of us ultimately shares together on the planet. This is a small world, one in which we are responsible for ourselves and for our neighbors. We are always in relation with others, and those relations should mirror commitments similar to the ones we make to ourselves as individuals. The only way to have a world free of genocide is to create a world in which people who are different get to know each other, and by virtue of honest, free exchange of ideas and cultural insights become more completely whole, more completely human, appreciative of all that we have and all that others have. In the end, we share our humanity, and the treasuring of human life, especially the lives of others. How can we kill each other when the "I" is as invested in "We" as it is in "I"?

My last comment here has to do with the practicality of the museum and its potential use by educators. The main thing to say is that if I had a chance to teach a work of literature from the Holocaust in schools again, I would use the Holocaust Museum's website to introduce students to important historical and social ideas embedded in the exhibits in order to teach the works more completely. This is a tremendous educational resource that helps students explore the deeper questions about what happened and what could happen again if we are not each of us vigilant in our cultivation of selves that grow into self knowledge and knowledge of others. And my main focus would be on helping students tap the rich resources here and in other places in terms of the lives of survivors. Their stories and lives, preserved in multimedia formats, have the power to change lives today.

DAWN MANN'S FINAL WORD

The Holocaust Museum curriculum creates a very unique, personal experience for individuals, which is one of the factors that makes it great. Upon entering, the museum visitor finds him or herself immediately immersed within a plea for social justice. The personal connection to my family fueled my interest in studying the museum. As I passed by each picture, each artifact,

I quickly realized that each had its own individual story. Whenever the Holocaust had been talked about during my school experience, the event itself was the story. Yes, the story of the Holocaust itself elicited emotions within me, but it was never presented to me in a way that shared and told the stories of each life lost or affected. This makes a huge difference to the observer, no longer just on the outside, but drawn in to the personal loss through genocide.

The entire experience became personal, touching the deepest emotions within me. Multiple times throughout my experience in the museum, I found myself wiping tears from my face because of the overwhelming empathy and shock I felt with every forward step I made through the exhibits. With each story that was being told, I found myself thinking of my Jewish family members and the stories of their Russian and Polish family members lost in the Holocaust. With every photograph I viewed, I would ask myself if any of the innocent faces presented before me were those of family members. The Jewish faith quickly became more than just a religion, but a culture, a way of life, a deep spirituality that was held closely within the millions of lives lost. The curricula that surrounded me helped me to make a deeper connection with my family members and their beliefs. The stories and memories of the Holocaust have had an impact on every aspect of my life today. There is not a day that goes by that I do not reflect on this experience. The critical call for social justice has been impressed upon my soul.

REFERENCES

Ellsworth, E. A. (1997). *Teaching positions: Difference, pedagogy, and the power of address*. New York, NY: Teachers College Press.

Kliebard, H. M., & Franklin, B. M. (2000). *Curriculum and consequence: Herbert M. kliebard and the promise of schooling*. New York, NY: Teachers College Press.

Marsh, C. J., & Willis, G. (1999). *Curriculum: Alternative approaches, ongoing issues* (2nd. ed.). Upper Saddle River, NJ: Merrill.

Morris, M. (2001). *Curriculum and the Holocaust: Competing sites of memory and representation*. Mahwah, NJ: Lawrence Erlbaum Associates.

Rugg, H. (1947). *Foundations for American Education*. New York, NY: The World Book Company.

CHAPTER 9

THE NATIONAL NETWORK FOR EDUCATIONAL RENEWAL: 25 YEARS COMMITTED TO EDUCATION, DEMOCRACY, AND RENEWAL

Lara A. Chatman and Thomas S. Poetter

Authors' Note: As a result of several difficult decisions regarding the topics of the chapters for this book, Lara and I worked together to produce this chapter. Ultimately, it became clear that I should generate the narrative voice of the piece since I have a long personal history as a member of the NNER. Lara provided strong research support for the chapter. We are happy to present it to you as co-authors.

In the early 1980s—while the rhetoric, politics, and in some cases, action around educational "reform" heated up following the publication of monumental documents such as *A Nation at Risk* (1983), which threatened that the "so-called" decline in public education would cause the nation to become less competitive with rising world economic powers—John Goodlad (1984) published his seminal study *A Place Called School* of course, the concerns

10 Great Curricula: Lived Conversations of Progressive, Democratic Curricula in School and Society, pp. 173–193
Copyright © 2011 by Information Age Publishing

about American education, which had been thrown baselessly around for several previous decades (Bestor, 1953; Flesch, 1955; Rickover, 1962), continued to be heaped on the system in the 1980s (Hirsch, 1987) and following (Finn, 1991), and really to no end today (Bracey, 2009). While Goodlad did not necessarily defend the state of American public schools, because the study was meant to illuminate the strengths and weaknesses of a vast and complicated system, he knew that schools—the people who work in them and those that are served—and institutions that work closely in conjunction with them such as universities, all held the keys, together, to the renewal of our citizenry, our polity, our economy, and our schools.

In the wake of momentum from that study, and after a storied career immersed in schools, teacher education, and scholarship, Goodlad and his associates launched the **National Network for Educational Renewal** (NNER) with the hopes of having an impact on the complex work of renewing our nation's schools while also renewing the institutions that prepare teachers for them.

So, for the past 25 years, through the National Network for Educational Renewal, John Goodlad and his associates have been working, mostly behind the scenes perhaps, but always literally on the front lines of American education P-16 and beyond, attempting to renew American education and our world in productive ways. This chapter tells the story of the NNER, explaining what it looks like and how it works, while also taking a look at its operations as an educational network focused on renewal, not the harder notion of "reform." To this end, Lieberman and Grolnick's important article "Networks and Reform in American Education" (1996)—which framed five organizational themes for the networks studied, and tensions that challenge the power and fragility of the networks, as well as four questions for further study—will serve as structural framework and guide for this chapter through which to describe and interpret the organization's development and current state. The NNER was one of the 16 educational networks studied by Lieberman and Grolnick in the mid-1990s, about 8–10 years following the founding of the NNER in 1986.

In terms of this chapter, then, first, we present some initial background about the network and how it works, and second, we take a look at the NNER today in terms of its position with regard to Lieberman and Grolnick's (1996) "tensions" in educational networks as well as their four questions for further study.

A BRIEF HISTORY OF THE NNER AND ITS CORE IDEAS

John Goodlad described the process of beginning the network:

> We decided that the three groups most responsible for the education of teachers, faculty in arts and science, in colleges of education, and in schools, hardly

talked to each other. We believed the three groups had to be brought together in a tri-partite way. So with a grant, we sent queries out to 25 states to see what interest they had in bringing these three groups together. We got an overwhelming amount of responses, from 50 teacher education programs, and we could not handle all the requests to participate. So we made it competitive and gave schools two months to tell us what they would be doing to get the three groups together, and we chose the original 10 institutions that began the NNER. Later, it expanded to over 20 partnerships around the country. (J. Goodlad, personal communication, March 2011)

Other groups interested in the "reform" of teacher education and schools emerged in the 1980s, such as the Holmes Group made up of prominent education college deans across the country, and they come up with specific strategies such as "fifth-year" masters degree internships for teacher certification programs (The Holmes Group, 1986). But the NNER had something different in mind. Instead, the new network sought to transform people and programs, involve leaders in the work of redefining purposes, synch commitment to purpose with the creation of representative programs of study and action, and engage everyone involved in the enterprise so that the purposes and the actual work could be renewed continuously. Goodlad describes the commitment to renewal, as opposed to reform, this way:

> The main difference between reform and renewal is that reform comes from the outside; renewal is a cultural process from the inside. (J. Goodlad, personal communication, March 2011)

Engaging topics of great concern in education among multiple constituencies has proven to be a worthwhile challenge over the more than two decades of the network's life so far. The work has always been grounded in key principles/ideas adopted by Goodlad and his associates to define the work at hand and guide the subsequent actions taken. The intellectual core of the work rests in what Goodlad calls the "Agenda for Education in a Democracy (The AED)." The AED is anchored by four moral dimensions, to which the fledgling network committed itself, that is:

- To foster in the nation's young the skills, dispositions, and knowledge necessary for effective participation in a social and political democracy.
- To ensure that the young have access to the knowledge, understanding, and skills required for satisfying and responsible lives.
- To develop educators who nurture the well-being of every student.
- To ensure educators' competence in and commitment to serving as stewards of schools. (Poetter, 2010, p. 10)

As Goodlad (2003) notes, the moral dimensions are supported by "twenty propositions referred to as postulates that identify about sixty conditions aligned with this mission, and a strategy of implementation and stewardship in the renewal of schools and the education of educators" (p. 1). The postulates became the testable propositions or ideas for what Goodlad called "proofing sites," or the NNER partnerships that emerged in two major waves, one wave of 10 original school/university partnerships in 1986, then a second wave of eight more in 1993. Miami University was one of the eight sites that were welcomed into the network in the second wave. Today, over 20 partnerships are part of the network and share in the work:

California State University Partnership
Colorado Partnership for Educational Renewal (COPER)
Colorado State University Partnership
University of Connecticut Partnership
Georgia Center for Educational Renewal at Georgia Southern University
Illinois State University Partnership
University of Southern Maine Partnership
The Brandon School/University Partnership (Manitoba)
Metropolitan St. Louis Consortium for Educational Renewal
University of Missouri Partnership for Educational Renewal
Nebraska Network for Educational Renewal
Montclair St. University and the NJ Network for Educational Renewal
Albuquerque Public Schools/University of New Mexico Partnership
The City University of NY and New York City Public Schools Partnership
Miami University Partnership
Wright State University Partnership
South Carolina Network for Educational Renewal
Arlington (TX) University-School Network for Educational Renewal
University of Texas El Paso (UTEP) Partnership
University of Washington Partnership
Wyoming School–University Partnership

Several other major commitments and ideas guide the work. One is the notion of "simultaneous renewal," the idea that constituents from multiple settings working together are engaged in the "necessary interplay between human adaptation and contingencies in a social setting designed to advance human well being" (Goodlad, 1994, p. 17). Renewal involves the process of inquiry, and requires of the "setting's stewards not just dialogue but reflection, reading, inventing, and rethinking" (p. 17). In order to foster renewal, The Center for Educational Renewal (CER) at the University of Washington and the Institute for Educational Inquiry (IEI), both founded by Goodlad and housed in Seattle, worked in close association with the NNER to win grants and begin programs to push an understanding and an implementation of the AED in network sites.

The IEI, now playing a lesser role in the work, has yielded most of its agenda to The Goodlad Institute housed at the University of Washington-Bothel under the direction of Tom Bellamy and to the NNER under the direction of Ann Foster, NNER's Executive Director. Both the Goodlad Institute and the NNER are separate and independent entities working together to advance the AED on the shoulders Goodlad's lifetime commitment to the simultaneous renewal of schools and teacher education.

Another key commitment is to cultivating connections among school and community-based partners across teacher education and the wider university community: that is, what the NNER refers to as the "tripartite"—three parts of the enterprise focused on the work of generating the next wave of excellent teachers and educators, especially constituted by school-based practitioners/leaders, faculty members in colleges of teacher education, and faculty in departments in the arts and sciences. The notion of the "tripartite" is a fundamental aspect of partnership work in the NNER. In process is a newer movement, led by Goodlad's thinking over the past decade, to encounter a fourth key leg of the work, that is the wider community, as it is constituted by community leaders and diverse groups who also have a stake in the renewal agenda in schools and teacher education. They represent a powerful, significant community that typically is under-represented in the work, and must be included in order for it to advance with any significance, meaning, and effect (Poetter, 2010).

Another key aspect of the work is NNER's democratic organization, with a polity comprised of multiple layers of groups that make decisions with/for the body. Representatives from each partnership constitute the Tripartite Council, which meets at the annual conference, engaging issues of interest and concern across the network from multiple perspectives including school, community, schools of education, and arts and sciences. The Tripartite Council provides advisement to the Governing Council, which in turn guides and councils the executive committee. The Executive Director and the Chair of the Governing Council, along with representatives from the tripartite across the network, make decisions together through the executive committee. Input is cultivated and valued across the network at all levels on all minor and major issues and concerns. As stated, the NNER hosts an annual meeting in one of its member sites where each of these entities meets and advises each other (Poetter, 2010).

From the beginning of the network's life, in order to learn the core values of the organization and its structure as well as have an impact on its daily work and spirit, Goodlad and his associates have sponsored and offered what is known as Leadership Associates Training in Seattle and across network sites. In these sessions, now lasting approximately one week all together but in the early days of the network for nearly 20 days in a year when supported by grants, participants are immersed in the literature of the movement and activities that illuminate the core values, practices, commitments, and hopes of the NNER. Participants, past and present, routinely speak of these experiences—where personal and institutional renewal ideas and practices get experienced individually and with others in unique, very strongly personal and intellectual ways—as personally, and ultimately institutionally, transformational.

There is much more to say about the structure and life of the NNER, even introductorily. Suffice it to say that this previous section lays the groundwork for further description and interpretation through Lieberman and Grolnick's (1996) hallmark framework for describing educational networks in the coming sections.

LIEBERMAN AND GROLNICK'S STUDY (1996)

One of the best and most influential studies describing the emerging networks for educational reform in the 1990s, "Networks and Reform in American Education" highlighted the fledgling phenomenon of organized educational networks taking shape across the national landscape in the 1980s and 1990s. One of 16 networks studied, the NNER was nearing its first decade of life and had encountered much success, having gathered up a great amount of footing as a successful network. In the study, the authors develop five significant organizational themes; present five tensions that illuminate the power and fragility of educational networks; and challenge themselves and the reader with four significant questions for further study.

The five organizational themes developed in the work are: Purposes and directions; Building collaboration, consensus, and commitment; Activities and relationships as important building blocks; Leadership: Cross-cultural brokering, facilitating, and keeping the values visible; and Dealing with the funding problem (pp. 10–26). The five tensions include: (1) negotiating between the purpose of the network and the dailiness of the activities that constitute network "work"; (2) dealing with the balance between "inside knowledge" and "outside knowledge"; (3) creating a structure to resolve contradictions between centralization and decentralization; (4) moving from informality and flexibility to more formal and rigid forms as the network grew; and (5) making decisions about how inclusive or exclusive membership policy should be (p. 27). The four questions for further study are: What is the role of prominent leaders? Temporary systems or new models for professional community? How can the work continue to be funded? What is the distinction between single focus/single role versus systemic focus/multiple role networks? How do we measure the impact of network participation (pp. 42–43)?

The remainder of this chapter is a narrative discussion positioning the NNER today with regard to the five tensions and deeper reflection on the status of the organization today with regard to each. Our intent is to provide enough descriptive detail about the organization, how it is structured, how it works, and the impact it has through a discussion of the tensions, as opposed to providing extensive descriptive details that support Lieberman and Grolnick's main organizational themes as listed above; their original article does that adequately enough. A reflection on the tensions, however, promises to yield deeper insights into the democratic, progressive nature of the organization's curriculum. The conclusion discusses the NNER in light of their four questions for further study.

MEANINGFUL OR EMERGENT PURPOSE/COMPELLING ACTIVITIES

Lieberman and Grolnick (1996) identified the NNER as having attracted adherents to its initial, continuing, and lofty goal of simultaneously renewing schools and teacher education. Because of the clear purpose of the organization, the challenge becomes creating activities and relationships that will cement the commitment of participants over time (p. 27). The NNER has faced this challenge through the years. For more than two decades, the impact of the Leadership Associates Training programs has been profound, expertly and strategically tying the purpose of the organization to meaningful activities. Participants come back from the sessions in Seattle, sometimes having connected with new colleagues from across the network as well as with professionals within their own sites in attendance, energized with a deeper understanding of the purposes of the work and the power of it when implemented while also possessing a newfound confidence for expressing the ideals of the organization on the home front in real time.

Engaging in meaningful professional development, learning about the organization, connecting with intelligent and like-minded people in these sessions captures, in a nutshell, the intent of the network and the notion of simultaneous renewal, that is that people connect when they interact together around deeply purposeful and intellectual activities, and gain the footing as a result to carry the work back to their own sites. This becomes a strong cycle, in which the communication and interaction through activities around the purposes of the organization creates networks within networks.

Ann Foster, executive director of the NNER, describes the leadership associates model this way, comparing the NNER to emerging economic growth networks while reflecting on the NNER's long history of success in building connections, relationships, and new activities: "Our sites, multi-hub small world networks networking within the overall network frame, keep the work moving forward and provide momentum and ultimately a core/periphery network where connections within the cluster of networks are strong and new networks can form because those most invested can then move to new groups to form new networks" (A. Foster, personal communication, March, 2011). This notion of people and organizations moving in a dialectic cycle around powerful ideas frames the model of action within the NNER, and reflects a recipe for communication and work that makes sense to the participants. Leadership Associates Training has always been a strong first step for establishing this substantive, organic flow. Ann adds: "NNER is a network rather than a hierarchical organization or a traditional membership organization. As a network we rely on networks within networks, where the work spreads locally in unique and powerful ways. Where individuals have participated in NNER leadership activities they return to their work place and lead efforts there so that the network grows organically or as an ecosystem, as John Goodlad would say. I think this is a critical distinguishing feature of the NNER" (A. Foster, personal communication, March 2011).

Of course, as Lieberman and Grolnick (1996) point out, however, a significant tension in the work of educational networks is the "struggle with the tension between activities that successfully involved the participants and the necessity to link these activities to the larger purposes of the network—thereby giving the work greater meaning" (p. 29). One trouble is that the carry back/carry over of the learning from the Leadership Associates Training experiences by individuals gets translated into the institutional structure and the work of individuals across complex organizations in different ways on such diverse home fronts. So, across more than 20 network sites there are varying degrees of continuity, for instance, with regard to the degree to which the core ideas of the network get translated into teacher education programs. Of course, there is a range of responses. Some institutions, for instance, have the core ideas of the NNER built into the documents supporting their programs, their syllabi for courses, and assignments that students of teaching engage in reflecting the network's ideals. On the other hand, some institutions have no more than a few faculty members who understand what the NNER is, let alone any formal connection to the actual teacher education program being implemented in the school/university partnership.

When Miami University nearly left the network as a result of administrative changes and a dwindling level of local commitment in the early 2000s, I attended my first NNER conference as a faculty member/partner in 2003 in Salt Lake City. What I discovered in a poster session in which each of over

20 networks site had a table set up to represent local progress on the AED across programs was this huge chasm between the nature of the work and its depth, or lack thereof, across the network sites. Some sites struggle—as a result of apathy or political strife or size of program or lack of leadership, etc.—and have little to show in terms of the connection between the larger purposes of the network and daily activities, and others are so immersed in the work on a daily basis that everything they touch seems to exude the core principles of the network. At Miami, for instance, where a core group of faculty are involved in the NNER—we have even housed the network's first scholarly journal during its first 3 years—the core principles of the NNER are not embedded formally in the teacher education program like they are, for instance, in other network sites (Erickson & Wentworth, 2009; Domine & Bello, 2010). Quite frankly, it is humbling to compare the institutional commitment and rigor with which the network influences the daily work across sites, especially if your own site constantly struggles upward and for every inch of footing along the way.

While this might be perceived as a weakness, instead, it suggests more accurately how things go in complex institutions like public schools and universities where so many competing forces work to have an impact on the formal and informal curricula of the setting. Meaning, institutional changes may be slow to reflect concrete ideas, words, or images of a movement like the NNER even when they may pervade the essence or even the actual practices in the site. That being said, it has always been on the front burner in our work at Miami to ramp up the formal connections between the work at hand in terms of programs and daily activities and the key component purposes that drive the thinking and the action in the network. How hot the burner gets and how much gets accomplished depends on many factors, not the least of which is the support that flows from other areas of the network that have made connections and improvements while living out the mission as a network site.

INSIDE KNOWLEDGE/OUTSIDE KNOWLEDGE

Lieberman and Grolnick (1996) draw a distinction between inside knowledge, or knowledge that is based on the experiences of practitioners in the field such as teachers and principals, and outside knowledge, the kind typically produced by university researchers working outside the day-to-day confines of schools, studying them from a distance (p. 30). The assumption is also made, of course, that knowledge of current reality and knowledge of what may be possible at least philosophically are both very important to the endeavor. While the inside/outside distinction may be apt, it may be too simple to make today and perhaps not as accurate as it was fifteen years ago. School and university positions and functions, especially in partnership settings, have morphed to some degree in terms of the proximity to the work and the sharing of tasks, such as the production of knowledge about practice. And after all, in the knowledge sharing and knowledge production traditions of the NNER, while flowing to some degree from the top-down in terms of the primacy of the work of Goodlad and his associates, the norm for activities across the network is collaborative, focused on sharing knowledge, perhaps even to the extent of privileging the inside knowledge of practitioners who work in the field on a daily basis. Lieberman and Grolnick actually comment specifically on this tension within the NNER, praising it for its lofty attempt at transforming the complex institutions of school and university simultaneously:

> ... the National Network for Educational Renewal, which is organized around postulates (or values) for schools and schools of education, ... works to connect problems of practice with ideas that are derived from these postulates. This network, perhaps the most complex of all that we studied, in trying to change entire institutions, works with a variety of clients. Its agenda is crafted by the individual school partnerships comprising the network, in combination with the outside knowledge of what changed institutions might look like, provided by the network staff. (p. 31)

In my long association with the organization, I have felt this inside/outside tension with regard to knowledge palpably. But to its credit, and maybe even leading to its ultimate successes, the NNER does not try to hide that differences with regard to knowledge, both in terms of understanding it and producing it, exist. In fact, it is in these differences and in the dialogue and work on them that the way forward emerges. The differences reflect the confluence of opinion, position, and ideas that must be deliberated on honestly and openly in order for us to make decisions, program changes, and create new ideas and practices. This, in essence, is the deliberative birthing recipe for democratic change in schools and universities. It works, in so much as those participating in it have the depth of facility necessary to make their way through conflict, as well as the time, and the openness to consider new ideas that are generated from the ground up, and commit to the process of doing what's best and right for all given the complex nature of organizations, rapid change, and the sturdiness (or not!) of core principles as they are tested in deliberative experiences (McCutcheon, 1995).

This type of work is about putting ego on the back burner, about allowing people to take calculated risks and make mistakes; about vetting new ideas and carefully making judgments about whether proceeding in action is prudent and might yield the desired ends. This is refreshing work today, considering that in most organizations almost all of the decisions flow from the top-down, regardless of the thinking that there has been some sort of modern-day leadership revolution among workers and managers in which sharing the work of moving forward with ideas and practices is collaborative.

Almost everywhere, it is not the case even if people say it is. In the NNER, it is true, in theory and in practice.

This became crystal clear to me while working on an initiative of the NNER that transcended the NNER to include community groups in the early 2000s. The Developing Networks Initiative (Developing Networks of Responsibility for Educating America's Youths), funded by the Kellogg Foundation and directed by the IEI, engaged multiple sites across the NNER in processes that included community members, faculty members from institutions of higher learning, and schools as they struggled together to determine how it is that schools, teacher education, and communities could work to improve the lives of children in communities of all sorts and sizes around the nation.

The project purposefully, and with great tension, continually put contending groups face-to-face to surface their issues, struggles, insecurities, and passions in order to figure out concrete ways in which to engage solutions to complex problems plaguing them in their own reality. The power of context, of voice, of inside knowledge all came into play as the groups, across multiple settings, tried to find ways to address issues and problems that on the surface seemed insurmountable. We know now that when we work together they are not insurmountable. We know now that together community members can solve complex problems and find ways to get along. We know now that some of the hardest work to do is to balance, analyze, and interpret for a new day all that we know about what we care about from the inside and outside. This was true as our own site made its way through the initiative, along with many sites across the network (Institute for Educational Inquiry, 2006).

The tension between inside/outside knowledge is held in healthy, high regard in this network for educational renewal. It seems on the surface, at least to those of us on the inside of the work, like a "no-brainer": that is, there is no inside without the outside, and vice versa. Of course, in our work together, we pull together to create meaning and knowledge from everyday experience, and bring to bear knowledge from philosophy, reason, scholarship, and research to inform and guide us. Any democratic unit, including a network with so many tentacles but deep, rich roots, would/should use the tension to enhance itself.

CENTRALIZATION/DECENTRALIZATION

Lieberman and Grolnick (1996) suggest that "an effective network organization creates ways to engage participants directly in the governance and leadership of the organization, while maintaining the flexibility to organize complex and potentially far-reaching operations" (p. 33). There has been no doubt over the years that the hub of activity through the IEI and NNER was Seattle, the home of John Goodlad and the "central" location of activities surrounding the network. And actually, places such as the house on Edgar Street that became the home of so many activities and meetings over the years, along with other iconic spots throughout the Seattle area, have a strong pull and meaning for people across the network who have become leaders internally and externally as a result as their association with the network. The attraction of the location is buoyed by participants' love of John Goodlad himself, the person who welcomed, challenged, and inspired so many of us to take his best ideas and work with them across so many institutions in the United States and Canada.

Centrality of place, however, has not trumped the idea that the network is much bigger than John, or the house on Edgar Street, or the institutional arrangements created to govern the network. Of course, as you can see from the previous list of member sites, the network has representation from every region of the United States. In fact, while there certainly are loci of power within the organization, at least in terms of influential members with positional power and institutional cachet, the proceedings of annual meetings, activities throughout the year, and on-site events typically embody the decentralizing notions of collaboration, voice, and openness to difference and diverse ideas of thought and notions of best practice.

Very purposeful governance arrangements have been made over the years to assure that all areas of the tri-partite, including members from schools, schools of education, and departments of arts and sciences would be included in equal numbers in all of the governing groups including tripartite council, governing council, and executive council. It is my experience that the "feel" of the organization, both by structural design and by the formation of personal relationships among members, is that it is accessible. Meaning, anyone approaching it, as a member or nonmember, is welcomed into the fold. No one is turned away. The technicalities of membership are addressed in a coming section. Suffice it to say that the structure and feel of the NNER lends itself to a decentralizing power, tied to central controls (by the NNER governing boards, the IEI—now only by habit, not formally—and to the Goodlad Institute) that are benevolent, open, and malleable. This allows for action and turbulence to bubble up at any point, and to be used to guide new directions in the work.

One remarkable play in this tension by the organization has been to maintain the site of its annual meeting at one of its actual member locations. This means that the meetings are not always held in glamorous travel/vacation destinations. The message is that the people, places, and sites throughout the network are important communities in and of themselves, and most worthy of being patronized, visited, and known. After all, the work is central, in the location. If renewal is to be achieved from the inside/out, then we have to learn to work with people where they are, and gain the advantage of standing on common ground, perhaps even literally, and especially when a network is spread out so far and connected most days by technology and not by face-to-face interactions.

FROM INFORMALITY AND FLEXIBILITY
TO FORMALITY AND RIGIDITY

Lieberman and Grolnick (1996) found in their study of 16 educational networks that "the consensus was that ideally, despite the pressures to expand, a network had to measure its success in the quality—not just the quantity—of its person-to-person connections" (p. 37). I think this commitment to the personal has been one of the driving motivations for my involvement with the NNER. In addition to decentralizing leadership, acknowledging and respecting the worth of each member and each site requires that members get to know each other. It is hardly an avoidable step, given all of the activities within the organization that foster dialogue at the annual conferences, across the network during activities throughout the year, and on special projects. It should be acknowledged, however, that some of the structures, such as the annual meeting, typically privilege the schedules and the norms of behavior of higher education colleagues. It is not easy for school-based or community-based colleagues to attend a conference during the week when school and work are in session, and the cost to travel to conferences tends to be beyond the reach of most teachers/citizens without significant financial assistance, which often comes from the university entity, creating uneasy power and access-to-resources dynamics.

That being said, however, it is clear that the early days of the network included expansion of the number of sites, and the proliferation of Leadership Associates Training opportunities to many diverse new members from across the tri-partite. People came from the new sites and melded into the fabric of the network over time, making substantive contributions to the national group while also simultaneously renewing from within. Throughout the period of expansion of sites, significant efforts have been made to welcome and enculturate new members into the organization. Like with many annual conferences, the NNER always sponsors a new member session to welcome and introduce new members to the work.

Over time, the effort to recruit and engage more school-based and community-based personnel is a priority of the network. There is a very important connection between schools, communities, and universities that can only be reached if there is an equal and reciprocating relationship for all. It can sometimes be a stretch for school and community-based citizens to take the same amount of responsibility for teacher education as university colleagues whose jobs are more tightly aligned with that mission. On the other hand, it is sometimes difficult to recruit university members to connect with schools and with community members and their organizations, since this type of work is not typically recognized in the academy as worthy of reward or credit, even in the fields of education. While these distinctions get driven further to the perimeter as time goes one, they still exist in context and sometimes act as impediments.

Organizations engaged in similar work to renew schools and teacher education, like the National Association of Professional Development Schools (NAPDS), have found a niche by acting as an open membership organization, meaning that anyone, regardless of institutional affiliation, including individuals, can join the organization and attend the annual meeting. The NAPDS has enjoyed a huge initial spurt of growth and credibility as a result of its inclusive program. This creates a larger organization, but it also means that it has to work harder to be intimate, since its only event typically is the annual meeting and no significant internal structures exist to foster constant networking among the members. The NNER, because of its smaller membership and by virtue of its relatively small size has a built in advantage for keeping the work less formal and less rigid than it might become with un-tethered growth. It is accurate to say that a high percentage of people who attend the annual NNER meeting and participate in its activities across the academic year know almost all of the central participants in the work. This creates a level playing field, keeps the members honest, and yields a high level of energy and commitment. When members know each other, they have to be supportive of each other and accountable to each other.

INCLUSIVITY/EXCLUSIVITY OF MEMBERSHIP

A response to this tension is related to the previous section, especially with regard to the expansion of the network membership. One local response is connected to the phenomenon of competitive entry to the network that governed the first two waves of membership in the NNER. In 1993, when Miami was welcomed as a "winning" applicant to the network as a new partnership site, and simultaneously then engaged the local area in a competitive process to select "member partner schools/districts," Miami did not select its local school district, Talawanda Schools, as a new partner. This produced an extreme amount of animus, not rooted out completely even to this day (though institutional memory, as they say, is typically "short," the slight does not now currently impede our work together in any way), even though the Talawanda–Miami Partnership now constitutes the flagship partnership in our network site. Perhaps, a function of the time period, and the culture of competition in higher education and schools, but the competitive angle certainly has morphed over the years as we have changed our orientations to each other significantly across universities and schools. And perhaps the current orientation of the NNER to support and monitor member sites, and not necessarily to grow, is related to an awareness, in light of the soaring membership in NAPDS, that gathering members isn't necessarily connected to the goals of the organization.

At a recent annual meeting of the NNER, new membership options were discussed with great interest in the governing council meeting. It is important given the difficult economic environment today for universities and schools to make sure that participants are getting "their money's worth," while also figuring out how to recruit new members "noncompetitively" when other member sites drop out, which has happened periodically over the past few years. The bottom-line revolves around answers to questions such as, "What do we want our network to be? Open to all? Open to the like-minded only? Open to diverse constituents who commit to core principles but may or may not be "similar" in approach, background, or style?" It seems fitting that a network that wants to renew from the inside/out needs both commitment and diversity. It needs to be committed to social justice as a core principle, which the NNER is and has been from its founding. It needs to be working to support members and encouraging their long-term connection, while also constantly cultivating potential new members. It needs to be aware that it is not alone on the journey, and reach out to other networks to energize members and deepen their sense of the importance of the overall project and their connectedness to many.

It is prestigious on several levels to be a member of the NNER, but it is also hard work to maintain membership, and dues must be paid to belong. There is constant tension in the work about membership, about inclusivity and exclusivity. While the structure of the network appears exclusive because of its size, it works hard to be inclusive internally, and is open to growth with interested parties across the country. This tension will always be with us, as long as we remain a small network, committed to core principles, and expecting a high level of implementation and participation among full members.

Perhaps, one answer to the vitality in the dialectic regarding local and national tensions over membership and activity lies in the nature of activities in sites themselves. All across the country, in places like Wright State University's Partnership in Dayton, Ohio, sites work to extend their influence locally, while holding on to core principles nationally. Extended sites such as schools and businesses get involved in partnerships and might not even know in the beginning how tied they are to core concepts off the ground. The power is in the context to transform and remake the network, constantly, with inside and outside forces at work simultaneously, renewing the field around them. Former Governing Council Chair and Wright State

School of Education Dean Greg Bernhardt describes this clearly in his description of the process of creating a new public charter school through the partnership:

> We are going to try to make the new STEM (Science, Technology, Engineering, and Math) School in Dayton, serving grades 6–12 and 30 school districts across three counties, into a demonstration school, showing how integrated, inter-disciplinary learning can occur across all the disciplines and how that's uniquely linked to economic development in a particular region. Increasingly, we will focus on how schools and the goals they are working on are not only focused first and foremost on preparing students for their roles in democratic society as good citizens, but also on increasing the links between school and the economic vitality of the region. If you don't cultivate opportunities for people to hold jobs then school districts suffer, parents move away, financial support dwindles, and schools disappear. (G. Bernhardt, personal communication, March 2011)

All members of the network want to work on the simultaneous renewal of schools, universities, and society. An increased membership, even vicariously, blossoms when network sites reach out. The work becomes less exclusive, more inclusive, with each project. And people and institutions become aware of their unique responsibilities as stewards for education and society because their roles are filled with potential for making a real difference in people's lives.

QUESTIONS FOR FURTHER STUDY

When I revisited Lieberman and Gronick's (1996) study for this chapter, it had been about 10 years since my last reading of it. When I was getting to know Miami's connection to the NNER then, I was pointed in the direction of the piece by a colleague and learned so much from my reading of it about the NNER and its connection in a broader sense to the fascinating phenomenon of educational networks taking shape at the turn of the century. I am indebted to the authors for their work in terms of the impact it has had on my orientation to the larger questions surrounding network creation and development. Their final questions at the end of their paper are fascinating, and a discussion of which stands to contribute to an understanding of the democratic and progressive orientation of the NNER.

In terms of "prominent leadership," which the NNER has enjoyed for nearly three decades from John Goodlad, its founder, and intellectual center, and inspirational personality, there is no doubt, of course, that prominent leadership has existed and continues to exist. While a strong leader founded the organization, the continuous efforts to democratize the organization, to spread leadership out, and build collaborative activities at the heart of the network reflect its democratic and progressive core.

In terms of whether the network is temporary or a new model for professional community, the answer has to be that it is a new model given its 25 year history, which exceeds the life of nearly all of the original networks studied by Lieberman and Grolnick, some of which have folded or re-fashioned themselves since the study. Of course, longevity does not necessarily lend itself to quality, since organizations can fade over time if they do not continue to renew themselves, but the very heart of the matter is renewal. I have a sense that if the work stopped being renewing, that entities would quit it, even if entrenched. The powerful commitments of real people to the core foundations of the work suggest that together they would find a legitimate way forward that was defensible, or abandon it for other endeavors. No matter the disposition, it would be decided through complex deliberation and democratic processes, with a socially just outcome, thus revealing the true spirit of the work and the commitments of members.

In terms of funding, it continues to be a struggle. As with most nonprofit education organizations, the pool for potential funding continues to shrivel, and especially, perhaps, for those espousing progressive and democratic principles. But hope springs eternal, though the days of multimillion grants from foundations interested in the work of the organization "as it takes shape," has been replaced by a means-ends investment orientation by most entities. The organization runs its daily operation on the dues of its members, and relies on outside monies for special projects. The organization was never dependent upon or run by grants, though they facilitated wonderful opportunities for so many over the years. I doubt that the organization will ever be beholden to money, and that id a good thing.

In terms of the NNER's orientation as a single or multiple focus network and its impact on the organization, it has had longevity as a multiple focus network. Many constituents are involved, and it is hoped that many more will become involved. This is unlikely to change, given the core set of commitments and principles embedded in the network and the rather exciting eclecticism of its leadership and its institutions. Interesting activities and inspirational/ transformational moments continue to pour forth from all corners of the network.

In terms of measuring the impact of network participation, this has always been a very difficult question for members to get their arms around. The complexity of educational networking typically defies quasi-experimental study designs. It is almost impossible to measure anything about the work definitively, since context is so critical to the work and there are so many variables at play. But the network continues to tell its story both internally and externally, though it exercises a rather neutral approach to

political maneuvering. Over time, I predict that the organization will continue to tell its story, while offering a progressive and democratic option
for participating in the renewal of American schools, communities, and
institutions of higher education that is open to all, and effective with a significant, powerful core of participants who continue to spread the word and
hope for renewal.

RESPONSE BY AMY YOUNG

When I think about democratic possibilities for our schools and students,
I feel hopeful: but not because I have any concrete ideas about what our
future educational system will look like. We are currently plagued with por-
trayals of "failing" schools and teachers, with films such as *Waiting for Superman* (Chilcott & Guggenheim, 2010), which blame people and places for
larger, systematic educational issues. We have witnessed the Texas Board of
Education vote to "add conservative values and historical interpretations to
the statewide social studies curriculum," thereby, altering the "liberal"
standard for textbook production nationwide. We have even seen Arne
Duncan's reform policies place schools in competition for "Race to
the Top" funding, a initiative that Duncan has admitted will create "a lot
more losers than winners" in the struggle for school improvement monies.
Even as I think about these blows to democratic educational possibilities,
I feel my heart tremble. These few examples are just surface level kinds of
buzzes about the current state of education in America; there is so much
more interacting and at-odds with core theoretical ideas about what it
means to learn and live in a democratic society in terms of media, practice,
curriculum, and policy. The future of education is incredibly muddy, but it
does not have to be bleak.

Part of what keeps me hopeful is organizations like the NNER, which
offer possibilities that can assuage educational cynicism. As Tom and Lara
mentioned, NNER is not about educational "reform" in a top-down or out-
side-in model. Instead, it endorses a process of grassroots, inside-out,
"renewal" as described by Goodlad, a highly significant distinction. America
has built an educational system so complex and rooted in bureaucracy,
administration, and capitalism that "reforms," as we currently understand
them, often serve to re-inscribe new, trendy, or revived, "traditional" practices,
that occasionally work in theory, but neglect real issues (for instance, the
necessity of living wages, affordable access to healthcare, the economic
recession, etc.) facing educators and students in various community and
cultural contexts. Renewal, as imagined by NNER, is about looking at the
mosaic of education, with a variety of players/stakeholders, assessing needs,

and collaborating in ways that are specific and transformative for the particular challenges faced, with educators, students, and democracy in mind.

This type of commitment from NNER to work in ways that are adaptive, rather than prescriptive, provides flexibility and opportunity for visions and renovations that are outside the margins of current reforms. Additionally, there is an energized feeling that accompanies "renewal," which recognizes the historical efforts of educators and communities in the creation of our educational system, while simultaneously providing spaces for reflection, critique, and hope for change of the existing structure. It is not a "face-lift" for education, or a way to cover up, tear down, or rebuild new reforms. Instead, renewal can be seen as an ongoing systemic and personal spiritual meditation, combining a focus on democratic educational potential and a respect for the "goodness" that currently exists in our students, teachers, administrators, university partners, and communities.

My hopefulness also exists in thinking about ways NNER could embrace democracy and education in new ways for the future. As Tom and Lara suggest, membership in NNER is limited and there are shifting parameters around its inclusion of partners. Although I understand these constraints, I would like to suggest that NNER seek out ways to broaden their impact, share their network resources, and embrace technologies that have become and will continue to significantly transform our ever-evolving democratic educational system. In particular, social media involvement might be one of those avenues. Though it is steeped in knowledge control and capitalism, it has become a medium for participatory democratic change, and is waiting for organizations like NNER to engage in its possibilities. Involvement in discussions and alliances to promote the ideals of NNER should not be reserved for those who have the travel funds to attend conferences, or who have the resources to write applications for acceptance into the Network. I appreciate the commitment that NNER has to real communities and its commitment to access; however, the spirit of NNER is one that is needed to be heard and felt in places where reforms are tiresome, educators are isolated, and communities are struggling to make sense of policy and curriculum.

Access and involvement with NNER could be imagined in different forms and mediums that reach out and connect with those who are seeking to find hope in this very muddy time. For example, the use of Twitter and Facebook as democratic accelerants cannot be ignored, as they represent virtual meetings of the minds, engaging and redefining "community" as spaces of collaboration, and used by NNER to share the vision of democratic educational renewal and encourage a recommitment to new "community" partnerships. But these technologies only scratch the surface of the possibilities: Foursquare, LinkedIn, MeetUp, YouTube, Digg, and others are also elbowing their way into educational spaces. The match between NNER and social media could be innovative and the hope for educational renewal could be the next viral revolution.

A FINAL WORD BY TOM POETTER

When Twitter was exploding last summer in terms of impact and use, several local radio personalities "pooh-poohed" it, making fun of it and calling it and all social media a fad and swearing not to waste their time on it. The next month they, like all of their competitors, were pursuing followers like mad to advertise their show in order not to fall even further behind! Things change quickly, but I am afraid that many of us do not move as fast as the radio guys, especially when we are wrong initially. And there is a knowledge gap, and a confidence gap with technology for some of us over 40. We are terribly careful with technology, still scared of Word shutting down without warning or losing a document somehow into the mysterious techno-sphere without seeming cause. But it would not surprise me if the NNER moved quickly to explore more effective ways for using technology in its work. For now, there is certainly a pull to continue business as usual, trying to meet face-to-face and talk on the phone. These are effective means of doing business, by the way. But the push out of our comfort zones cannot be resisted for much longer, or we run the risk of becoming an anachronism. Who wants that?

One key issue at hand is one that Amy nails in her response. How can we use new ways to advance democracy and progressive approaches to buoy it in the world, on the ground, in everyday life in communities and schools?

One way is to increase thoughtfully the number of participants, while increasing simultaneously the level of satisfying interaction among the main players for renewal who inhabit the network sites across the NNER and who are trying to reach out and impact real communities. This is a real challenge. The trick is being uncomfortable with the status quo, and wanting more. Sometimes you have to go on the offensive when things look bad, like the economy and the general outlook for public education, let alone for people who are progressive or who think purposefully raising children to live in a social and political democracy requires direct action in schools and community. We cannot sit back, but move ahead, perhaps even by taking some risks and failing here and there. Nothing is going to get better, and we are not going to have any stake in the game at hand, if we sit back. There is little time or political/educational advantage in that approach. We need to move.

REFERENCES

A nation at risk: The imperative for educational reform. (1983). Washington, DC: The National Commission on Excellence in Education.

Bestor, A. (1953). *Educational wastelands*. Champaign-Urbana, IL: University of Illinois Press.

Bracey, G. (2009). *Education hell: Rhetoric vs. reality*. Alexandria, VA: Education Research Service.

Chilcott, L. (Producer), & Guggenheim, D. (Director). (2010). *Waiting for 'Superman'* [Motion picture]. United States: Paramount Vantage and Participant Media.

Domine, V., & Bello, J. (2010). Stewarding urban teacher education in Newark: In search of reflection, responsibility, and renewal. *Education in a Democracy, 2,* 155–168.

Erickson, L., & Wentworth, N. (2010). Implementing the agenda for education in a democracy into a teacher education program. *Education in a Democracy, 1,* 119–141.

Finn, C. (1991). *We must take charge: Our schools and our future*. New York, NY: Macmillan.

Flesch, R. (1955). *Why Johnny can't read–and what you can do about it*. New York, NY: Harper.

Goodlad, J. (1984). *A place called school*. New York, NY: McGraw-Hill.

Goodlad, J. (1994). *Educational renewal: Better teachers, better schools*. San Francisco, CA: Jossey-Bass.

Goodlad, J. (2003). Old wine in new bottles. *NNER NEWS, 2*(3), 1.

Hirsch, E. D. (1987). *Cultural literacy: What every American needs to know*. Boston: Houghton Mifflin.

Institute for Educational Inquiry. (2006). *Engaging with the community: Developing networks of responsibility for educating America's youths*. Seattle, WA: IEI. Retrieved from http://www.ieiseattle.org/EngagingwiththeCommunity.pdf

Lieberman, A., & Grolnick, M. (1996). Networks and reform in American education. *Teachers College Press, 98*(1), 7–45.

McCutcheon, G. (1995). *Developing the curriculum: Solo and group deliberation*. White Plains, NY: Longman Publishers.

Poetter, T. (2010). Creating institutional memory for this journey: Opening Calisthenics. *Education in a Democracy: A Journal of the NNER, 2,* 7–14.

Rickover, H. (1962). *Swiss schools and ours*. Washington, D.C.: Little, Brown & Co.

The Holmes Group. (1986). *Tomorrow's teachers: A report of the Holmes Group*. East Lansing, MI: The Holmes Group.

CHAPTER 10

FREEDOM SUMMER 1964: TRUTH, RECONCILIATION, AND JUSTICE—HOW A MISSISSIPPI COMMUNITY LIVES THE LEGACY OF FREEDOM SUMMER

Kevin M. Talbert

This is a tale of two cities. Well, really it is the tale of one city, divided by four and a half decades. It has seen the worst of times and the best of times. And it has an important story to tell.

This is the tale of two cities, one White and one Black.

This is the story of America, visioning itself as a "shining city on a hill," all the while allowing large parts of itself to be a very real example of the "valley of the shadow of death."

This is a story of a struggle for freedom, a struggle that neither began nor ended in what has been called the "long hot summer" of 1964. This is a story that does not end. This is a true story, and a story that lives beyond the pages of this book, a story that continues to be written everyday.

10 Great Curricula: Lived Conversations of Progressive, Democratic Curricula in School and Society, pp. 195–214
Copyright © 2011 by Information Age Publishing
All rights of reproduction in any form reserved.

195

The Mississippi Summer Project of 1964, known commonly as Freedom Summer, can be read as a "great curriculum" (Poetter, Introduction, this volume) for a number of reasons. As with all of the curricula discussed in this book, studying Freedom Summer can provide a window for self-reflection, for learning about ourselves as Americans, scholars, teachers, and learners. It is a great curriculum because it is a lived curriculum (Marsh & Willis, 2007) and as a lived curriculum has endless layers of nuance with rich potential for study. Freedom Summer is a great curriculum because of what happened. It is a story filled with drama, tragedy, love, struggle, and redemption. Finally, it is a great curriculum because of its gravity, because of the significance of what happened and because of what continues to happen as a result.

PHILADELPHIA, NESHOBA COUNTY, MISSISSIPPI, 1964: A PEDAGOGY OF HATE AND SILENCE

"Mississippi is the only state where you can drag a river anytime and find bodies you were not expecting. Things are really much better for rabbits—there's a closed season on rabbits." (E.S. Martinez, 2002, p. 218)

"In Mississippi you never ask, 'What is the meaning of life?' or 'Is there any point to it all?' but only that we may have enough life to do all that there is to be done." (E.S. Martinez, 2002, p. 219)

To characterize Mississippi as "the most racist state in America" would be too simple. Certainly, this perception prevailed in the early 1960s and partly explains why the state was chosen for the Freedom Summer Project in 1964. Mississippians knew their state was perceived to be backwards, poor, inferior to most other states, particularly those in the North and East. In part, this explains their resentment towards the workers who came to conduct the Freedom Summer Project, and to the media who came to chronicle their experience. Of course, their resentment is also attributable to their guilt, their self-conscious culpability, and their self-awareness of the racism at work among them.

But Mississippi was not completely overcome by racists; there were dissenters. There were people who desperately wanted to see change. Some were struggling for it; others wanted to struggle, but were afraid to do so publicly. As one participant reflected on the reason Mississippi was chosen, he noted that, "A long look at Mississippi can help us understand our own communities and neighboring communities, north and south, because Mississippi is not another country" (Holt, 1965, p. 11).

While this story is about what happened in Mississippi in the summer of 1964, it is also about what was happening throughout America, though perhaps more subtly in many places. The events of Freedom Summer shone a spotlight on Mississippi's struggle to overcome itself. No doubt the very presence of focused national attention helped propel change where it had been nearly impossible previously. Today, studying the events of Freedom Summer can shine a light on us, exposing our own continued struggles to overcome ourselves.

Race defined life in Mississippi. In many ways, there were two Mississippis, one White and one Black. And both White and Black understood the dynamics of this relationship and were expected to comply. Any Black who tried to elevate his status too much might face stern consequences for being an "uppity n—." And any White citizen who seemed too anxious for racial equity faced being labeled a "n—lover" and being shunned or worse by the community. This racial inequity was largely accepted but rarely spoken. The image that Mississippi liked to show to the outside world was one of racial harmony, where both Black and White accepted this differential position. Many in the state narrated a story of racial harmony, suggesting that the Black population actually thrived quite well in this position, and was happy.

The truth was that the Black population of Mississippi had seen some economic improvement since World War II. Florence Mars (1977), a resident of Philadelphia, Mississippi, in Neshoba County, writes in *Witness in Philadelphia* about the racialized social order of that time: "Despite the gradual improvement in the Negro's circumstances, the overriding fact was that the Negro race had a certain place, separate and inferior to that of the White race" (p. 45). Mars reflects that even the church preached, and practiced, segregation (p. 20). She also illustrates that as the general prosperity of the Black population increased, however gradually and slightly, the disparity between White and Black decreased. This proved an increasing threat to White hegemony and prompted a visceral response from many White Mississippians, including increasing incidents of violence.

Since the Brown versus Topeka Board of Education decision in 1954, the state of Mississippi had been intensifying its efforts to maintain legal and institutionalized segregation across the state. For example, in December 1954, citizens of Neshoba County and across Mississippi voted for a state constitutional amendment that would abolish the state's public school system if integration became imminent (Mars, 1977, p. 56). In the 1963 race for Governor, Paul Johnson, Jr. (then Lt Governor) was elected on a racist platform, using references to "n.....s, apes, coons, and possums" (a twisted substitution for the National Association for the Advancement of Colored Persons [NAACP]) in campaign stump speeches. While Johnson was Lt. Governor, he blocked James Meredith's attempted matriculation to law school at the University of Mississippi. In response to Meredith's effort to enroll, local radio stations blared *Dixie* and *Go Mississippi*, as well as a new song known as the *Never, No Never* song (Mars, 1977, pp. 74–76).

Juxtaposed against a well-known anthem of the Civil Rights Movement, *We Shall Overcome*, one can get a clearer sense of the racially charged atmosphere of life in Mississippi. The political structure of Mississippi was saturated with ardent segregationists and racial purists, from Senator Eastland, the state's senior senator who held the highest seat on the Judicial Committee (which was charged, in part, with oversight and implementation of Civil Rights legislation), to the Governor's office, all the way down to local law enforcement and the White Citizens Councils, which often worked in concert together with the Ku Klux Klan.

"In the early part of 1964 a new fear crept into the consciousness of Mississippi. The population heard that during the next summer the state was to be invaded by thousands of 'civil rights agitators' and 'beatnik college kids'" (Mars, 1977, p. 79). The leadership of the state treated it as an "invasion." They significantly increased the number of law enforcement officers in the state. Ever mindful of its perception by people outside the state, and maintaining its idyllic self-image, Mississippi made it known that it did not welcome these trouble makers from northern cities who were coming to disrupt their way of life. Use of words like "invasion," "outsider," and "agitator" to describe anyone working for racial equity is interesting to think about as a pedagogy of hegemony, rhetoric employed to great effect to create clear lines of demarcation between good, loyal Mississippians and bad ones. While legal changes had been slowly coming to the state, the social structure had changed little, and the struggle to change the social order was vigorously resisted.

Violence was increasing as the summer of 1964 approached. People were beaten and churches were burned. Florence Mars recounts cross burnings that occurred in and near her hometown:

> On the evening of April 5, 1964, 12 crosses burned simultaneously in Neshoba County. Six were burned in Philadelphia—five in the Negro quarters and one on the courthouse lawn; and six were scattered over the county in predominantly Negro communities. The *Neshoba Democrat* quoted Sheriff Rainey: "Sheriff Lawrence Rainey said it was believed that outsiders came through this area and burned the crosses and were gone before anybody could see them. He said he definitely felt that the burning was not done by local people and that it was an attempt by outside groups to disrupt the good relations enjoyed by all races in this county. (Mars, 1977, p. 80)

One must ask how these "ghosts of Mississippi" were able to simultaneously, without being caught, burn crosses across the county. Sheriff Rainey was known for his harshness towards the county's Black population. He would later be involved in the murder of the three civil rights workers who had come to Philadelphia to investigate a suspicious church fire.

Before telling the story of the church burning and the tragic murder that followed, I must interject a moment to remind the reader that, though its voices are not strongly represented in Mars' narrative as a *Witness in Philadelphia* nor in the *Letters from Philadelphia*, Blacks were not passive victims in Mississippi. Julian Bond, in his introduction to the *Letters* notes, "They were and are protagonists, fighting for their daily lives, fighting to determine their own future" (Bond, in Martinez, 2002, p. xxiii). Many Black Mississippians did not passively accept their inferior status, but struggled to change the racial order. That their stories remain largely untold is the result of neglect by historians and other scholars, sometimes willful, unfortunately. One must not think that because the stories of Black Mississippians have been less frequently told for mass consumption that their contributions were insignificant or not worthy of study. Self-reflectively investigating the pedagogy of silences within practices and dispositions of research is essential for all writers who make claims to truth-telling and socially responsible scholarship.

Mickey Schwerner had been volunteering in Mississippi for some time already by June 1964. He had been in Philadelphia, Mississippi, meeting with local Black residents about organizing a Freedom School. Mickey's activities caught the attention of the local White Citizens Council, the local law enforcement, and the Klan. He was a marked man around Neshoba County.

James Chaney was raised in Meridian, Mississippi, which is not far from Philadelphia. He also had experience organizing and advocating locally for civil rights, though much of James' experience with racism in Mississippi came because he was Black.

Andrew Goodman had only recently volunteered for the Summer Project. He left New York with the support of his family and went to Oxford, Ohio, where the training sessions for the Mississippi Summer Project were being conducted. While there, he met Schwerner and Chaney; when they heard the news of the burning of the Mt. Zion Church in Philadelphia, where Mickey had recently been trying to create a Freedom School, Schwerner and Chaney prepared to leave Oxford to travel south to investigate. Andrew volunteered to join them; it would be his first experience with community organizing.

On the morning of June 21, 1964, the three young men left the Council of Federated Organizations (COFO) headquarters in Meridian to drive to nearby Philadelphia to meet with the congregation of Mt. Zion Church and to take affidavits about the suspicious burning of the church. On their way out of town, the local Deputy Sheriff, Cecil Price, stopped them on a charge of speeding. Their real crime was breaking the social protocol of Mississippi, since two White Jewish men and one Black man were working together, "agitating" for civil rights. The three men were held for about

6 hours before being released at about 10:30 p.m. and told to return to Meridian. They were never seen alive again. Sometime shortly after their release, they were murdered. Officially, they had "disappeared." Their bodies would not be recovered until August 4, 1964.

There have been different accounts of the details of the murders portrayed throughout the last four decades. The most famous account was shown in the movie *Mississippi Burning*. Some of Philadelphia's residents today critique the movie's sensationalized "Hollywood" portrayal of life in Neshoba County and of the murders, and are especially critical of depicting the FBI agents as the heroes of the story. Ever mindful of its image to the outside world, part of the town's curricular mission today (as I will detail later) is to "set the record straight" about what happened. I will not offer any further details of the murders, except to say that they were very brutal. I do not wish to further sensationalize the killings and I realize that sometimes, because the details are so violent, that the larger message of the causes, impact, and aftermath of the killings become overshadowed.

Locally, the murders were not acknowledged. Most said it was a hoax cooked up by COFO (the organization overseeing Freedom Summer) to get national publicity and increase fundraising. Florence Mars comments on the mood of the town in the days immediately after:

> Wherever I went the disappearance was the topic of animated conversation. The mood of the town was jovial; everyone thought it was a hoax. Although the rest of the country might fall for it, Neshoba County knew better: "COFO arranged the disappearance to make us look bad so they can raise money in other parts of the country." Besides, "Cecil Price said he and Richard Willis followed the station wagon to the edge of town and watched it disappear south, toward Meridian." That's all there was to it. Neshoba County would not be taken in by the stunt. It seemed to me the effort was forced, the conversation a little too loud, the assurance exaggerated. (Mars, 1977, p. 87)

Mars also notes that there was no statement of any kind from the city administration or from church groups expressing sympathy or concern for the welfare of the three men. She began to realize that the 6 hours detainment was not a coincidence, that it was designed to give those involved in the murders time to assemble and then execute their plan.

There were some in the town who expressed their outrage at what had happened and knew it was not a hoax. One local gentleman, Buford Posey, called the FBI a few days after the murders to suggest he knew that the sheriff's office was involved, as well as a local preacher named Edgar Ray Killen. He was dismissed because most in the town considered him an eccentric, though this did not prevent them from running Buford out of town. Mars also notes that many of those who knew that the disappearances were no hoax—and that murders had occurred—were women, and many of them

Catholic (Mars, 1977, p. 98). "When we publicly expressed the view that this was no hoax, we were all met by a common response: Are you for COFO?" (p. 98). Obviously, the White power structure in the town was controlling the message, and demonizing those who spoke against their power. Mars began to work secretly with the FBI to try to root out those responsible, and consequently was under surveillance by the Klan at one point herself.

The murders were not publicly acknowledged by the city for more than four decades. Even today some people in the community think it is best not to "drag up the past" or that it is best to "let sleeping dogs lie." The only acknowledgement at the time of the murders came from the pulpit of the First Methodist Church, by Reverend Clay Lee. He preached a sermon near Christmastime in 1964, 6 months after the murders, in which he said "he would be derelict if he did not direct attention to the responsibility that Philadelphia, and in particular, the congregation of First Methodist Church, had to rid itself of the Herod spirit. He reminded the congregation that men must answer for their omissions as well as their actions" (Mars, 1977, p. 146). After four decades, the city began the process of ridding itself of its Herod spirit and of accounting for its omissions and its actions.

FREEDOM SUMMER: A PEDAGOGY OF POLITICS AND HOPE

Freedom Summer needs to be understood against the context of the larger Civil Rights Movement. The Movement is largely assumed to have begun in the mid-1950s with the Brown decision and with the Montgomery bus boycotts. The purpose of the Movement, of course, was to initiate change to destroy legally supported segregation and racism across social and political institutions. By the early 1960s, the Movement received focused national attention due to the efforts of the Student Nonviolent Coordinating Committee (SNCC), the Southern Christian Leadership Conference (SCLC), the Congress on Racial Equality (CORE), the NAACP, and countless other groups and individuals working and sacrificing for racial justice. Although in many ways Freedom Summer was the nexus of the civil rights movement, the fact is that Southern Blacks had been organizing and working on their own behalf for years. "[I]n many instances, however, SNCC staffers were the first paid civil rights workers to base themselves in isolated rural communities, daring to 'take the message of freedom into areas where the bigger civil-rights organizations fear to tread'" (Bond, in Martinez, 2002, p. v). SNCC, which had been founded in 1960 during the sit-in movement, sought to change the political order of the South and was among the first organizations to press for Black voter registration and the creation of independent political parties. The organization realized that in order for

Black citizens to have the full fruits of their citizenship, and for legal changes to become reality, enfranchisement was essential.

The SNCC volunteer Robert Moses initiated the first plans for a statewide voter-registration campaign in Mississippi in 1961. "The state of Mississippi became a laboratory for SNCC's unique methods of organizing" (Bond, in Martinez, 2002, pp. vii–viii). Though initially met with resistance by the state, by 1963, SNCC was preparing for a statewide "Freedom Vote" campaign, in which 80,000 Blacks cast votes for their own representatives for Governor and Lieutenant Governor (Bond, in Martinez, 2002, pp. viii). This was the groundwork for the Mississippi Summer Project of 1964 that would come to be known as Freedom Summer. The project was officially coordinated by COFO, which was a conglomeration of SNCC, CORE, SCLC, and the NAACP. However, SNCC provided most of the money and volunteers. About 800 White students, primarily from colleges throughout the North and West, volunteered for the summer project. "They helped build the new political party SNCC had organized, the Mississippi Freedom Democratic Party (MFDP); registered voters; and staffed 28 Freedom Schools" (Bond, in Martinez, 2002, p. ix).

The organizers understood that a comprehensive plan for racial justice needed to include both enfranchisement of the Black population, and also the creation of a generation of Black leadership in locales across the South. "[A]t the core of our efforts was the belief that Black people had to make decisions about and take charge of the things controlling their lives; the effective movement was grounded in grassroots local leadership. We were organizers in Mississippi, not leaders, even if at moments we led" (Cobb, 2008, p. 69).

"Initially intended to highlight the brutality inherent in Mississippi's culture and to register large numbers of disfranchised Black voters" (Street, 2004, p. 273), the Movement quickly evolved beyond the practical necessity of registering Black voters (and hopefully finding viable Black candidates for political offices) to include a comprehensive plan to expand social, economic, as well as political freedom. In June 1964, training was held at the Western College for Women in Oxford, Ohio, to prepare the nearly 800 students who would be volunteering that summer.

The young people who gathered in Oxford, most from elite universities, volunteered for a number of reasons. Many were not completely sure exactly what was in store for them that summer. Many had never been to Mississippi and knew very little of just how difficult it would be there. One student reflected on her decision to volunteer in a letter to her parents: "Convictions are worthless in themselves. In fact, if they do not become actions, they are worse than worthless—they become a force of evil in themselves.... I think you have to live to the fullest extent to which you have gained an awareness or you are less than the human being you are capable of being ..." (Martinez, 2002, p. 27).

The training the volunteers experienced in Oxford was part survival boot camp and part crash course in community organizing. SNCC leaders, particularly Bob Moses, emphasized the seriousness of the task ahead and the very real possibility that they would suffer arrest and, worse, violence, upon arriving in Mississippi. Volunteers learned how to survive a beating, covering their head and curling in a way to protect their vital organs. They learned expected procedures for speaking to police, and the protocol for checking in with the local office in the event of trouble. As the training progressed, many of the volunteers became keenly aware of the gravity of their commitment, and some began to consider whether they wished to continue. Few left, however. They understood that "there is a battle to be won now today ..." (Martinez, 2002, pp. 24–25). The orientation was preparing them for the battle ahead.

That the official training curriculum enacted at Oxford, Ohio, had an impact on the volunteers is clear. So did the lived curriculum. While at Oxford, news arrived of the disappearance of three volunteers who had been there the previous week: James Chaney, a young Black man and native of Meridian, Mississippi; Michael "Mickey" Schwerner, a veteran of SNCC with significant experience in Mississippi already; and Andrew Goodman, who joined the other two when he heard they were leaving to go South. The three young men had left Ohio to travel to Philadelphia, Mississippi, to investigate a suspicious church burning at a site where Mickey had been trying to organize a freedom school. Rita Schwerner, Mickey's wife, spoke to the group, and prepared them for the worst: that is that they had likely been murdered. One young woman, after hearing of their disappearance, reflected on SNCC's policy of nonviolence, which would be the standard for all volunteers in Mississippi:

> ... We have been told over and over again of brutality and beating and murder. Hank says none of us really believe it inside.... Part of it is the nonviolent philosophy, especially the part I now understand, which I did not before. That is the part that teaches you to love your "enemy," how to feel true compassion for the cop who is using a cattle-prod on you, how to understand him as a human being caught in a predicament not of his own making. I think, although I am not explaining it to you that I now know how. When I came I thought that M. L. King and his "love your enemy" was a lot of Christian mysticism. Now I can see it as a force and support, helping those who understand it. It makes me think that maybe I can take what is coming this summer ... (Martinez, 2002, pp. 33–34).

Others were less certain: "Bob Moses just told us now is the time to back out. Should I? I do not know—I am scared shitless. I do not want to go to Mississippi" (Martinez, 2002, p. 38).

Both the SNCC organizers and the volunteers were aware of the national attention focused on their project. They hoped that the national attention might finally spark real social change, but they also were realistic about how the project and its volunteers were perceived by many across the country. A Summer Project volunteer reflects: "[T]he big story out of Mississippi this summer ought not to be about my participation in the movement, or even my death. The big story ought to be Life in Mississippi. If that life is ugly, then its creators must be villains, and those who endure must be beautiful" (Martinez, 2002, p. 22).

THE PHILADELPHIA COALITION: A PEDAGOGY
OF RECONCILIATION

In stark contrast to the past, today Philadelphia, Mississippi, is a town eager to share its history. The local chamber of commerce advertises a tour of historic sites in Neshoba County, including a driving tour of important sites during the Freedom Summer of 1964. I visited and took the tour myself. The tour was guided by a local community organizer who shared both the history of the town and his personal experiences with race in the community as a lifelong resident of Philadelphia. I intentionally traveled a similar path from Oxford, Ohio, to Neshoba County that Schwerner, Chaney, and Goodman had taken in the days immediately before their disappearance. Today, there is a sign and a memorial on Western Campus of Miami University in Oxford that commemorates the training sessions for Freedom Summer that occurred there and recounts the disappearance of the three young men who had left there to investigate the burning of the Mt. Zion Church in Neshoba County. Knowing how my university represents the events of Freedom Summer, and the murders that occurred, I was curious how Philadelphia represented its history through the driving tour.

There is a brochure that accompanies the driving tour that identifies the sites, gives synopses of the events, and shows pictures and recounts stories of local residents who lived the events of Freedom Summer. The brochure also tells the stories of some current residents, those who are the "next generation" of residents, those who have borne the fruits of the freedom struggle. I have found that, unlike some communities that acknowledge their past but seem to live in it, Philadelphia is a community that does not live in the past. Neither does it deny the past as it once did. Rather, it admits the past, and rather than living in the past, uses it as an avenue to move forward to create a new and better present and future.

One might wonder how strong the connection is between Neshoba County today and Freedom Summer of 45 years ago and why I would choose to suggest that the two stories are so intertwined. Neshoba County today still seeks its freedom, for Black and White, as well as the local band of Choctaw (the car the three civil rights workers were driving when it disappeared was discovered after a tip by a local resident, who was said to be a member of the local Choctaw Tribe), through the efforts of a local community organization called the Philadelphia Coalition. This is a community straining to heal itself, to set the record straight, to make amends for past sins. They realize the necessity of acknowledging those sins in order to move forward together. Philadelphia, Neshoba County, Mississippi, is today living the legacy of Freedom Summer. Said one of the community organizers I met when I visited, who is a member of the coalition: "This is how I repay the debt to Schwerner, Goodman, and Chaney."

The Philadelphia Coalition originated in early 2004, a group formed to organize the ceremony to commemorate the 40th anniversary of the Chaney, Goodman, and Schwerner murders. During the first meeting, something interesting happened. At one point during that initial meeting a White member arose to spoke and offer a suggestion, and darting glances were exchanged among the Black members of the group, though no one voiced objection. At another point, the same phenomenon happened when a Black member of the group spoke, and again no one voiced discomfort. At the end of the meeting, two of the group's leaders, one White and one Black, who had each noticed this interesting dynamic were talking together and wondering aloud, "What that was all about?"

Through their own dialogue, they became aware that the members of the group, especially White and Black members, misunderstood and dis- trusted each other and that when each spoke, the other heard through the contexts of each group's racialized experience in that community. Many of the White members hesitated to speak and/or listen frankly out of guilt and shame for the city's racial heritage. Many of the Black members hesitated out of mistrust and/or broken loyalties. These two men realized that though each side had been speaking and listening politely to each other in the meeting (and in the community, for that matter), they had not really been fully hearing each other, because neither fully understood the other.

At the next meeting, the men shared their revelation and suggested that, for the next few weeks, they suspend their regular agenda and simply dialogue with each other, telling stories to relate each person's unique experience with race growing up in their community. For both White and Black members, this was a self-revelatory experience. In particular, the White members of the community began to free themselves from the shame and guilt they held onto as they realized that the Black community does not hold all Whites personally accountable for the racist acts of a few. The next few weeks of dialogue and listening with each other allowed the members to learn things they did not know about people they had known for years, largely because they were never spoken out loud. These were the first steps by the community to overcome the pedagogy of silence that had domi- nated for the last four decades.

From those early meetings, the Philadelphia Coalition emerged more unified. The members came to understand that, as a group and as a community, in order to move forward with any remembrance ceremony of the murders, and to heal as a community, they needed to publicly acknowledge their past and call for justice, something the community had never done. The coalition initiated plans to work with the Attorney General of the State of Mississippi to seek indictments against the eight surviving citizens who were believed to have been involved in the murders. In May 2004, the coalition issued a statement, excerpted here:

> With firm resolve and strong belief in the rule of law, we call on the Neshoba County District Attorney, the state Attorney General and the U.S. Department of Justice to make every effort to seek justice in this case. We deplore the possibility that history will record that the state of Mississippi, and this community in particular, did not make a good faith effort to do its duty.
>
> We state candidly and with deep regret that some of our own citizens, including local and state law enforcement officers, were involved in the planning and execution of these murders...
>
> Finally, we wish to say to the families of James Chaney, Andrew Goodman and Michael Schwerner, that we are profoundly sorry for what was done in this community to your loved ones. And we are mindful of our responsibility as citizens to call on the authorities to make an effort to work for justice in this case. Continued failure to do so will only further compound the wrong...

Pursuit of justice for the murders was a way for the community to hold itself accountable. For the Coalition, confessing the past and asking for justice were the first steps toward community reconciliation. They were not the only steps, however. There are detractors today who wonder why the Coalition does not continue to press for justice for other murders throughout the state. Coalition members emphasize that their organization is not a legal organization. They are committed to seeking justice and are willing to work with other organizations, but emphasize that their mission is to work within their community to improve itself.

Of the eight names given to the grand jury, only one person was indicted, Edgar Ray Killen. A local preacher and an influential member of the local Klan, Killen was the chief suspect. Understandably, the trial was arduous for the community. Once again Neshoba County was under the national spotlight. Ultimately, Killen was convicted of three counts of manslaughter and sentenced to three consecutive 20-year terms. He was 83 years old at the time of his conviction. The jury, which was racially diverse, could not agree on murder convictions. More than four decades after the murders, community members still rose to speak as character witnesses on Killen's behalf, including the city's mayor, a revelation that shocked the courtroom and community leaders, who had no idea that the mayor would support

Killen. Interestingly, Killen also still apparently had enough influence to bribe or threaten at least three jury members, as he implied on tape to a documentary film crew. He spoke during the trial with absolute certainty that he would not be convicted. While this was undoubtedly partly arrogant bragging, it was also attributable to his expectation that fear and loyalty to him would prevail. The convictions were returned on June 21, 2005, 41 years to the day after the brutal murders. Two community organizers with whom I spoke about the trial both noted their satisfaction as well as relief, particularly because they felt there were significant bumbles by the prosecution during the trial.

Part of the lived curriculum of the Philadelphia Coalition's efforts today is its conscious desire to reclaim the city's story. The coalition recognizes the town's negative reputation from the murders. Yet, its mission is not simply "image control." They rightly decry the sensationalized Hollywood accounts of the murders and of their community and the image of their community's brutality that lives in popular culture. They want the truth to be told about the murders, but they also want the truth told about people like Florence Mars, Reverend Lee, and forgotten others who spoke and fought for justice. They want the story told of the city's progress toward racial justice. The Philadelphia Coalition is committed to moving forward, but needs to reconcile itself to its past to do so. In 2005, the coalition worked with the state legislature of Mississippi to initiate legislation to mandate that curriculum on the civil-rights movement be included in all schools throughout the state. Members of the coalition recognized that many of the local young people knew virtually nothing about the Movement, or about what happened in Mississippi during the 1950s and 1960s.

On my recent visit to Mississippi, I spent more than two hours in the car with two members of the Philadelphia Coalition, one White, one Black, on our way to a local premiere of a documentary titled *Neshoba* (Dickoff & Pagano, 2008). I find it an elegant comment on the lived curriculum of Mississippi today that two White men and one Black man could travel together across the state without fear of harm, a fitting representation that the state has progressed since Schwerner, Goodman, and Chaney were murdered.

The award-winning documentary, which took more than four years to make, recounts the story of the trial of Edgar Ray Killen. The directors were granted personal interviews with Killen and he is shown speaking throughout the film. Scenes with Killen speaking about the murders and the trial were stirring; his words, filled with racist invective, condemned him. The film also tells the story of the Philadelphia Coalition and its efforts to seek justice in the case. Interspersed throughout are interviews with Killen's family, local community members, and the victims' families. One senses from the film that Neshoba County is still a community coming to grips with its past. Some community members suggest "it's better left in the past." Some speak in support of Killen and his character. The film shows the intense emotions stirred by the case and, particularly, the intense emotions of those community members who recognize the evil perpetrated by their town and their guilt and urgent desire to see justice.

I viewed the film, which is touring national independent film festivals, in a crowded theater near Jackson, Mississippi. Viewing the film with members of the community, with coalition members, and the general public, was an illuminating experience of the lived curriculum as well. Generally, the community members' and coalition members' reaction to the film was positive. A number of the people in the film, excepting Killen's family and supporters, were present for the screening. Though the directors were not natives of Mississippi, they did spend considerable time in Neshoba County and developed close relationships with many community members.

The coalition members with whom I traveled to view the film brought press releases along, the statements issued at the first call for justice, after the verdict, and from early 2008 that issued a continued call for justice for those still at large in the Neshoba case. For the Philadelphia Coalition members, the film was a pedagogical moment, one that could initiate dialogue about the past as a step to working together in the present. Through its efforts, the Philadelphia Coalition is fulfilling the vision of the leaders of Freedom Summer who sought to create a generation of Black leadership in local communities and to create a world where Black and White could work together toward more democratic community life.

A PEDAGOGICAL INTERLUDE

There are numerous possibilities for how one might read the events of Freedom Summer and the efforts of the Philadelphia Coalition as a curriculum. The frames I have chosen, the pedagogy of silence, the pedagogy of hope, and the pedagogy of reconciliation, I intuited from the Philadelphia Coalition's own words, its own apparent curricular standpoint. I also derived the frames from my experience of the story, through research and through my visit to Neshoba County to see where the events occurred and to talk to those involved today in the community's efforts toward reconciliation. I also offer these frames as ways of viewing the curriculum as "great." Each of the three chosen frames provides numerous potential avenues for further inquiry; in fact, they may raise more questions than they answer.

I turn briefly to an explanation of these frames. The pedagogy of silence has two interrelated dimensions. First, it includes the county's silence in acknowledging the murders and its complicity in the culture of hate. For the Philadelphia Coalition, such a silence feels not just like denial, but like a subconscious endorsement. One might liken it to a disease that goes undiagnosed; it festers and destroys, manifesting in numerous symptoms that evidence general lack of health. Efforts to treat symptoms without treating the disease's source are ultimately fruitless. The second dynamic of a pedagogy of silence is the way that hegemony seeks to silence opposition, to silence those it dominates. In this case hegemony, actualized as White supremacy, functioned to suppress through physical and ideological violence those who opposed. Labeling the volunteers as "agitators," "communists," or "— lovers" is an example of just one ideological tool exemplifying White supremacists' attempts to silence opposition.

The pedagogy of hope reflects the vision of Freedom Summer organizers as well as the larger Civil-Rights Movement. Hope is manifested through praxis, which is the idea that oppressed groups may resist their oppression and achieve freedom by awareness of their oppression and its consequences, understanding hegemony's influence upon them, and then reflectively using that knowledge to work to overcome oppression and domination and to make a more just and democratic world (see Freire, 2000). Certainly, the current work of the Philadelphia Coalition also illustrates a community's praxis. The coalition recognizes the forces of hegemony at work in their community and actively seeks to subvert that hegemony (the pedagogy of silence) to work toward community cooperation and justice.

The pedagogy of reconciliation, perhaps self-evident in the narrative I have constructed, includes both the community's reconciliation to its past and also reconciliation to one another. Revealed at least partly as the obverse of the pedagogy of silence, reconciliation is also the product toward which the pedagogy of hope is directed. The Philadelphia Coalition recognizes that for the community to act for justice in the present it had to first rectify the silence that had prevented justice and acted as a wedge between community members. The pedagogy of reconciliation began for the coalition at that early meeting where it recognized the need for community members to hear each other, to allow each other to literally speak against the silence that impeded their understanding. Freire (2000) explains, at length, the necessity of dialogue to the liberatory project.

CONCLUDING SEGUE

I conclude with an excerpt from the Coalition's March 2008 call for justice; I do so to let the Philadelphia Coalition have the final say in this portion of the chapter, to give it the opportunity to own its story, to set the terms of its own life, its own curriculum:

> We challenge our fellow citizens to join us in an honest appraisal of the past, creating a truth process to tell the story. Knowledge brings truth and the truth brings freedom. Today, we have a cause for hope because our community came together to acknowledge the evil that occurred here and to assert that we will no longer accept it as a description of who we are. Our purpose for the future should be: to seek the truth, to insure justice for all, and to nurture reconciliation through education. And so we promise in our own community to see this journey through to the finish line.

RESPONSE BY TOM POETTER

I chose to end the book with Kevin Talbert's discussion of Freedom Summer in part because it frames the wider community/school curriculum and experiential continuum that the book intends to navigate with you the reader. Of course, this chapter highlights the community's role in curriculum. The Philadelphia Coalition has a curriculum of engagement and action that tells a powerful story and that meets people on the ground, where they are. And the wider story of the curriculum of civil rights—that plays out in Kevin's account, and in history, and in our ongoing struggles as a people with issues surrounding race and how we will live and learn together in a pluralistic, democratic society—continues to challenge us. This chapter highlights several issues/phenomena that should be of interest, concern, and action for school leaders, for teachers and school administrators, and for community activists.

One critical element is the not so unusual reality that what happens close to home tends to be under-taught and under-appreciated. Many have commented that the hard won spoils of the civil-rights movement sometimes tend not to be appreciated by those who reap the benefits, both White and Black, perhaps in part at least because the stories and lessons tend not to be handed down explicitly through school experiences to our children. Creating distance from the sometimes too close reality of "home" tends to be a common, if unintended strategy of decision makers in schools. We tend to avoid controversy and conflict when we can, so that dealing with local issues or larger societal issues, especially when groups have taken sides, becomes difficult for teachers and administrators to take on (McCutcheon, 1995). In most cases, it is the adults who struggle with addressing hard issues; the wonderful reality is that students can take them and actually long for the challenge most times. Students would often rather face the difficulty than let it remain clouded in mystery or secrecy.

The questions are: what critical community story remains untold, under-interrogated, and/or unimagined in your setting? How can you claim and reclaim it, using it to advance the social learning as well as the academic learning of your students? How can students and teachers and schools not only advance learning within the school, but also move the social agendas of creating deeper knowledge, and healing, and a more democratic way of life out into the community?

One thing we can do as curriculum leaders in schools is to carefully navigate the possibilities of confronting tough issues, hurts, and fears in the curriculum with students, first by asking them what they know about the topic at hand, what they would like to learn about it, and what they might do to take action if they could (Beane, 1998). In the case of the reality described in this chapter, the work done by the Coalition to address civil rights head on by creating a legitimate, open forum for conversation and action—such as creating the driving tour and participating in it as citizens interpreting the past through their current realities and forging a committee that actually goes deeper into dialogue and meaning making—opens a door to thinking about the powerful possible connections between the world beyond the school walls and what could go on inside them.

The story hits close to home because Miami University and Oxford, Ohio, are now celebrating and confronting their connections to Freedom Summer in ways that were not thought possible just a decade ago, in ways similar to those working toward history in Philadelphia, Mississippi. The 40th (2004) and 45th (2009) anniversary celebrations of the events of that summer held here in Oxford and how they have had an impact on our university, our wider community, and the world have been watershed moments in the history of our locale, helping us to not only teach the historic push for civil rights in our local classrooms, but also helping us confront the real racism and barriers to promoting equity that existed and still exist in our own social order, so seemingly distant from Mississippi, but in reality, not so much (for more information about Freedom Summer visit www.muohio.edu/freedomsummer2009).

But the most prominent, practical takeaway element for me, however, has to do with the lessons taught and questions raised by the distinctly American characteristics of time and commitment to leadership that play out in Kevin's depiction of Freedom Summer and its aftermath in Mississippi. In this case, then, I want to draw parallel the lives of those continuing the work through the Coalition to one of our great American Patriot Heroes, John Adams.

Those of you who have read David McCullough's (2002) *John Adams* or have seen the HBO mini-series (2008) starring Paul Giamatti and Laura Linney can very well imagine where I am going with this. You know now of

Adams' innumerable sacrifices for the colonies and for the new United States, especially his significant sacrifice of a private life for a public life and the dangers incurred by decisions to represent Massachusetts in the new Continental Congress and to sign the Declaration of Independence. What strikes me so about McCullough's depiction of Adams is the incredibly courageous colonial sense of time and commitment that would make each of Adams' decisions to travel to Philadelphia from Boston or cross the Atlantic life changing decisions that would involve months if not years of uncertainty, despair, and potential demise. This notion of traveling willfully despite the risks, even into oblivion, and the concomitant commitment to somewhat nebulous ends all at the same time, strikes me as tremendously American and courageous, and uniquely connected to the journeys of Freedom Summer.

Just as Lewis and Moses and countless others led a Civil-Rights Movement to overcome social inequity amidst palpable dangers, and as hundreds of college students poured into Mississippi even after the murders of their colleagues in 1964, and as the Coalition in Philadelphia, Mississippi, continues to interpret the past for a new present and future despite those who would suggest that burying it all does just as good, so too did John Adams stare down the challenges of the day, in the long-term, by moving. He did not sit still, but responded when called to action. Was he always certain of next steps? Certainly not. Was he committed to truth, and to justice, and the causes of freedom? Certainly so. So he had to move. Sitting still would have been immoral, unthinkable.

In all of these cases, the protagonists commit themselves long-term and at great peril to the American dreams of equity, justice, and truth for all. So too must school leaders see the big picture of their commitments to children and to the wider community. Sometimes there are good fights worth waging because they represent for us watershed moments that we cannot turn our backs on. Sometimes, we cannot survive as leaders by "waiting things out"; sometimes history and life require that we make a decision, alone or collaboratively, based on foundational principles, and take action. How do we construct a theory and action for leadership in schools? What issues or principles or ideas are we tied to long-term, that we would not turn our backs on in a time of conflict or disaster? What hard decisions will we be willing to make, even if we put ourselves squarely in harm's way? Patriots come in all shapes and sizes and colors. Who is willing to risk their life and fortune? Who is willing to travel the dark road tainted by violence? Who is willing to stand up for children and their rights to be challenged, and to know, and to be taught well and ethically in a safe, democratic place day-after-day?

All of these questions are related, and our lives as school people not ever distant from the foundational American project, the one that leads to liberty, and to death. Where will the new life be in America? Will there be a role for schools, and teaching, and curriculum? Will there be a role for you to play?

THE LAST WORD BY KEVIN TALBERT

Often those things that are of greatest need closest to home are the most overlooked by school leaders. School leaders sometimes look to learn from the specific contexts of the local community for possibilities for change. But I would add that school leaders, be they teachers or administrators, should not just seek to solve the problems most relevant locally, but that they should also be conscious of using the assets available to them in their local community—especially the people at hand—to solve those problems.

Too often schools act similarly to "little Mississippi's." They jealously guard their image to "outsiders" and act to resist influence by people outside the school walls, asserting its right to act on its own behalf. While certainly the cultural landscape so often denigrates the work being done in schools, school leaders must recognize not only the opportunity, but also the necessity of building cooperative relationships with other stakeholders in the local community. School leaders need not only be paid employees of the school, but in fact could be parents, local business leaders, local civic leaders, indeed any person with a vested interest in making our schools more democratic. Valuing the lives of those closest at hand, in the school and in the wider community, and recognizing them and committing to work with them to improve the discourse and experience of those within the school walls, is one of the most difficult and yet most rewarding curriculum steps that can be taken by school leaders.

Also, I would like to add that I agree that the Philadelphia Coalition's work does parallel that of John Adams, as well as that of all those who have spent time moving toward peace and justice in our society. Certainly Adams displayed courage and sacrifice as he repeatedly left his family to serve his state (later his country). And Adams chose to forfeit his private life for a public life. I do wish to note, however, that Adams' ability to make such choices was somewhat of a luxury afforded by his social and economic status. Though not a wealthy man, he had a measure of financial security that afforded the opportunity to make such a sacrifice.

Hidden from the narrative are all of those people of Adams' day who were denied the option to participate in public life because they lacked financial security. Those who participated in Freedom Summer showed similar courage and sacrifice, but it would be an error not to privilege those who daily lived in courage and resisted on a daily basis in the setting over time. On a daily basis, the Coalition lives out a commitment to courage and justice. Catalysts for change are important, but so are those who stick in the setting, and on a daily basis make the world a better place. My hope is that this story is remembered as their story.

REFERENCES

Beane, J. (1998). *Integrated curriculum*. New York, NY: Teachers College Press.

Cobb, C.E., Jr. (2008). *Organizing freedom schools*. In C. M. Payne & C. S. Strickland (Eds.), *Teach freedom: Education for liberation in the African-American tradition* (pp. 69–74). New York, NY: Teachers College Press.

Dickoff, M., & Pagano, T. (2008). *Neshoba*. Pro Bono and Pagano Productions.

Friere, P. (2000). *Pedagogy of the oppressed* (30th Anniversary ed.). New York, NY: The Continuum International Publishing Group.

Holt, L. (1965). *The summer that didn't end: The story of the Mississippi civil rights project of 1964*. New York, NY: Da Capo Press.

John Adams: HBO Mini-series. (2008).

Mars, F. (1977). *Witness in Philadelphia*. Baton Rouge, LA: Louisiana State University Press.

Marsh, C. J. & Willis, G. (2007). *Curriculum: Alternative approaches, ongoing issues* (4th ed.). Upper Saddle River, NJ: Pearson Education.

Martinez, E. S. (Ed.). (2002). *Letters from Mississippi: Personal reports from civil rights volunteers of the 1964 Freedom Summer*. Brookline, MA: Zephyr Press.

McCullough, D. (2002). *John Adams*. New York, NY: Simon and Schuster.

McCutcheon, G. (1995). *Developing the Curriculum: Solo and Group Deliberation*. New York, NY: Longman.

Street, J. (2004). Reconstructing Education from the Bottom up: SNCC's 1964 Mississippi Summer Project and African American Culture. *Journal of American Studies, 38*(2), 273–296.

EPILOGUE

Thomas S. Poetter

This epilogue is an attempt to pull the book together and to challenge the reader to view the text curricularly, both in terms of the text as a curriculum and in terms of the text as a device for getting at deeper curriculum issues at stake in the world of curriculum theorizing and practice. I am attempting to be as clear as possible here, but cannot make any guarantees that the writing will not drift some as I follow the story that is suggested and imbedded in this project.

As an author, it is rare, at least for me, to feel such joy and energy at the end of a scholarly project. Many times in the past, I have actually been glad when a book project is over, and not just because of the thrill associated with finally seeing it in print. For one thing, the material typically becomes stale as you go over and over it again and again. You can find yourself in a seemingly endless stupor, just wishing to get on to the next project, but not with this book. This project has been a totally different experience, especially given the opportunity as a professor of curriculum to help the authors work through their initial ideas, research activities, chapter drafts, and then final chapters. It has been a remarkable experience for me, and I think I can speak for the authors as well that it has been a journey worth taking that we would take again in a heartbeat. It has also embodied many aspects of a progressive curriculum, especially with the open-inquiry-oriented project at its core.

THIS BOOK AS A LIVED CURRICULUM

The way I feel about this book has a lot to do with the fact that the book embodies a lived curriculum of its own, at least on two levels. That is, what you are consuming as a reader is a curriculum artifact and more, since each person who reads it, and each group that discusses it, creates new meaning as a result. I have been using the following definition of curriculum, that is, curriculum is "the discovery of personal meaning" for several decades in my work (Combs, 1976; Burke, 1993). It comes from Combs, who used theories of perceptual psychology to frame his notions of educational humanism, and other progressive humanists such as Goodlad and Associates (1979), who did extensive work theorizing the "experienced curriculum," all opening up the possibility that the curriculum is only truly alive when it manifests itself in the experience of learners and the meaning they make from that experience. These experiences tend to be idiosyncratic, often unspeakable, but no less real, powerful, and most often, educative. When readers experience the text, and become something new and different as a result of having consumed it and worked with it, they are creating a new lived curriculum.

And deeper, the authors experienced a curriculum, starting with the first day I passed out the syllabus for the course, suggested a research project focused on "great" curricula, and set out with students to actually produce a book-length work that took more than two years to complete from start to finish, way beyond the boundaries of the original course. The curriculum played out as authors struggled to finish chapters, meet my expectations and guidelines, even beyond the timeframe of the course. We grew closer as a group and in our shared venture to produce scholarship found new opportunities to interact socially and professionally. We were able to create a new life together with texture that we would not have been able to achieve if it had not been for this project. So we experienced a lived curriculum as a group and as individuals that continues to have legs.

THIS CURRICULUM FEELS "UNDERCOOKED"

This having been said, it is still clear to me that both the authors and the reader may perceive the chapters to be somewhat "undercooked," as author Christopher L. Cox explained to me his own feelings about his own work as we were working through drafts of his chapter on curriculum of the 2009 Inauguration. After all, just like the chapters published by Eliot Eisner in his great volume *The Educational Imagination* (1979) by his doctoral students at Stanford University, for the most part, his students had not yet received their degrees, and were working with Eisner to produce "educational criticism" as part of their graduate work with him. It is certainly foolhardy to think that students who read and work in the curriculum field can only learn from material that is definitive, produced by "experts" with degrees, and wholeheartedly polished by experience and age.

In fact, it is the experience of following the inquirer into the field of study, tracing his or her steps, if you will, through the writing, that has a wonderful potential to generate deeper questions and rich dialogue, no matter the scholar. Perhaps, there is growth even with missteps and bungling. We hope this is not the impression left with you here, but it bears saying nonetheless that we do not feel like these chapters or this work is "over" in any sense, just because it is published and being read. There is plenty left to do, even on the chapters presented here. Even as we present them as consumable, we all understand that they are "in process."

REVISITING "GREAT"

I also want to address again briefly and in closing what we mean by "great" in this volume, though Kevin Talbert in the preface and Kevin Smith in his chapter on the one-room schoolhouse offer tremendous insights on our collective notion of the term "great" as a heuristic device for taking us further into the curricula at hand, and I work on "great" at some length as well in the introduction. I think this line of thought will reveal, ultimately, what we have been "cooking up" here. It is fair to say that we do not mean "greatest" when we use the word "great." Meaning, we are not trying to argue that these are the "greatest" curricula in the history of the world, or even the "greatest" at work and alive right now in history. Perhaps they are, maybe not, since there are many other worthy other progressive candidates for the list, we just did not study them.

What we mean is that the examples given here are "great" examples of progressive curriculum in action in the world, and that when implemented and lived they lead to outcomes that are sensitive to and illuminative of the potential for education and schooling and community life to yield a greater understanding of democracy, and of the individual's own progress toward becoming more completely human, and of the potential for teaching and learning and the opening up of opportunities to create a more just, diverse, and tolerant society.

So, this is a book about "great" progressive curriculum at work in the world, and we hope that at the end of your reading you have a sense of how they are or are not great, and also that you are making sense of that which is curricular in your own midst in terms of it stacking up to our examples.

This type of thinking opens one up to the possibilities of curriculum theorizing in the world, and perhaps of creating more humane and just opportunities for learning and growth in the real world. But I want to take a next step and suggest what we are actually doing by "cooking up" these chapters, beyond just using them as objects of inquiry in order to say something about the world.

"COOKING UP" A PROGRESSIVE STANCE TO CURRICULUM THEORIZING AND PRACTICE

Let me be clear that I am worried for the future of education and schooling, especially of public schooling in the United States, and want to say a few words about the road to demise I see playing out in experience and what the curriculum field can do about it, and perhaps what cases like those presented here can do to stem the tide. For sure, that is a tall order, and we do not want to overshoot by too much. But we also want to be a part of the solution, and not the problem.

As you know, schools are becoming more and more like test factories than anything resembling progressive schools, in which individual interests and concerns are cultivated, and students are challenged by teachers and the community to connect what they are learning to the world outside the school's four walls. Instead, schools are coming to be even more, if any of us thought it possible, the embodiment of instrumental, technical, mechanistic, and irrelevant thinking and action mis-educationally for children and society. Schools have been ferociously attacked from the outside as ineffective and worse. They have no means for defending themselves, since they are of the public and are supported by the public, but they are under fire, mercilessly so, and in my opinion, often without just cause (Bracey, 2009).

Schools are subject to corporatization, privatization, and management of "reforms" that outsiders place on them in order to control them, their processes and their products, in order to captivate a certain status quo (where everyone knows their "place") and the capital that follows them. It hardly needs to be said that the curriculum reforms of the past decade have led to (1) the standardization of discrete bits of knowledge across subject areas that barely hold together and are nearly indefensible as worth knowing or as reflective of an "educated" person, and to (2) the chronic, nearly inescapable obligation of teachers, as a result, merely to teach to the test. What do we expect teachers to do when the test becomes the currency by which teaching effectiveness is judged?

When the curriculum becomes rigid, embodied in textbooks and other curriculum materials, and mostly scripted for professional teachers to deliver without question, as if they do not know any better, everything begins to fail. Why would upwardly mobile citizens subject their children to this state-mandated nonsense that is being passed off as strong standards-based education in public schools? They cannot stand for it, so they leave, walking to other opportunities in the private sector, including the public ones that will become private in due time (the world of private/public charters, magnets, and payment vouchers) because they can. Impoverished schools and programs, ultimately, will be left to oversee citizens with the least ability to escape. They will be stuck even worse so than they are now. Of course, it is complicated, but there is so much despair that even in higher education, especially in the curriculum field, there is a clear falling away of those willing to work on the problems at hand constructively.

A DIFFERENT RECIPE

On the one hand, there has been an exodus from concern for the plight of public schooling by curricularists in universities, many who originally found their way into the curriculum field through teacher education. But they found it impossible to teach or even act ethically, knowing that their students, who would ultimately become teachers, would never be able to live out the truths they were learning in their classes. They found themselves more distant than ever from public school colleagues, teachers and administrators, who went along for the ride to keep their jobs and to earn new ones, even to the point that a strongly critical graduate school program could not save them. Discouraged, politically out of the power loop at almost every level, they quit thinking about or caring about schools. They lost status or gave it up to organizations like the Association for Supervision and Curriculum Development (ASCD). As a result, they possess no voice for change, renewal, or meaning making in America's public schools. They are smart, they are writing, but even if their work dips into the condition and plight of schools, no one listens, except scholars of their own ilk.

Then there are colleagues in higher education and in schools that tend to the whims of the state and the powers that be and continue to teach that curriculum work is merely the work of aligning standards and objectives with desirable outcomes, and designing assessments to measure whether or not the desired ends are met adequately. This is technical work, often ensconced in the rituals and the beliefs of a subject area. So we have curriculum specialists in math education and social studies education, for instance, along with many other fields. And each of those fields has reigning standards, and experts to be trained to help teachers meet those standards effectively, efficiently, and without question. Legions of curriculum professors align themselves with the status quo as embodied in these emerging fields of curriculum study, by discipline and subject area, and have no vision of their work as transformational, or ethical in terms of aligning with a philosophy that values the individual and views experience and knowledge as powerfully embedded in the world and not just in a subject area. They are not progressive by any means, but merely traditional conservatives doing their best to deliver the product the state demands. We will see them come out in legions as the new "common core" curriculum takes shape across states in the next decade. It is inevitable it seems (Dillon, 2011).

And then there is a breed, made up of people like me and the students in our program, who still think that while schools surely are not completely defensible as educational institutions since they possess so much room for growth, they still offer the best way forward for a democracy to educate its young, foster respect and know-how across many layers of society, and build community. Where better to pass along our values? Where better to establish norms for behavior and habits for success in society? Where better to cultivate an American polity out of the many, working to become, at each moment, more one? Where better to extend opportunity when other institutions close it off? And, if schools can be established, preserved, and grown as places of worth, they need to reflect a commitment to students as human beings, who have interests, concerns, and knowledge before they even show up at the door, with backgrounds and lives to tap as significant resources, and who can be educated to use what they know is great about our country and about ourselves and not be completely dependent on what the textbooks say, and what the legislators say is important to know, and what the tests say about their worth.

I think of us as occupying a "no man's land," stuck between front lines, un-enamored with the status quo yet unwilling to flee. We believe that schools and communities are vital, educative bodies, and that forces are out to kill them off, debase them, destabilize them, from the inside/out and the outside/in. We want to emerge from this position and argue that there is a different way forward.

Those of us in this category, educational progressives of many types, sizes, backgrounds, and beliefs, believe that it is possible for schools, teachers, students, administrators, and citizens to reclaim their educational experiences in schools and in society by treating their work together as curricular, asking questions along the way and operationalizing principles that value the individual, pursue interest and concern, and attend to the connection between what is taught and learned and their impact on society, for real, beyond the doors of the classroom and school.

Subject areas do not stand on their own as important, but only in so much as they serve the ends of solving problems and developing new knowledge. Teachers are facilitators of a wide range of learning possibilities and a wide range of students, not just of students in a certain grade learning only one subject at a time. Students seek answers to questions that burn within them about the world they know, and carry and pickup the knowledge they need to solve problems and participate in democracy as citizens along the way. Assessing learning has more to do with learning in action than it does with knowing certain things. It is more about knowing "how," than just knowing "what" in a tightly controlled way. Of course, "what" you know is always important. The trick is how you get the "what" that serves and illuminates the ends at hand, hopefully ends that will transform the world, making it more equitable and just.

What I wish to argue is that curriculum work that does not forget that there is a great human spirit embodied in the lives of individuals and communities, and that their lives reflect a deep sense of self and community, tradition and possibility, might just help us to navigate forward in a more progressive manner. How better to do that, or make it possible for people who have never experienced a progressive educational event, than to present examples of curriculum that are progressive, even controversially so, so that individuals such as the readers of this book and the supporters of curricula such as those featured here, might take a look around them and begin to argue and fight for the rededication of schools and communities to a more progressive orientation to their work that is educative?

I am hopeful that this scholarly project, in some small way, can reinvigorate proponents to put examples and possibilities forward that run counter to the arguments that schools are lost and not worth attending to or that schooling of a traditional kind with a limited view of knowledge, teaching, learning, and curriculum is the only legitimate way forward.

WHAT CAN WE TAKE AWAY FROM THESE EXAMPLES THEN?

It is clear to me after supervising the work of the authors of this volume and after working with the chapters over many months that we can say several things about these sorts of "great" curriculum, in general, for the reader. I offer these insights as an individual, and invite your further analysis and critique, especially as you discuss them individually as cases and in total as a group.

PROGRESSIVE VALUE CERTAIN ENDS
THAT OTHERS TYPICALLY DO NOT

It is safe and easy to say, though very controversial and perhaps at the core of where criticism will take its aim at us, that what the curriculum in most of these settings is trying to accomplish with learners has mainly to do with producing learning that is individualized, even idiosyncratic. Certainly, this is the case in the school-based examples, though almost all have to play within the reality of the present day testing craze. Eagle Rock is private, and sets its own standards for graduation while working within in the State of Colorado to recognize graduates. Central Academy, the One-Room Schoolhouse in Croydon, The Algebra Project locations, and the NNER sites all deal with the reality of testing, from young grade school students through teaching candidates seeking certification/licensure and beyond. Their work lies mainly in the public sector. But none of the sites caters to the test. Instead, they let the test come to them and address it by doing what they do best all along. The theory is that doing their best educationally with and for students, in the manner and with the ends they have in mind as primary, will produce enough value for the students to score "naturally" on anything mandated and standardized by outsiders.

In the case of Central Academy, test scores have remained high for students as compared with the district's more traditional settings, for instance, though they battle daily the incursion that the testing movement presents to them as the district struggles to tighten the grip on students and teachers on a daily basis, fearful of not scoring and therefore making sure of it by parsing the objectives of each subject into learning events that will be tested and ultimately used to judge them and the value of their work.

The community-based curricula are magnificent and fascinating in this regard. Take for instance, the Freedom Summer curriculum of Philadelphia, Mississippi. The ends today are much different than they were in 1964. To transform a culture of hate for a culture of tolerance, of understanding, of forgiveness, and of forward-thinking represents the best of democracy at work to produce unum out of pluribus. Still suffering and with problems, nonetheless, the community soldiers on with dignity, vulnerable to criticisms for past bad acts but proud of progress it makes on a daily basis to treat the past honestly, and to create a new present filled with hope and opportunity. In essence, what is happening today reflects the deepest, most profound hopes, in process of improving, that those who led the movement through despair perhaps could have hoped for.

WE CAN'T GLORIFY OR VILIFY BUSINESS APPROACHES
AND USE THEM PRODUCTIVELY

We purposefully wanted to pull in corporate business models where progressive principles are playing out in the curriculum, even on a small, specialized scale, so that we could show how there are progressive ideas embodied and working even in the most unlikely places. It is safe to say, as a rule in our group and perhaps across our program, that we do not use or worship management approaches in schools or in the community that are just business-based, focused merely on profit, and typically technical. But to ignore things happening within organizations, even businesses, is to miss an opportunity to inquire, and to make judgments and learn about remarkable aspects of reality that might inform us in the present or future.

Danny studied McDonalds, and I studied Little League International, so that we could explore how progressive ideas get embodied and practiced even within the corporate grind. On the one hand, I recounted how a progressive, community-oriented effort to establish Little League over seven decades has produced a lively, growth-oriented, yet contested curriculum. Of course, Little League faces many challenges, including the emerging power of corporate interests at the expense of or for the exploitation of its very clients, the players and their families. After all, it is safe to say that corporate interests put an end to the original input and impulses of its founder, Carl Stotz, way back in the 1950s. Subsequently, it is not hard to miss the millions of dollars in advertising and revenue that come into play when teams make their way to Williamsport to conduct the World Series in full view of millions of fans on television.

It is also safe to say, whether Little League International's Board of Directors realize it or not, that maintaining a program as a servant of the wider community that is filled with opportunity, openness, and democracy might necessitate the subjugation of corporate interest. As the corporate interests and power become more prominent in Little League, I submit that its health and well-being may be challenged, without due care to the potential consequences. Time will tell. The truth is that participants, millions of them, benefit immensely by playing baseball/softball. It is the responsibility of the Board of Directors and all participants in Little League, including players, parents, and community supporters and friends, to maintain and protect the continuation of this benefit.

And, of course, on the other hand, McDonald's started as a corporation, and over time birthed powerful and progressive means for educating employees, connecting with the community, and providing meaningful economic opportunities to millions of citizens. In Danny's chapter on McDonald's, he is clear to say that he understands the neo-liberal aspects and implications of McDonald's current and past behavior as a behemoth, multinational company. It is impossible to deny McDonald's corporate past and present, and not to see that its approaches have produced little benefit, except those unto itself, in some areas. But it is also shortsighted not to recognize that within the corporate structure there is this amazingly powerful and progressive engine. People get chances, and make the most of them, and learn and teach each other in a relatively safe, innovative environment, all the while working in an arena that is connected to sustaining the world, feeding it, providing jobs, maintaining order, hope, and opportunity, and providing relief and comfort as well to the most needy, especially the sick and suffering in hospitals. I think it is a fascinatingly complicated case, and that Danny describes it well. It is up the reader to judge, and to extend the inquiry. I am glad Danny had the courage to take it on, and we are proud to have presented it here, though it is potentially tremendously controversial.

Since so many students in education will wind up working in business, and there are aspects of education that are business-oriented, from teaching to administration, it does no good for us merely to denigrate business, really. It is what it is, and different in many regards from education. So we must critique it, in order to understand it, ultimately so that we can put any good ideas we come across to use for defensible ends, corralling it to our purposes, at least in so far as we can work with and analyze the anomalies business presents for educational situations. This is a critical aspect of sound educational research and critique, and we try to put this commitment in action here.

THE STUDENT IS THE STARTING POINT, GETTING AT THE "LIVED CURRICULUM"

Even McDonald's starts with the customer. The Holocaust Museum with the individual visitor. Little League with the player. The Inauguration with the individual viewer/citizen, witness to history. The Civil Rights movement with a core/corps of individuals willing to sacrifice safety for moral ends, justice, fairness, opportunity, and inalienable rights that belong to each of us fully, and if not, then truly to none of us. Community movements and their curriculum that we highlight here are heavily focused on the individual, how important he or she is in the turning dialectic of history. We are all part of a polity, a society, yet independent to a certain degree, free to make choices within the conditions that define order. The truth of the matter is that schools have mostly lost sight of a commitment to the importance and the power of education for the individual, and how critical it is for anything beyond basic skills and basic knowledge accruing to the learner as a result of schooling.

Recommitting to the individual, what he or she needs or what he or she wants to know, is a critical commitment to make in the context of progressive curriculum and pedagogical arrangements. After all, the value of the "lived curriculum," perhaps, the only educative measure that matters, whatever the story is of the individual learner who experiences a curriculum, is extraordinary, at least as far as we are concerned. This is the incontrovertible finding that has to be drawn from the stories of the "lived curriculum" told here, about the endangered but valuable lives of those who become family in the one-room schoolhouse, a place where individual students do not get lost in the shuffle of school and make a considerable contribution to each person's education in the process of becoming a community of peers over several years together; about the children of Central Academy and The Algebra Project, who participate in a progressive education that places them squarely in the middle of the community, working with adults and peers to figure out how the knowledge they are gaining has to do with making a life in the present and future that is community-oriented, morally just, and democratic; and about the students at Eagle Rock, who are not relegated to boot camp for past bad acts, though they might have to sleep outside, but who get challenged to face the past, present, and future by engaging with adults who care about them and want to know, under certain conditions, what they want to see happen in their lives as they work daily to reclaim lost ground.

Critics will no doubt argue that exploring the "lived curriculum" of students just does not translate to scale. "How can we figure a way to measure the results of that? What would it prove anyway?" Right. Great questions. Dianne Suiter makes the commitment in her work as the principal of one of the last progressive, public schools in the entire nation to the assumption undergirding the entire enterprise: doing education right, no matter who is sitting in the seats, depends on the full exploration of the "lived curriculum" of each child. This is an undeniable commitment of the work at hand for the progressive educator, and she proves, just like so many great progressive teachers and leaders of the 20th century proved, that it works! It works in terms of results. It works to scale. More important, it is morally defensible, and the right thing to do, especially if we know how!

Students in these schools, because they have agency, grow outside of themselves, work with smart and dedicated teachers who push them to make meaning and to study rigorously their concerns and interests, not only in order to grow as individual students capable of becoming citizens and making a productive contribution to society, but also to score on the test! They get grades, they score on standardized tests. They are not hurt by being educated this way. They are being helped. They are receiving the same kind of education that wealthy, elite aristocrats want for their children. Engaging in a progressive education done well, in which the lived curriculum of everyone is explored in-depth and with passion, purpose, and meaning always yields. The Eight-Year study taught us that (Aikin, 1942). Deb Meier taught us that through her remarkable run with progressive schools in New York City (Meier, 1995). Central Academy teaches that. Eagle Rock teaches that. The NNER teaches that, through its constant attention to the power of each partnership site to generate ideas and actions for renewal and change from the inside/out. Why cannot we listen? Pay attention? Why cannot we attend to these successes? Perhaps, they are remarkable, given the times we live in. But they are not "exceptional," that is outside our own reach. We need to renew our approaches in order to honor where we need to begin again in American public education and in our society? With the individual, with the local setting. It's that simple.

CURRICULUM AND PEDAGOGY ROLL TOGETHER, AND EVERYTHING IS CURRICULAR

We do not make a hard and fast distinction between curriculum and pedagogy in this text. Our assumption, collectively, is that teaching and curriculum turn on each other. So for instance, when thinking about the curriculum plans of the teacher in the one-room schoolhouse, we understand that her plans on a daily basis, the ones official and written out, the ones embodied in curriculum artifacts for use like worksheets and books, etc., will get used, engage students, but will also be transformed by the lived experience of the curriculum at hand, each day and each minute in the classroom, and in a different way no matter what she does, by each child.

And we know that a major impact on the curriculum that students "live" in that setting will be affected by the interactions that students have with peers, community members, and the teacher as learning takes place there and even outside the setting! So learning, in this setting, and in so many that we know of and all of the ones documented here, has a strong "expressive" element, to use Eisner's phrasing, meaning that what happens in the classroom, intended and not, but always on purpose, cannot really be scripted but simply gets expressed as the educative situation plays out as people, processes—that is, as life itself—gets played out (Eisner, 2004).

Many, many factors come into play, and the only way to make sense of it, hard and fast, is to accept that as students participate in the learning setting, they live a curriculum that is idiosyncratic to them, and are affected simultaneously by curriculum materials and by teaching. And, it is obvious to us that all of these things cannot always be separated out from each other. The implication of this for research, planning, and teaching is that it matters what we plan to do and how we plan to do it, but education also depends on the learner, and on complex interactions among teacher, student, and milieu that cannot always be anticipated. This does not mean that the outcomes—expressive in the sense that the actors are always human beings—cannot be anticipated, and that quality learning experiences cannot be planned for. It is just that we sometimes get something we had not planned for, and that is not always bad.

The bottom lines have to do with engaging the learner, fostering intellectual activity, and making purposeful connections to/in the world. When these things happen, curriculum and pedagogy come alive. That is why we as a class and as a body of scholars in this text always talk about curriculum being everywhere, it is embodied in the experiences of learners doing educative things in nearly every setting we live and move in as long as the experiences of the learner lead to growth as it is embodied in action that is morally defensible (the training of pickpockets excluded, of course! See Dewey, 1932).

ASSOCIATED LIVING, MOVING TOWARD DEMOCRACY

The possibility of advancing aspects of a social democracy, creating the kind of world we want to live in, where "democracy is more than a form of government; it is primarily a mode of associated living, of conjoint communicated experience" (Dewey, 1932, p. 101), operates at the heart of nearly all these curricula. Certainly, for instance, in the case of what is happening in Neshoba County today, the fallout long-term from Freedom Summer 1964 and the civil rights movement in general, the subsequent conviction of Killen (Tucker, 2005), and the recognized need to both deal with the past and move on, have all created the kind of raw tension where community often emerges. It is fair to say that the coalition that is building community in Neshoba is remaking its community and society, in hopes for the better, as a stronger, more unified, more understanding place where people can live better lives together, in association with each other, in relationships, despite ongoing struggles and issues. This is one of the key ends of democracy, something to be fought for and treasured, a minor miracle of great proportions, since out of the dust of inequity and injustice has come some golden measure of fairness, civility, and relationship, in a word, democracy, though it is not perfect, or even ideal.

The same is true, to some degree, for each of the curricula here. Forms of associated living abound, in moments of clarity for the purposes at hand as people work together to deal with the unspeakable, as in the lives shared and touched at the Holocaust Museum and on a tour of Neshoba County with a member of the coalition; in shared commitments to a common good that is more than a dream but a reality approached on a daily basis, as in the learning created and shared in places that buzz with voices and projects among the Central Academy and the Algebra Project students, or among residents at Eagle Rock engaged in an intense tutorial; in the cultivation of voice and innovation, at a McDonald's training session around the food preparation table or at a local Little League's board of directors meeting in December.

What is at stake for all of us as educators is the promise to educate ourselves and each other under conditions that lead to more intense associated living, where common interests are explored and we develop the social habit of freer interaction across multiple groups with multiple agendas and purposes (Dewey, 1932, p. 100). We cannot be better if we are not challenged, even to the core of our most treasured beliefs. How can we hold to existing tenets and still be accepting of and challenged by others'?

This leads to an obvious statement that must be made that will be highly contested. Progressives believe that the way people interact in a democratic environment, where the conditions are such that citizens are free to explore interests and interact intensely with others, reflects the best that we are and the best we can be. This is hotly contested, with present day policies in education and government focused, at least rhetorically and with much power, on the individual over and against the social good that individuals might create together. "Don't tread on me" is the slogan of the day, not "e pluribus unum." We do not have a hard time accepting individual interests, but we do have a hard time accepting multiple relations, and engaging in free, equitable relationships with each other.

Because we do not know each other, are scared to do so, are threatened by that, we live in isolation, and therefore, we live out of association with each other. As a result, we are less democratic, less progressive, less American, if you will. We are certainly less unified, and we breed more hatred and distance and misunderstanding than we do learning and love. These are sad outcomes for people evolving in the 21st century, and in the 3rd century of a republic.

SO RELATIONAL DYNAMICS BECOME MORE IMPORTANT, EVEN CENTRAL

We live together, so acting like a family and being in relationships that mimic strong family ties have certain advantages. Of course, we see the outcome of intense social relations developing in school and community that lead to family-like feelings, as is the case with the one-room schoolhouse, at least the one that Kevin Smith studied. The pull of family, the reality and imagination of it at work on a daily basis in a small town where everyone knows each other even better as a result of their association with this amazing school and as the school faces extinction, like so many remaining one-room schoolhouses do across North America, is so strong that it becomes a significant and powerful argument, in and of itself, for saving the school.

The school creates family in community, stretches each member, and creates extra value for life, the good life. Family is so important.

Of course, Victor's family did everything it could at Eagle Rock to help him finish high school. Eagle Rock creates family where family sometimes is broken in the student's life. This is controversial action, pulling children out of lives that have meaning and value, no matter how horrible and crazy they seem on the surface, and remaking the world with them. For instance, in special education, advocates fight for students to remain as long as possible in the least restrictive environment, in the place where students identified as needing special services have the best chance of stretching/ advancing their lives in terms of knowledge and social relations, becoming citizens as a result of the intense value that associated living brings to them and to those who engage them (Rotuno-Johnson, 2010). There is so much value in these ends that removing a child from that environment for treatment or services has negative consequences and is often avoided at all costs.

But here the pendulum seems to have swung too far against the student, and the school, acting as progressively and as responsibly as it can, seeks to swing it back, taking stock of the student's life, where he or she wants to go, and charts a path reverberating with freedom and order toward sound ends in a completely separate place. Relations, places, homes, family become distant. This is a new way. And they do it so well that the students often seem more capable of creating a new reality for themselves that overshadows the damages of the past, and offers hope for a long, strong life that is productive in the world, perhaps even in the one left behind originally.

The tension over the distance between the past and the present does not rankle, it concerns everyone involved, which I think gives it so much texture as a progressive entity, pushing and pulling at what is possible given everything that has happened and is at stake for the student and the wider community. When you are in their midst at Eagle Rock, you feel the pull of family, and the creation of meaning out of experience tangibly. It is a powerful site of transformation, and many visitors to the school, and the students it serves, continuously confirm this in their stories.

TENSIONS OVER CLICHÉ'S, LIKE "PROJECTS," AND "SECOND CHANCES"

It is no doubt irresponsible and irresistible all at once, just like it was in Kilpatick's day, at least according to Dewey, to argue simply for students to do projects in school settings and everything will be progressive, educative, sound (Saettler, 2004). Of course, there is some truth to it, but also not so much. Teaching progressively is one of the hardest things to do in education/ schooling. Anyone who has tried to leave the notes of lectures and control of the classroom setting behind and tried to listen to students and allow them to control the direction of learning knows how hard it is to do! In fact, most people educated for teaching treat the notion of a progressive approach as quaint, historical, or as unusually impractical. Some teachers who assign projects to students without working twice as hard to teach during the development of their work are probably doing more harm than good. And the student is not the absolute center of the universe: knowledge, problem-solving, and structure all play a part. A great progressive classroom is not about "anything goes" or indulging the child. Far from it.

It is important to understand that the curricula described and interpreted here are active, and engaging, and put the learner/participant at the center of things, producing knowledge, not just consuming it, and the curricula often involve extensive project work. So the NNER is a network, in the true sense of the word, relying on local sites to engage in projects reflecting the Agenda for Democracy in Education, sometimes with the support and direction of the national body and other sites, but sometimes on the talent and motivation inside the site to move forward. At Central Academy you will find a "classic" progressivism at work in classrooms, where students work individually and in groups on projects solving problems nearly all the time they are together in school. Each shift at McDonald's, each season of Little League, each driving tour of Neshoba County conducted by a member of the coalition is a project, new each time, filled with endless possibilities, room for innovation, and new opportunities for the participants to make meaning that might just be transformational, for the individual and maybe even for the community at large.

When we engage in projects we plan, and enact, and live a new curriculum, giving learning meaning as it is found in experience that bumps up against, transforms, or becomes "the real world." The real world is not all about tiny bits of knowledge that do not fit together, or despotic clutches of time and space at work and play where second chances are few and far between. Nothing could be further from the truth. In many ways, the real world is progressive, a place where knowledge and experience have a flow, a more holistic feel, a contextualized set of nuances that guide action and next steps. And people alive today know very well about second chances. Tests do not determine the outcome of every next step; instead, real assessments guide next steps, send us forward, provide a second chance.

When you see a set of students presenting their findings after conducting an inquiry in a progressive school, you will often get to a point where peers and guides ask the students to take another shot at the work and go deeper, explore a different direction, complete the project. Unlike standard, traditional curriculum assessments, which typically place the test at the end and quickly move the "learners" to the next unit, regardless of performance, leaving prior learning, if there were any, behind, focusing now on the new and the next, progressive attempts to assess occur throughout the project and sometimes beyond its very life; this book itself as a project artifact from a course is a case of that type of approach. Worse than a one-time test with poor results, students might be forced to enter a "remedial" curriculum when they score low, and get left behind while their classmates steam ahead. Instead, groups and individuals move in progressive camps when the work is completed. No one gets left behind; everyone learns, progresses, moves, albeit at a different rate, in different ways. But students do not get left behind. This is a critical commitment in progressive education; it stands in contra-distinction to most traditional formulas. Projects, and second chances abound, as well they should.

How powerful is it when students are allowed and encouraged to inquire into the world as it is taking shape in events right now? Very powerful, as we know from Chris Cox's chapter on the Obama Inauguration. In it, he frames the energy that progressive educators have always known is at hand when the world erupts: Look at it, study it, own it as part of your experience. This entry into the world makes us more human, more understanding, more aware of the many viewpoints and practices alive in the world that may be of us, yet distance, or other, and accessible if we look. Plus, looking at reality as it takes shape puts us closer to the action than we ever could be before, especially through technology and media. Now is here, we should embrace it!

CURRICULUM INQUIRY CHALLENGES

Of course, as we close this volume it is important to say, again, that we hope you will be inspired to conduct curriculum inquiries of various types and with various orientations after reading along with us. Engaging curriculum questions and phenomena in the world, and writing about our experiences with them, puts us closer to the field Schwab (1969) envisioned, where the arts of the practical are engaged across the field in meaningful ways, and deliberation becomes a central way of life, emboldening our work together and strengthening our democratic way of life, the extent to which we live together associatively.

It is also important for me to say how remarkable the student-authors in this volume are to me. They faced the challenge of taking a course that usually lasts a semester for more than two years. Of course, there are benefits to them, not the least of which is the opportunity to engage in a supervised inquiry that is published. In the end, I want to briefly discuss how they confronted two difficulties that they overcame to make this volume work.

First, they confronted access issues. Just getting into the site, quickly and in a way that allowed them to generate data and stories to use in their writing, proved to be a challenge for almost all the authors. Several attempts at access were stymied early on, or dragged out seemingly interminably. This has always been a sticky point in qualitative research (Van Maanen, 1988), and the trick of knowing when to cut bait or stick with fishing, especially with only one semester at-hand can be nervy stuff. I credit the students for working meticulously and purposefully toward access and believe that the chapters would not have happened without the authors' skillful negotiation of access in so many interesting sites of inquiry.

Second, looking takes effort. It is different than reading books/research and writing a paper. Generating data, dealing with nuance, sorting through so many stories to be told, and just being in the field with other human beings looking and asking questions creates a different sort of tired, a fatigue that most of the authors had not even experienced in teaching, which is hard enough! At any rate, the class had a sense of what it is like and what it takes to be a researcher. Educationally, I can only hope this pays dividends when they take on their primary inquiry, the dissertation, for graduation from the program.

And finally, though I mention this in the front matter, I appreciate and thank our Department of Educational Leadership, and Miami University for so generously supporting us as a writing team. As I document elsewhere, there are barriers to conducting educational research with students that must be negotiated and always overcome (Poetter, 2010). We did overcome them, and we appreciate your attention in this volume and hope that your reading of it stirs debate and deliberation that advances the field. We also hope that you found the various examples we present, across so many different parts of the community, as helpful in seeing that curriculum is everywhere, and important to theorize about, plan, enact, and live (Marsh & Willis, 2007).

REFERENCES

Aikin, W. (1942). *The story of the eight-year study with conclusions and recommendations.* New York, NY: Harper & Brothers.

Bracey, G. (2009). *Education hell: Rhetoric vs. reality.* Alexandria, VA: Educational Research Service.

Burke, R. W. (1993). *Perceptions of the twelve-step program as curriculum* (Unpublished doctoral dissertation). Indiana University, Indianapolis, IN.

Combs, A. (1976). *A perceptual psychology: A humanistic approach to the study of persons.* New York, NY: Harper & Row.

Dewey, J. (1932). *Democracy and education: An introduction to the philosophy of education.* New York, NY: The Macmillan Company.

Dillon, S. (2011, April 28). Foundations join to offer online courses for schools. *New York Times*, p. A12.

Eisner, E. (2004, 4th ed.). *The educational imagination: On the design and evaluation of school programs*. New York, NY: Macmillan.

Goodlad, J., & Associates. (1979). *Curriculum inquiry*. New York, NY: McGraw-Hill.

Marsh, C., & Willis, G. (2007). *Curriculum: Alternative approaches, ongoing issues* (4th ed.). Upper Saddle River, NJ: Pearson Merrill Prentice Hall.

Meier, D. (1995). *The power of their ideas: Lessons for America from a small school in Harlem*. Boston, MA: Beacon Press.

Poetter, T. (2010). Taking the leap, mentoring doctoral students as scholars: A great and fruitful morass. *Teaching & Learning: The Journal of Natural Inquiry & Reflective Practice, 24*(1), 22–29.

Rotuno-Johnson, R. (2010). Democracy and special education inclusion. *Education in a democracy: A Journal of the NNER, 2*, 169–182.

Saettler, P. (2004). *The evolution of American educational technology*. Charlotte, NC: Information Age Publishing.

Schwab, J. (1969). The practical: A language for curriculum. *School Review* (November), 1–23.

Tucker, N. (2005). The twist in conviction of Killen makes sense there. Retrieved from *www.chron.com*

Van Maanen, J. (1988). *Tales of the field: On writing ethnography*. Chicago, IL: University of Chicago Press.

ABOUT THE AUTHOR

Thomas S. Poetter is Professor of Curriculum Studies in the Department of Educational Leadership at Miami University in Oxford, Ohio. Since 1994, Poetter has been engaging students in inquiries into theory and practice in curriculum and teaching. His first book, *Voices of Inquiry in Teacher Education* (1997, Lawrence Erlbaum) challenges teachers to view inquiry as a key orientation for a lifetime of professional practice in schools. Since then, his students have authored and co-authored many books and articles as a result of coursework taken with him at Miami including book-length works such as *Critical Perspectives on the Curriculum of Teacher Education* (2004, UPA) and *No Child Left Behind and the Illusion of Reform* (2006, UPA). Recently, Poetter outlined his curricular and pedagogical approaches with students in "Taking the leap, mentoring doctoral students as scholars" (*The Journal of Natural Inquiry & Reflective Practice*, *24*(1), 22–29). A longtime public school advocate and partner, Poetter continues to write and teach with remarkably talented, focused students at Miami in the areas of curriculum, teaching, and public education renewal.